The Glory of '86

The Glory of '86

The Year Boston Ruled the Sports World

Tom Van Riper

ROWMAN & LITTLEFIELD
Lanham • Boulder • New York • London

Published by Rowman & Littlefield
An imprint of The Rowman & Littlefield Publishing Group, Inc.
4501 Forbes Boulevard, Suite 200, Lanham, Maryland 20706
www.rowman.com

86-90 Paul Street, London EC2A 4NE, United Kingdom

British Library Cataloguing in Publication Information Available

Library of Congress Cataloging-in-Publication Data

Names: Van Riper, Tom, 1963– author.
Title: The glory of '86 : the year Boston ruled the sports world / Tom Van Riper. Other
    titles: Glory of 1986
Description: Lanham, Maryland : Rowman & Littlefield, [2024] | Includes
    bibliographical references and index. | Summary: "The Glory of '86 tells the
    remarkable story of one of the most memorable years ever for sports fans across New
    England, when the New England Patriots, Boston Celtics, and Boston Red Sox played
    in the Super Bowl, NBA Finals, and World Series"— Provided by publisher.
Identifiers: LCCN 2023040335 (print) | LCCN 2023040336 (ebook) | ISBN
    9781538175699 (cloth) | ISBN 9781538175705 (epub)
Subjects: LCSH: Sports—Massachusetts—Boston—History—20th century. | New
    England Patriots (Football team)—History—20th century. | Super Bowl—History—
    20th century. | Boston Celtics (Basketball team)—History—20th century. | NBA Finals
    (Basketball)—History—20th century. | Boston Red Sox (Baseball team)—History—
    20th century. | World Series (Baseball)—History—20th century.
Classification: LCC GV584.5.B6 V36 2024 (print) | LCC GV584.5.B6 (ebook) | DDC
    796.09744/61—dc23/eng/20230925
LC record available at https://lccn.loc.gov/2023040335
LC ebook record available at https://lccn.loc.gov/2023040336

For the Watertown crew

Contents

Acknowledgements

I would like to thank all the players, team executives, reporters, and others for taking the time to do interviews for this book. Former New England Patriots Steve Grogan, Garin Veris, and Craig James; former Boston Celtics Bill Walton, Jerry Sichting, and Scott Wedman; and former Boston Red Sox Rich Gedman, Roger Clemens, and Dwight Evans were very gracious with their time.

The insights of media veterans who covered these teams in the 1980s— Bob Ryan and Lesley Visser of the *Boston Globe*, Bill Ballou of the *Worcester Telegram & Gazette*, Steve Krasner and Jim Donaldson of the *Providence Journal*, Bob Lobel of WBZ TV, and John Molori of *Patriots Football Weekly* and *Boston Baseball Magazine* were invaluable in putting this book together.

I must also acknowledge former Patriots' general manager Pat Sullivan, former Celtics' general manager Jan Volk, former Celtics player and scout Rick Weitzman and (still) Celtics public relations man Jeff Twiss for their time and assistance. (Mr. Twiss even pulled double duty, helping to secure interviews with former players while offering his own memories and insights as well.) Special thanks go out to Bill Wanless of the Triple-A Worcester Red Sox for his assistance in arranging an interview with Rich Gedman, who is now the Worcester hitting coach, and to Diana Holland at the Roger Clemens Foundation for arranging an interview with Roger.

And finally, thanks to New England natives Rich Chaiton, John Cascione, and Paul MacDonald for adding the fans' perspective to Boston's magical year of 1986.

Prologue

January 5, 1986
Los Angeles Memorial Coliseum
Los Angeles, California

Marcus Allen took the pitchout from quarterback Marc Wilson at about the 15-yard line and ran to his right toward a gaping hole. He put on a burst of speed and then leaped as he approached the goal line, shaking off safety Fred Marion's half-hearted attempt at a hit as he fell into the end zone for a touchdown. The L.A. Coliseum rocked as the television audience back East winced. That feeling of dread was beginning to set in across New England.

The Los Angeles Raiders were rolling. After spotting the Patriots the game's first touchdown, L.A. had hit back hard with three straight scores. Early in the second quarter, the same Raider club that had handled the Patriots pretty easily in Foxborough back in September led the AFC Divisional play-off game 17–7. Just before the game, NBC studio analyst Pete Axthelm had told host Bob Costas that he believed the Patriots, hot as they had been since the middle of the season, had effectively played their Super Bowl the previous week in their wild card round win over the Jets and that the magic figured to run out against the talented Raiders. He liked L.A., not only to win but to cover the 5½-point spread. New Englanders may not have liked Axthelm's take, but was he right? It was starting to look that way.

The Raiders were winning the battles in the trenches while their stars were playing like stars. One possession earlier, Allen had ripped off a 14-yard run to help set up a 16-yard Wilson touchdown pass to wide receiver Jessie Hester. On New England's first play after the ensuing kickoff, All-Pro defensive lineman and Charlestown, Massachusetts, native Howie Long scooped up a fumble by running back Mosi Tatupu to give the Raiders the ball right back inside the Patriots' 20-yard line, leading to Allen's touchdown run. In less than two minutes, the Raiders' four-point deficit had become a 10-point lead. Long was wreaking havoc on the defensive line; Allen was well on his way to another 100-plus-yard rushing game. If not for L.A.'s Fulton Walker fumbling an early punt to set up a quick New England touchdown, the score would've been even worse.

One man who wasn't wincing or, for that matter, showing any emotion whatsoever, was Patriots' head coach Raymond Berry. The only time he seemed to look up from his notes and move on the sideline came when he walked a few paces to quietly offer Tatupu a reassuring pat on the shoulder after his costly fumble. No worries, plenty of time left.

In the NBC booth, Dick Enberg and Merlin Olsen mused about what Berry could do to turn things around, with Olsen figuring he might abandon the methodical game plan and look for a big play. But on the next Patriots' drive—nothing doing. Running back Craig James immediately ran right for 16 yards. Two plays later, it was James corralling a short toss from quarterback Tony Eason and rumbling 24 yards to the Raider 37. On second down Tatupu—perhaps buoyed by Berry's encouragement on the sideline—found a hole on the right side and steamrolled ahead 22 yards to the 15-yard line. Another James run moved the ball to the 9.

On the next play the Pats got the break they needed. Howie Long's aggressive move toward the line of scrimmage just before the snap got him flagged for an offside penalty. Long argued for a bit with the referee, and for good reason. Replays showed that New England's Pro Bowl tackle Brian Holloway had moved first, drawing Long offside. But, of course, referees don't catch everything. The call stood, giving New England a first down. The Raider defense stuffed the next 2 plays. But on third and goal from the two, James ran left and followed big John Hannah, the great veteran offensive guard still going strong at age 34. As Hannah cut down L.A. safety Stacey Toran, James waltzed into the corner of the end zone for a touchdown.

The Patriots were within three and looking rejuvenated. On the kickoff, Ed Reynolds laid a hit on return man Fulton Walker that knocked the ball loose, although Matt Millen alertly recovered Walker's second fumble of the game for the Raiders on the 19-yard line. But Millen's hustle only delayed the turnover by a couple of plays. After the Patriot defense swarmed Allen for a four-yard loss, a Wilson pass on second down intended for receiver Dokie Williams near the right sideline was picked off by corner Ronnie Lippett at the Raider 28. It was already Lippett's second interception of the game as he made the Raiders pay for their strategy of picking on him to avoid Pro Bowl corner Raymond Clayborn on the other side of the field. The ensuing drive fizzled, but Tony Franklin's 45-yard field goal tied the score 17–17 with under two minutes left in the first half.

The Raiders did manage to take the lead back before the half ended. As tough a day as Marc Wilson was having (3-for-10 for 34 yards thus far with two interceptions and a lot of headshakes and other gestures of frustration), his best throw of the day found tight end Todd Christensen downfield for 30 yards into New England territory. It was the key play in a drive to the Patriots' 15-yard line as the clock wound down. A Chris Bahr field goal gave the Raiders a 20–17 lead at halftime.

The Patriots were in a good spot, though. After flirting with disaster for a stretch, they trailed by just three. Eason was not lighting up the stat sheet—only 55 passing yards in the first half without a single completion to a wide receiver as Raider cornerbacks Lester Hayes and Mike Haynes consistently blanketed Eason's big play men, Stanley Morgan and Irving Fryar. But Eason had avoided any interceptions while engineering a conservative offense led by James's 53 rushing yards that had kept the ball for more than 18 of the first half's 30 minutes. Add three takeaways of the ball by the defense and special teams and you could see why New England was able to put up 17 points in a half of football despite few big plays on offense.

In the second half, the Patriots' defense came out looking like the unit that had allowed the sixth-fewest points in the NFL in 1985. The Raiders' opening drive reached midfield thanks mainly to a couple of solid runs by Allen that boosted him over the 100-yard mark for the game. But right after that, New England's defensive looks confused Wilson so much that he burned through not one but two timeouts, leaving L.A. with just one for the rest of the game. On the next play, linebacker Don Blackmon and defensive end Garin Veris broke through to sack Wilson for a big loss. Boos rained down from the Coliseum faithful.

After a bizarre sequence in which the two star running backs, James and Allen, exchanged fumbles, the Patriots had the ball on their own 32. An Eason pass underneath to James got them to midfield. And then, finally, a big play to a wide receiver as Morgan shook loose and caught Eason's throw across the middle in stride at the Raider 35. The play almost went for naught as the slippery ball that seemed to be plaguing everyone was poked out of Morgan's hands from behind by Lester Hayes. But Irving Fryar quickly jumped on the loose ball at the 26-yard line to keep the drive going.

Two strong runs by James behind Hannah and Holloway gained 18 yards to set the Pats up with a first and goal on the 8. The Raider defense stiffened near the goal line, ultimately forcing Eason to throw a bit too long on third down toward a well-covered Fryar near the back of the end zone. Franklin came in to boot the short field goal that got the Patriots even, 20–20.

Among the 11 players lined up for the Patriots' kickoff team was a rookie backup safety named Jim Bowman, a little-known second-round pick the previous spring out of Central Michigan. No doubt, Bowman's spot on the roster had been largely secured by his all out, hard-nosed play on special teams. It was Bowman who had recovered Fulton Walker's fumble of the first-quarter punt that had set up New England's first touchdown.

Franklin drilled his kick downfield. Raider return man Sam Seale muffed the catch on his 5-yard line as the ball sailed right through his arms, hit his midsection, and bounced forward. Seale was still okay at this point, with enough time to grab the ball off the ground before the kickoff coverage got to him. But in his haste to make up for lost time, Seale scrambled around for a moment while holding the ball out with one hand. Mosi Tatupu swooped in and drilled Seale at the 10-yard line, knocking the ball loose and sending it bouncing back toward the goal line. The State of Massachusetts and half of Rhode Island screamed, "fumble!"

The scramble for the ball was strictly a competition among guys in white jerseys—not a single black Raider shirt to be found. Ultimately it was the hard-charging Bowman who pounced on the ball in the end zone. Up went the referee's hands to signal touchdown. Up went thousands more hands seeking high-fives in the bars and living rooms of New England. The Patriots had the lead.

A little more than a quarter of the game remained, but the sagging shoulders in black told the story: The Raiders were a beaten team. The New England defense kept Allen, who had run them ragged for 121 yards through the first three quarters, under wraps during the final quarter. That put more pressure on Wilson to bring Los Angeles back with his arm, something he just wasn't going to do. With a little under eight minutes left, he threw behind Allen downfield and watched his third interception of the day land in the hands of safety Fred Marion, who returned it to the Patriot 45.

Leading 27–20, New England kept the ball on the ground and chalked up two first downs to run the clock under four minutes, the biggest play coming when James peeled off 14 yards up the middle on third and 12 to pick up a first down and keep the drive moving. The two timeouts the Raiders had used up in the third quarter were looming large as the Patriots continued to chew up clock. The Raiders finally used their last timeout after stopping New England on third down on the Raider 37 with 1:51 left. L.A. got the ball back on its 20-yard line after Rich Camarillo's short punt bounced into the end zone.

The Raiders seemed to have a last gasp when Wilson, after missing on his first two throws and then completing a short one, found Allen open on a do-or-die fourth-down play and then watched Allen turn upfield after the catch and run 20 yards to midfield. But to the dismay of the Coliseum crowd and the relief of Boston-area TV viewers, the play was called back on a face-mask penalty charged to Raider offensive lineman Mickey Marvin back at the line of scrimmage. The Raiders were backed up with a fourth and 17 at their 13-yard line with 1:03 on the clock.

Then the fitting end to a game decided by so many crazy bounces of the football. Wilson's final throw of the day overshot intended receiver Jessie

Hester but wound up right in the arms of teammate Dokie Williams, who was just a few yards behind Hester near the right sideline. But the surprised Williams couldn't control the ball cleanly, and the drive was over. A couple of kneel-downs by Eason ran off the final seconds and made it official. The Patriots had shut out the Raiders in the second half to come away with one of the biggest wins in franchise history, 27–20. Craig James, who finished with 103 yards rushing to nearly match Marcus Allen, was named outstanding player. The Patriot sideline was so giddy that GM Pat Sullivan, son of the owner, used the occasion to taunt Howie Long for his pregame putdown of the Patriots and prediction of victory. The Raiders' ornery linebacker Matt Millen responded by whacking Sullivan on the head with his helmet, setting off a mini fracas near the New England sideline. That night, a smiling Sullivan wore the scar like a badge of honor as he exited the team plane in Boston.

The Patriots were headed to the AFC Championship Game for the first time ever. To reach the Super Bowl, they would have to defeat the Miami Dolphins in the Orange Bowl, their perennial hellhole where they had lost 18 times in a row. So a win would snap two dubious skids at once—19 years of the Super Bowl era without an appearance and 18 years of losing to the Dolphins in Miami. Could they do it? Despite the history, it was hard to see why not. It was only the fifth day of 1986, but there was a clear vibe in the air. This year felt different.

Introduction

I developed my first kinship with Boston during the fall of 1976, the bicentennial year, when my father took me on a road trip from Long Island for a weekend getaway to tour the historic sites. Actually, check that—my fandom really goes a few years further back to fourth grade social studies and those first textbook discoveries of the Revolutionary War. I was a true American history geek, riveted by the grammar school versions of Lexington and Concord, Bunker Hill, the Boston Tea Party, and Paul Revere's ride. And so, by middle school, when the trip happened and it all came to life, Wow! Stepping onto the Lexington Green where the first shots of the war were fired, looking up at the tower of the Old North Church on Salem Street where those two (if by sea) lanterns had hung, walking through the Granary Burial Grounds on Tremont Street where Revere, John Hancock, and Sam Adams were buried, it really didn't get much better for an amateur history buff.

But it was more than just the famous spots. It was walking through the open-air market at Haymarket and through the just-renovated and reopened Quincy Market. As much as I love New York—and there is no city on the planet that oozes the kind of raw power and energy that New York does—Boston resonated with a unique character of history and modernity at once. It was comfort food, like New York without all the excess. Big enough to be a major urban center and small enough to feel comfortable and get around easily; sure, the traffic is no picnic, but trust me, you can drive from Providence to Boston in about the same amount of time it takes to ride a couple of subways from South Brooklyn to Midtown.

That first New England peek in 1976 only lasted two days, but I had a pretty good hunch I'd be back.

Of course we all knew that Boston was a major sports town, and we knew all about their teams. But growing up I was never particularly caught up in any sort of Boston–New York rivalry. Yankees–Red Sox didn't resonate much when I was a young kid for two reasons: (1) The rivalry was mostly dormant at the time as the Baltimore Orioles dominated the American League East;

and (2) I was a Mets fan and Yankee hater, so I kind of liked the Red Sox. By 1978, when the rivalry had been revived, the Bucky Dent homer crushed me almost as much as any kid from Framingham or Dorchester.

There wasn't much of a true rivalry between the Jets and the Patriots because both were mediocre during the early-to-mid-70s and constantly looking up at the Miami Dolphins. The Bruins and Rangers always had a pretty nice NHL rivalry dating back to their early "Original Six" days, but since I didn't pick up hockey quite as early as other sports it pretty much passed me by. By the time I really got into the sport at around age 11 it was the two-year-old Islanders, playing 20 minutes from my Long Island home, who were my team, while expansion and realignment had separated the Rangers and Bruins into different divisions.

The only hot rivalry of the day between the cities came from the NBA, where the Knicks and Celtics squared off in the Eastern Conference Finals for three straight years, from 1972 to 1974. That rivalry would soon sputter after the Knicks sunk into mediocrity later in the '70s and were displaced by the Philadelphia 76ers as the Celtics' true eastern rival. But boy was it wonderful while it lasted. Some of my fondest sports memories come from the days sitting in front of the television with my dad watching the Knicks of Frazier, Reed, and DeBusschere battle the Celtics of Cowens, Havlicek, and White for the right to go to the NBA Finals. The Knicks' Game Seven win at Boston Garden in 1973 on their way to a championship marked the only time the Celtics ever lost a seventh game at that hallowed arena until the Sixers of Julius Erving and Mo Cheeks pulled off the feat nine years later.

Still, as much as I was pulling for the Knicks, I never felt the rivalry in the traditional vicious sense. It was more of a fun family feud. The reason: My dad, a New Yorker through and through, was a Celtics fan. Why? He hailed from the same St. Albans, Queens, neighborhood as Bob Cousy. Some of his young childhood days had been spent meeting up with friends at the local schoolyard to watch Cousy, already a local legend at Andrew Jackson High School and a future Holy Cross and Celtics star, do his thing in neighborhood pickup games.

So really, despite the circumstance, I was okay with the Celtics. I particularly liked the way Dave Cowens and Jo Jo White played. And after the Celtics disposed of the Knicks in five games in the 1974 Eastern Finals, I rooted alongside Dad for them in the NBA Finals against Kareem Abdul-Jabbar and the Milwaukee Bucks, a great series in which the Celts lost a potential Game Six clincher at home in double overtime but then came back to take the title by winning Game Seven on the road.

It was seven years later that I let out a primal scream in our family kitchen upon opening the envelope from Boston College to discover that I had been accepted into the class of 1985. It felt like the luckiest day of my life, figuring

I had been a borderline candidate. For the next four years—and, as it turned out, a little way beyond that—Boston was my pseudo home. And what a sweet time it was to be a BC Eagle. In addition to the usual college stuff—dorm life, studying, intramurals, weekend parties, Green Line rides into downtown— our class had stumbled onto the start of a golden era of BC sports. There were the three Sweet 16 appearances for the basketball team in four years as we relished our underdog status against the likes of Georgetown, St. John's, and Syracuse during the formative years of the Big East Conference. To us, Patrick Ewing, Chris Mullin, and Pearl Washington had nothing on John Bagley, Michael Adams, or Jay Murphy. College didn't get much better than squeezing into the upstairs student section of 4,400-seat Roberts Center, the precious campus bandbox where the team almost never lost.

And, of course, there was football. Entering school, we were happy enough that our team was the only major Division I program in town, allowing us to see Penn State, West Virginia, and other nationally prominent squads visit our campus. What we didn't have were any great expectations for our perpetual middle-of-the-road program to actually win a lot at that level. We figured on having to settle for hammering Holy Cross every year while hoping to be reasonably competitive against the rest of the schedule.

That is until, out of nowhere, one of our own classmates—a short, barely recruited local kid from nearby Natick named Doug Flutie ("Wait, you mean that guy we just played pickup basketball with?")—would quickly rise through the quarterback depth chart and lead the team to three nationally ranked seasons and three bowl games, grace the cover of *Sports Illustrated* twice and, while he was at it . . . break the career NCAA passing record, win a Heisman Trophy, and captivate the whole country. During the fall of 1984, which closed with the Miami Hail Mary and the Heisman presentation a week apart, Doug Flutie wasn't just the biggest athlete in Boston—he was the biggest athlete in America. So ridiculous were the demands on his time that Johnny Carson and David Letterman couldn't even book him.

Not that he was too busy to do his classmates a solid, though, even when Flutie Mania had hit its absolute peak. On Thursday night November 29— six days after beating Miami on a last-second nationally televised 48-yard heave to Gerard Phelan and two days before the Heisman ceremony in New York—Flutie agreed to stop by our campus apartment to tape an interview for a sports marketing project that a friend and I were doing for a class (my friend Steve won the coin toss and got to conduct the interview while I sat off to the side along with my roommates). Sitting in a cheap dorm chair with a couple of lamps moved around as lights, Doug leaned forward and with maximum energy answered every question clearly and thoroughly as if he were on the set of ABC News. After concluding the interview in five minutes or so—we had promised him it would be quick—we figured he'd run right out.

Instead, he kicked back and hung out with us for the better part of an hour, talking football and, well, football ("I've seen 'the play' about fifteen hundred times," he joked at one point). Talk about a senior year highlight—Flutie may have sent his regrets to Carson and Letterman, but he made it to Mod 21A.

We rang in 1985 at a big dance emporium in Dallas called Billy Bob's before watching Flutie get a win over Houston in his last college game at the Cotton Bowl the next day.

But while it was all loads of fun for BC students and alumni, we could sense that the excitement only spread so deep throughout the area. This wasn't the South or the Midwest, where college sports were almost religion. Boston was an eastern city and a major professional sports town. BC sports were all well and good, but they weren't taking any space in the local papers away from the Celtics, Patriots, Red Sox, and Bruins. My own perusing of the daily sports pages had expanded from *Newsday* and the *Daily News* to include Boston's *Globe* and *Herald* during the school months. Leigh Montville, Bob Ryan, Peter Gammons, and Will McDonough, among others, were my new go-to columnists. For an out-of-towner, the chance to occasionally scrape up a few bucks to catch a game at Boston Garden or Fenway Park was pretty awesome—the sports section of all that Boston history. And another reminder of why you were glad that you didn't wind up going to college in some sleepy town in Pennsylvania or upstate New York.

Yet while Boston was a sports-crazy town, the vibe always seemed a bit different. Fans were always more fatalistic than optimistic. Always waiting for the other shoe to drop, as they say. The Celtics were the exception, always carrying high expectations because of the championship pedigree that went all the way back to the late 1950s. By the start of the 1985/86 season they were a few years into the Larry Bird powerhouse era and already had a couple of recent NBA titles in the till.

But the Red Sox and Patriots, despite boasting some strong teams, had combined for zero playoff wins over the previous decade. In fact, the Pats hadn't won a single postseason game since joining the NFL in the 1970 merger with the AFL. The Red Sox lived with the ongoing "curse" of 1918 which they had just barely failed to erase in a tight 1975 World Series loss to the Cincinnati Reds. Both clubs had been through some recent ownership turmoil. Red Sox partner Buddy LeRoux had made a move—ultimately unsuccessful—to wrest control of the club from Jean Yawkey while Patriot owner Bill Sullivan and his son Chuck reeled from a bad bet on the music business when their financing of the Jackson 5 Victory Tour lost millions, leading to the eventual sale of Sullivan Stadium and the team before the 1980s ended.[1]

Local Channel 4 sports anchor Bob Lobel recalls: "The Pats and the Sullivans were always kind of a soap opera."

On the field, both the Sox and Pats were coming off mediocre seasons the year before their big runs, neither offering a reason for fans to think that anything special was brewing. The Bruins were better—several strong teams in the 1980s with Ray Bourque and Rick Middleton—but they hadn't won a Stanley Cup since Bobby Orr's heyday in the early 1970s.

"You need to look at this in the context of what came before and what came after; 1986 was special," says Lobel, a man who covered it all. Indeed this was the year in which the Sox and Patriots played in their only respective World Series and Super Bowl over a roughly three-decade stretch.

As much as New Englanders were sports nuts, they'd been conditioned to expect the worst while hoping for the best. The Patriots losing to the Raiders in the '76 playoffs on a couple of hideous calls by the refs? Naturally. Bucky (bleeping) Dent sending the Sox home in '78? Of course. The Bruins done in by a too-many-men-on-the-ice penalty in Game Seven of the '79 semifinals at Montreal? Sure, what's next?

The year 1978 had been particularly galling. In the spring the Bruins lost to Montreal in the Stanley Cup Finals just as the Red Sox were building a big lead in the American League East. By October the Sox had blown the lead that had once ballooned to 14½ games over the Yankees by losing an excruciating tiebreaker on Dent's cheap home run. Wrapping things up, the Patriots, AFC East champs in the fall of '78, fell into some turmoil after coach Chuck Fairbanks announced near the end of the season that he was on his way out to take over at the University of Colorado. The Pats were promptly thumped at home by the Houston Oilers in their first playoff game. All of this was still recent enough to feel fresh in the mid-1980s.

I graduated from BC in May 1985 on a beautiful sunny day inside Alumni Stadium, the site of Doug Flutie's heroics and our numerous tackle football games in the snow. Flutie wasn't graduating, having deferred his final semester to toil for Donald Trump's New Jersey Generals in the USFL, but he made it to the ceremony to give us all a wave.

A month or so later I moved with three of my college buddies into the upstairs of a two-family house in nearby Watertown, Massachusetts, a few miles west of downtown Boston. It was our first foray into the real world as we began those first post-college jobs. The setup made for a quasi-extension of college but with more reasonable hours—you could always blow off early class to sleep in, but you couldn't blow off that first hour of work, now could you? With two New Englanders and two New Yorkers, we spent a lot of time imitating each other's accents, quipping about how local weatherman Bruce Schwoegler talked, among other things, and of course watching a lot of sports.

What we couldn't have foreseen at the time was that we were settling into young adulthood during the tail end of what we would now call the old

Boston. The traditional, pre-gentrified Boston. Tip O'Neill, Ted Kennedy, John Kerry, Mike Dukakis, Ray Flynn, and Bill Bulger—brother of notorious local criminal James "Whitey" Bulger—were the big politicians.

The massive "Big Dig" infrastructure project hadn't started yet. Public transportation was a lot simpler. Charlie Card? Please, no. It was change or tokens for the T, which cost 75 cents a ride.

Filenes, Woolworth's, and Jordan Marsh anchored retail in Downtown Crossing. Waterfront icons Jimmy's Harborside and Anthony's Pier 4 still ruled the seafood world downtown. Meantime groups of students from BC, BU, Tufts, etc. who couldn't afford such fine dining would scrape together 10 bucks and a case of beer to stand in line at No Name, a fish and chowder assembly line with no liquor license tucked into a row of unsightly buildings on the pier. Popping open the Budweiser while strolling the switchbacks of the line and continuing as hurried waiters threw plates of scallops and clams in front of you at a big round table in the middle of a massive dining room was about the best Friday night party available off campus.

The '80s yuppie craze was in full swing in the downtown financial district and out in the Route 128 corridor that was flush with tech jobs at DEC and Wang. Molly's on Brighton Avenue was a big happy-hour spot. Many recent college grads who stayed in the area and liked to pretend that their entry-level corporate salaries were a lot higher than they were flashed their Gold Cards at Faneuil Hall, at Narcissus and Copperfield's ("Cawpa Fields" in local parlance) in Kenmore Square, Faces in Cambridge, and Daisy Buchanan's in the Back Bay, where Bruins, Patriots, and Red Sox players were known to sometimes rub elbows with fans. For those not into Madonna, Tears for Fears, Michael Jackson, or other MTV-age music there was the 1950s and '60s nostalgia craze at the Jukebox near the theatres on Tremont Street. And for a more casual night out, there was always candlepin bowling at Sammy White's in Brighton.

Indoor smoking was not only allowed, it was practically encouraged.

The Boston of the 1980s was a hot property in the entertainment world. *Cheers* was the biggest show on television, complete with cameos from Kevin McHale and Wade Boggs paying visits to fictional owner and former Red Sox relief pitcher Sam Malone. The show's popularity made the Bull & Finch Pub on Beacon Street near the Public Gardens, the place used for the *Cheers* exterior shot, a bigger tourist attraction than the Old North Church, Paul Revere's house, or anything else on the Freedom Trail. The networks also brought us *St. Elsewhere*, set at a fictional Boston hospital, and a pretty bad show called *Spenser for Hire* starring Robert Urich, which had a good run of mid-80s popularity thanks to all the location shots around town that people liked to talk about around the water cooler the next morning.

Washington Street downtown was still the Combat Zone, the definitive urban red-light district that was a decade or so away from petering out once Chinatown expanded and rising property values eventually drew developers eager to build more upscale digs.

The nearest corner convenience store was likely to be a Store24, not a 7–11. Southie was still genuinely working-class Irish, and the North End was still genuinely Italian—mass condos and trendy coffee places were still a way off. It would be about a decade before a Bostonian would see a Starbucks, like the one that now sits directly across the street from Whitey Bulger's old hangout, Triple O's in South Boston, which itself is now a trendy restaurant called Fox and the Knife. Bulger and his gang were still at their peak in the mid-80s, running Southie with an iron fist and using their corrupt relationship with the Boston FBI to grow their power throughout the city. But that was in the shadows, most of us wouldn't know about all of that until the stories came out years later.

In sports, too, the old Boston ruled the day. It was the 1980s, but it could have been the 1950s. The Boston Marathon still didn't pay prize money. Dynamic owners who would transform the Patriots and Red Sox into powers and practically turn Boston into Title Town USA in the 21st century—Robert Kraft and John Henry—weren't around just yet. No one ever used the term "Red Sox Nation."

It was the Boston of Fenway Park before the Green Monster squeezed in extra seats and donned a giant Coke bottle right above. A Fenway Park of organ music, monotone Sherm Feller on the public address mike ("number fourteen, Jim Rice, left field, Rice . . . "), and cruddy men's rooms adorned with single room-length troughs along the walls instead of individual urinals. It was the Boston of Boston Garden with its lack of air conditioning and dead spots on the floor. The Boston of the Yawkeys and Sullivans and almost invisible Celtics owners named Harry Mangurian and Don Gaston. The Boston of Red Auerbach. And a Boston with Johnny Most, Ned Martin, Bob Montgomery, Gil Santos, Mike Gorman, Bob Cousy, Fred Kusick, and Johnny Pierson behind the microphones calling the action.

In 1986 a field box at Fenway cost $11, a bleacher seat $4. The Sox drew well, but like most teams on most nights during that era, they didn't sell out. Unless it was a big series you didn't feel any urgency to get your tickets in advance—you went when the spirit moved you. Walking up to the ticket window 15 minutes before game time on a summer night was still one of the most popular ways to get to a game. If you had time, you'd pregame or postgame at Who's On First or the Cask 'N Flagon in Kenmore Square. At Boston Garden, $8 got you into the balcony for a Celtics game, and for $14 you could sit much closer. At 14-year-old Sullivan Stadium out in Foxborough you could sit on one of the cold metal bleachers on fall Sundays for under 20 bucks.

There were no all-sports radio stations. You got your sports news from the *Globe* and the *Herald* and from local news talking heads like Bob Lobel, Bob Neumeier, and John Dennis. These were the last local media superstars before we were glued almost full time to regional sports networks and checking our phones for scores and highlights. Actually, the first regional sports network, NESN (New England Sports Network), was up and running by the mid-80s with a lot of Red Sox and Bruins games. But many of the games were still on Channel 38, a local institution beloved for its sports, movies, and nightly *Odd Couple* reruns.

As far as winning—it was hard to do against 1980s competition. Take a look at all the dynasties or mini-dynasties that came out of the '80s—in addition to the Bird Celtics, the decade showcased the Magic Johnson Lakers, Joe Montana 49ers, early '80s New York Islanders, and late '80s Edmonton Oilers. The three Boston titles during the decade (all by the Celtics) could have been many more had they not run into some of those buzz saws. Those Laker, Islander, and Oiler teams combined to block four possible Boston titles in the final or semifinal round during the '80s. Throw in a few one-hit wonders that didn't bring home extended championship runs but whose places as all-time single-season clubs are very secure: the 1983 Philadelphia 76ers, 1984 Detroit Tigers, 1985 Chicago Bears, and 1986 New York Mets.

Those last two teams stifled potential Boston championships in the 1986 Super Bowl and World Series, leaving the Celtics as the only team of the trio to take the whole enchilada that year. But just to reach the Super Bowl, NBA Finals, and World Series within a year was rarefied air. The feat had only been accomplished once before, by Philadelphia in 1980 (Philly actually made it 4-for-4 that year, with the Flyers, Sixers, Phillies, and Eagles all reaching the last game of the season—only the Phillies won).

Bob Lobel remembers how much all the success that year drove competition in the city's newsrooms and television stations. More special features to put on the air, more travel to big events. And it all cost money. "We were constantly fighting battles with management to get to do the types of things we needed to do," he says. "Management wasn't happy with all of this because they had to spend money. We went places we wouldn't have been going to. The more competitive they got the more competitive we had to get. Did it pay off in the ratings? Probably, but it's hard to say."

Fighting for all those eyeballs meant getting creative. Lobel and his team liked to clip together pieces set to music, such as the Red Sox division-clinching celebration set to Lionel Ritchie's "Dancing on the Ceiling." As he recalls, "It was, how many ideas can we come up with?"

One of the prime people Lobel and other newsies dealt with was Jeff Twiss, the Celtics PR man who joined the organization in 1981 and took over public relations the next year. Juggling requests for interviews, promotional events, and tickets became a whole new ballgame in the 1980s, he says. "The whole front office had about 25 people at most, today it's more like a 100." Twiss wasn't running a big PR staff which NBA clubs have these days; it was one full-time assistant and, he says, one other person who would occasionally help out. What they did have were a lot of were young, unpaid interns. "We kept them busy," he says.

Other journalists and players who were there remember.

Lesley Visser, sportswriter with the *Boston Globe* and by then a part-timer with CBS Sports: "You were used to greatness from the Celtics, but the city hit the jackpot that year, hit the Mega Millions."

Dwight Evans, Red Sox right fielder: "Boston is just a great sports town. We're all spoiled now and this was the beginning of it."

Scott Wedman, Celtics forward: "You felt like royalty to a degree. The fans had a high basketball IQ and appreciated good basketball. You didn't want to be half stepping with those fans. I became a better player in Boston even though I wasn't playing the same minutes because of the fans and because of the talent around me."

Roger Clemens, Red Sox pitcher: "It was fun. Everything started to click for us. Once the city got behind us it really got rolling."

Craig James, Patriots running back: "I always felt much loved, much appreciated by the fans. Playing in New England required a tough mentality. I played hard. I think they appreciated that. I had a great relationship with the fans."

Bill Walton, Celtics center: "I had always loved going to Boston as a visiting player. I went there to play with Larry and for Larry, and for all the other guys. The fans just made you high. It was a privilege to play with the Boston Celtics."

John Molori was a Boston College communications major in the mid-1980s who would go on to cover Boston sports through *Patriots Football Weekly*, *Boston Baseball Magazine*, and several area newspapers. A product of Methuen, in the northern Boston suburbs, he was able to see the 1986 success in the context of what came before during his young fan boy days—all that promise followed by frustration by the Sox and Patriots.

"The first team I really got into was the 1976 Patriots. Ben Dreith's name is like Bucky Dent," Molori says of the NFL ref who flagged Patriots lineman Sugar Bear Hamilton for allegedly roughing Raiders' QB Ken Stabler to keep Oakland's winning drive going in the '76 playoffs. The phantom call still irks Patriot fans, even if they did get their revenge on the Raiders years later on the Tom Brady "tuck rule" call.

"It was the first time for me as a fan that a team other than the Celtics got there," Molori says. "The Patriots in the Super Bowl, the Red Sox in the World Series, it was exciting. I remember that my roommate and I went to this souvenir shop on Yawkey Way. I bought this t-shirt that said 'Year of the Champions' with all three teams. The Boston mentality was always waiting for the other shoe to drop, but that year it didn't happen." Well, it happened once the Patriots got to the Super Bowl and once the Red Sox got to the World Series, but you catch his drift.

But the really interesting thing about watching the Boston teams compete in 1986 was the way they did it on their terms. Back then it was easy to see the Red Sox, Celtics, and Patriots as franchises lagging behind the times, as not exactly "with it" in the world of modern sports. Outdated facilities, few free agents, little marketing. New England was a traditional place, and the people liked that in their sports teams too. The Green Monster and Parquet Floor were as much a part of local tradition as Bunker Hill. The Celtics were long known for keeping their head coaching hires "within the family," a practice that by definition lost them chances at better candidates who had come up in the business with other teams. Of course, there was no arguing with the Celtics' results most of the time, and they did bend the tradition at the start of the 1980s by bringing in former Cleveland coach Bill Fitch, who had an excellent four-year run highlighted by a 1981 title.

It was mainly the Sox who seemed to be in something of a bind with Fenway Park, a beloved landmark and great place to see a game but also a small box of a park that often produced one-dimensional teams playing a slugging, station-to-station game even as the sport moved into an era of speed and contact. The result was a team that was often good but rarely great. Everyone loved Fenway, but did it put the Sox at a competitive disadvantage?

You didn't hear a lot of loud music at the games—dead air during stoppages in play was just fine. At a time when ESPN and MTV were just entering their primes and driving the first true convergence of sports and entertainment across the country, Boston seemed happy to keep things as they were. No mascots or enthusiastic public address announcers trying to stir up artificial excitement. Red Auerbach's iron rule kept dance teams far away from Celtics games, a custom that wouldn't change until his death in 2006. In Boston they kept it real. The fans were knowledgeable and didn't need any added entertainment. The game *was* the entertainment.

The Showtime Lakers (and the Laker Girls), Super Bowl Shuffle Bears, and curtain-calling-after-home run-Mets weren't to be emulated, they were to be defeated. The Bostonian attitude was: Get out of here with that stuff. You can have the bells and whistles, we'll stick with tradition. You can have GQ Pat Riley and tough guy Mike Ditka, we're good with maybe the three blandest, quietest coaches in sports—Raymond Berry, K.C. Jones, and John McNamara.

The glory of '86 had a little bit of everything. A dominant champion, a couple of exciting and unexpected runs, and some season-ending disappointment.

Essentially all of the city's sports history rolled into one year. The cast of characters ran the gamut, from the familiar stars and franchise faces (Bird, Rice, Boggs, Hannah) to the injection of prime young talent coming into its own (Clemens, Hurst, James, Tippett, Fryar) and the veteran walking wounded making a final big run (Grogan, Buckner, Walton).

At the Watertown apartment, our secondhand sofa and chairs in front of the rabbit-eared box TV were the best seats in the house to watch it all unfold, from Bowman's fumble recovery to Dave Henderson's homer. From the Patriots nearly winning 14 straight heading into the Super Bowl to the Celtics' 50 wins in 51 tries at Boston Garden (and Hartford Civic Center) and right on through the Red Sox's run deep into October. Before Brady and Belichick, before Pedro, Big Papi, and Curt Schilling's bloody sock, before KG and Paul Pierce, there was 1986. If you liked sports, it was a glorious time to be in Boston.

PART I

August 1985 to January 1986

Chapter 1

Late Summer/Fall 1985

Raymond Berry's first training camp as the New England Patriots head coach figured to be interesting. At age 52 he had exactly eight games of professional head-coaching experience under his belt since being selected to take over the team the previous October after players and management alike had soured on taskmaster Ron Meyer, the head coach since 1982.

Berry was an improbable choice. It wasn't that he didn't command plenty of respect in football circles—Berry had been a Hall of Fame wide receiver with the Colts in the 1950s and '60s and then a longtime receivers coach with several NFL teams, including the Patriots from 1978 to 1981. But Berry had never coached above that level—never got a shot as an offensive coordinator—and hadn't been on a sideline at all for three years. To see him suddenly appear as an NFL head coach, particularly right in the middle of a season, was unorthodox to say the least. Owner Bill Sullivan had huddled with his son Patrick, who had been inserted as general manager the previous year, and with player personnel chief Dick Steinberg to discuss what the club needed in mid-1984 in the wake of a near-revolt over Meyer, the former college coach at SMU whose disciplinarian ways weren't selling real well with pro players. Meyer had also taken it upon himself to fire respected defensive coordinator Rod Rust, which was pretty much the final straw for management.

Recalls Patrick Sullivan: "There was a lot of discussion among my father, Dick, myself. We had a winning record (5–3) but I knew we weren't going anywhere. I said we should take a long shot here. We needed someone who the players have respect for, a spiritual guy. Given the circumstances, coming off a couple of years of Ron, he was the right guy. And Ray was local, still living in the Boston area."

The players did have a natural respect for a guy who they saw as one of their own. Veteran leaders Steve Grogan and John Hannah were quick to support the choice. Hannah in particular was key, according to Sullivan. "Hannah said he's someone the team can respect," Sullivan says. "If Hannah didn't buy in, we couldn't have done it."

Remembers Bob Lobel, covering the team for Channel 4: "All those veterans, Grogan, Hannah, Steve Nelson, they were all good guys, regular guys. And they all loved Raymond Berry, they thought he was the best."

It was Hannah, the seven-time All-Pro, who had ridiculed what he saw as Meyer's amateurish ways which included operating separate buses for the offensive and defensive players. Reporter Jim Donaldson, who covered the Patriots for the *Providence Journal* back then, remembers that "Meyer had the offensive and defensive buses, and Hannah would say, what is this, high school?" Donaldson's own observation of Meyer was that he wasn't a bad sort, but had a sneaky way about him. His success at SMU ultimately brought a huge cost—a virtual shutdown of the program a few years after Meyer left when improper payments to recruits were uncovered. "I liked Ron Meyer but he was a bit of a snake oil salesman," Donaldson says. "He won at SMU because he bought players. I once asked him how much he paid for Eric Dickerson and he said 'Well heck, Jim, I just paid him enough to put gas in his car.'"

It's funny how things can work out. Without Meyer's tenure, which the team longed to escape from after two and a half years, there would have likely been no Ray Berry. And Meyer's hiring in the first place came as a direct result of the nightmare of 1981, when the Pats finished 2–14 under Ron Erhardt, a guy with a solid track record (19–13 over the previous two years) who was known to have a keen offensive mind. Erhardt would later go on to earn a pair of Super Bowl rings as an offensive coordinator with the Giants.

But the fall of '81 brought his New England downfall, even if by dumb luck. It was undoubtedly a fluke season, one in which the Patriots competed almost every week but dropped eight games by a touchdown or less, five of them by a field goal or less. Punctuating the snake-bitten season was a late November loss in Buffalo on a last-play 40-yard Hail Mary that beat them 20–17. Even though it was easy to see that the '81 Patriots were not nearly as bad as their record, a 2–14 finish looks ugly in the standings and brings a lot of pressure to make a coaching change. Erhardt and his entire staff, which included Ray Berry, were shown the door in favor of Meyer, fresh off his 10–1 record and number five national ranking at SMU. Within a couple of years Meyer had won a few more games than he'd lost but he'd worn thin on everyone enough to compel the front office to bring in the anti-Meyer, Raymond Berry.

And so by October 1984, the players had their man. Or really, their men. One of Berry's first orders of business was to reinstate Rod Rust as defensive coordinator. A 57-year-old veteran who had been coaching football since the 1950s and coaching pro defenses since the mid-1970s, Rust was known for his ability to confuse offenses with different looks and to aggressively go for the ball to create turnovers. You'd be hard-pressed to find anyone who didn't like his methods. Even the offensive players noticed. "Rod Rust was a very intelligent guy, the players really respected him," says Steve Grogan. "The defense really played well. In '85 they really took off."

Berry, Rust, and Co. finished up the 1984 season by splitting their remaining eight games to finish 9–7, just missing the playoffs. To the fans, it was pretty much same-old, same-old. Once again the Patriots were okay, but they weren't knocking any doors down. For the eighth time in nine years, they had finished .500 or better, but without so much as a single playoff win to show for it. Why would 1985 be any different?

Maybe because, as much as the Patriots were mostly muddling along on the field during the early-to-mid-1980s, they were quietly doing a lot of good drafting. The 1985 roster would have 32 players drafted by the team between 1980 and 1985, including 17 starters. Hence, a roster filled with young veterans, most with some experience under their belts but still a few years shy of 30—the peak performance years.

Leading the draft operation was Dick Steinberg, a former college assistant coach and pro scout who had progressed to Director of Player Personnel and quickly gained a lot respect in the industry as a talent evaluator. His philosophy was one that has mostly become passé in today's NFL but really worked for him: Raw athletic ability trumped positional need. "Dick was always afraid a coach [who of course always wants to win as many games as possible as quickly as possible] would want to draft for need. But Dick took the best available athlete, football is a game of athletes," says Donaldson.

Steinberg's first draft in 1981 netted five players who would start for the 1985 team: offensive linemen Ron Wooten and Brian Holloway, tight end Lin Dawson, running back Tony Collins, and outside linebacker Don Blackmon, an athletic player with strength and speed who Steinberg nabbed in the fourth round out of Tulsa. "Great size, athletic, a real smart football guy, not an ounce of BS," says Sullivan of Blackmon, who would go on to a coaching career after his playing days.

Wooten, out of North Carolina, would ultimately develop into a full-time starter at right guard and anchor the right side of the line, making him a sixth-round steal. How did that happen? Credit the rumor mill, the industry chatter that was common at draft time. Some teams apparently thought that Wooten, a very bright guy and a chemistry major at North Carolina, had no more than lukewarm interest in the NFL. Recalls Sullivan: "Wooten should have been a third-round pick but there were whispers that he was going to medical school. He had no plans to go to medical school. Any draft would always have some of that cloak-and-dagger stuff."

Holloway would go on to three Pro Bowls during an eight-year career, the first five of which had him lining up next to Hannah on the left side of the line. One guy who wasn't a fan, though, was Donaldson. And he's pretty blunt about it. "Holloway was never as good as he thought he was. He was self-serving," he says. So why the three Pro Bowls? "He went to Stanford and he talked a good game. Holloway was pretty good, but those other guys on the line were better."

The Patriots also picked up punter Rich Camarillo out the University of Washington as an undrafted free agent in 1981, a key weapon who would go on to a long career as one of the league's best.

The 1981 debacle on the field yielded the Pats the prize of the first overall pick of the 1982 draft. They didn't exactly hit the jackpot. Their pick was Kenneth Sims, a 6'7", 270-pound defensive end from the University of Texas. The choice didn't surprise many people. Sims was a two-time All-American thought to have the size and ability to dominate the pro game. He never got there as he dealt with periodic injuries that limited him to 74 NFL games in eight seasons. It's not quite fair to call Sims a bust, because he turned out to be a useful player who would wind up having his best season for the 1985 Super Bowl squad. But he never reached the heights that a club envisions for an overall top pick. He certainly wasn't the first or last. Even with all the preparation in the world the draft never stops showing you that it's an inexact science.

Steinberg and his staff may not have nailed the top pick, but they still nailed the 1982 draft. Exactly 40 picks after Sims, they selected a guy who turned out to be so good that he could have been the top pick himself: outside line-backer Andre Tippett out of the University of Iowa. At 6'3" and 240 pounds and seemingly without an ounce of body fat, Tippett was a black belt in karate and a picture of strength, speed, and balance. Much like Don Blackmon on the other side, only better. With Tippett and Blackmon, the defense was now armed with quick outside linebackers on both sides who could chase down runners trying to turn the corner and who could get to the quarterback.

Anyone watching Andre Tippett play in the mid-80s would be hard-pressed to say he wasn't the equal of Lawrence Taylor, or at least very close. Before he was done, Tippett would sack the quarterback a hundred times in his 11 seasons, including 16.5 times in 1985 when he finished half a sack behind Chicago's Richard Dent for the league lead. "A truly scary character," says Donaldson. "He could use that speed and weight to his advantage through martial arts. If a tackle was left by himself Tippett would just blow by him. In effect he would tie up three guys."

In the fifth round the Patriots plucked Fred Marion, an All-American safety out of Miami who was thought to be a tick too slow to go higher. But Marion would go on to be the starter at free safety for nearly all of his 10 years in New England and pick off 29 passes, seven of them in his 1985 Pro Bowl season. Good instincts and anticipation of where receivers were headed mostly made up for his lack of blazing speed. "Very cerebral," Donaldson calls him.

In the aftermath of the 1982 draft Steinberg picked up an unpolished gem when he signed undrafted nose tackle Dennis Owens out of North Carolina State. The longshot Owens made the squad out of camp and wound up starting 44 games on the defensive line during a five-year run. He wasn't a star, but he clogged the middle against the run and picked up 11.5 sacks during his career. Your basic solid interior lineman. "Smart and aggressive and very coachable," Sullivan says of Owens. "Sometimes the undrafted guys are more coachable."

More solid talent arrived in 1983. The third round brought offensive tackle Steve Moore from Tennessee State, who would become a starter. In the 10th round Steinberg got Nebraska nose tackle Toby Williams, who played at defensive end after turning pro and had a big 1984 season before missing most of '85 with injuries. And two rounds earlier the Pats had found cornerback Ronnie Lippett out of the University of Miami. Lippett had played in the same college defensive backfield with Marion where they combined to intercept 20 passes across 1980 and '81 as part of the group that first led the Hurricanes' rise to dominance in the early '80s. "A tough guy and a perfect cover guy" is how Sullivan describes Lippett, who not only made the club as an eighth-round pick but started all 16 games as a rookie when he stepped in for All-Pro Mike Haynes, a 1983 contract holdout who was ultimately traded to the Raiders. Lippett would wind up playing in 122 of a possible 144 games during a nine-year career, leading the NFL in interceptions in 1986.

As a little bonus, Lippett also brought an intangible benefit: extra desire to beat Don Shula and the Dolphins. Once when he was in college, Lippett and a few of his Miami Hurricane teammates went to watch a Dolphins practice only to have Shula object and boot them all out. His resentment proved to be a pretty good motivator: Lippett would go on to intercept Dan Marino seven times during his career.

Above all else of course, the 1983 draft was most notable as the year of the quarterback. The Patriots were one of six teams, all in the AFC, to grab a QB in the first round. Picking one spot after the Buffalo Bills took Jim Kelly at No. 14 (and with John Elway and Todd Blackledge also off the board but Dan Marino and Ken O'Brien still on it), the Pats drafted Tony Eason, a talented passer who had just set a school record by throwing for more than 3,600 yards during his senior year at the University of Illinois. Eason's big senior season earned him eighth place in the 1982 Heisman Trophy balloting, including five first-place votes.

Eason would sit behind Steve Grogan for most of his rookie year, but the following couple of seasons would bring some competition and debate over the tough, beloved veteran and the promising, smooth-throwing youngster. There were a few occasions during 1984 and 1985 when one would replace the other as the starter. Sometimes it was a coaching decision, sometimes it was an injury that forced a coach's hand and therefore brought no real controversy. The best part was that the two men seemed to get along just fine, with Grogan willing to work with Eason to help bring him along. So despite the natural competition, the Patriots never seemed to get bogged down in enough of a "quarterback controversy" to derail a Super Bowl run.

As much as the club padded its talent base pretty well in those early '80s drafts, there was only one player—Andre Tippett—who truly brought superstar talent, a weapon at the next level who could change the course of a game. That changed in 1984 when Steinberg and the front office decided that they had built enough depth to give up multiple picks, and a nice wad of cash, to land some big guns. Welcome to the New England Patriots offense, Irving Fryar and Craig James.

The club rolled the dice by dealing multiple picks in a trade with Tampa Bay to get the number one overall pick which they used to take Fryar, the electric wide receiver/punt returner from the University of Nebraska. He had been a huge part of the 1983 Cornhusker squad with Mike Rozier and Turner Gill, one that many were calling the greatest college team ever until they were upset 31–30 by Miami in the Orange Bowl to lose the national title. Fryar was an athletic marvel who caught passes (40 receptions that year including eight touchdowns), ran the ball on reverses a couple of times a game (23 carries for over 300 yards and two more TDs), and blocked not only willingly but enthusiastically for his Heisman Trophy–winning tailback, Rozier. Talk about best available athlete. "Fryar graded off the board, he had size, speed, and he didn't mind contact," says Donaldson. "He was fast *and* he liked to hit people." The same really couldn't be said for the Patriots' other speedy receiver, Stanley Morgan, still a major deep threat at age 30 but a guy who apparently preferred to run and catch and leave the tough contact to others. "Once during Ron Meyer's tenure he was looking kind of unhappy in the locker room, glancing at Meyer who was across the room talking to someone," remembers Donaldson. "I asked him if something was wrong and he says 'Mother f— wants me to block.' Irving *loved* to block."

Fryar instantly became the most dangerous punt returner the Patriots ever had, averaging almost 10 yards a return as a rookie and then a league-leading 14 yards per return in his 1985 sophomore season, including two long touchdowns.

Meantime the team took advantage of an opportunity to get Craig James, an uber-talented tailback from SMU who had signed with the Washington Federals of the USFL the previous year. The Pats had used a seventh-round pick to take James in 1983 in order to retain his NFL rights should things not work out in the shaky upstart league. And that's just what happened. After a decent rookie year in 1983, James suffered a knee injury in the spring of '84 as the team and the league struggled financially. James was released from his contract, almost out of necessity, in time to sign with the Pats for the 1984 season, reuniting him with coach Ron Meyer for his first half-season.

Sullivan recalls the big 1984 talent upgrade: "We took an aggressive approach acquiring players. We traded up to get Irving Fryar. Then getting Craig James was a bit complicated. The Washington owners wanted out of that contract. But one thing we had to do to sign him was remove all these discipline clauses. I told our lawyer that Craig could kill the president and still get paid."

The 1985 draft became the next reminder of the uncertainty factor. The Pats' first pick, center Trevor Matich out of Brigham Young, never made much of an impact. Their second-round pick, defensive end Garin Veris out of Stanford, certainly did. Getting playing time right away as a pass rushing specialist and then taking on every-down status late in the season after an injury to Sims, Veris's quickness on the D-line bought him 10 sacks during his rookie 1985 season, second on the club to Tippett.

All the young talent that Steinberg built up in the 1980s wasn't exactly thrown to the wolves or expected to carry the team by themselves. The Pats still had a core of veterans that gave the club that much-needed center of gravity, a group that could help the young players and still had enough left physically to contribute plenty themselves: on the offensive side, Grogan, Hannah, Morgan and center Pete Brock; on defense, lineman Julius Adams, inside linebackers Steve Nelson and Larry McGrew, strong safety Roland James, and cornerback Raymond Clayborn.

Most were products of a period of the 1970s when Steinberg was a scout for the club under general manager Bucko Kilroy, who had first devised the athletic rating system that Steinberg would later employ. "Dick was a bright guy, and he could really find talent. But Dick's mentor was Bucko Kilroy. I've always maintained that the best Patriots teams were 1976, '77 and '78," says Sullivan of the string of Kilroy clubs that went 31–13 over those three years but suffered the frustration of a narrow playoff miss in 1977 and early exits in '76 and '78.

Clayborn, from Texas, would go on to a career as one of the NFL's best cover corners, still going strong enough in the mid-80s to cover the likes of Miami's Mark Duper and Mark Clayton and the Jets' Wesley Walker in the big division battles. Nelson was a midwestern guy out of North Dakota State who was simply a tackle machine and the defensive glue at inside linebacker. Nelson got up on ball carriers enough to make a hundred or more tackles in 9 of his 14 seasons. In 1978, the first year that the NFL bumped its schedule to 16 games from 14, Nelson exceeded *two hundred* tackles and intercepted five passes.

And then there was John Hannah, so dominant on the offensive line that almost no one would say he didn't stand as the greatest Patriot ever until Tom

Brady came along. Nicknamed "Hog," Hannah was a stud out of Canton, Georgia, who played for Bear Bryant at Alabama in the early 1970s before New England took him with the fourth overall pick in the 1973 draft. One of his teammates on the 1971 Bama squad was future Red Sox third baseman Butch Hobson, a backup quarterback for the team that went 11–0 but missed out on a national title by getting blitzed 38–6 in the Orange Bowl by Nebraska. Hannah was a two-time All-American at Alabama.

He hailed from a big family football tree. Hannah's father Herb had also played at Alabama and then a season with the New York Giants, and his younger brother Charley followed him to Alabama before playing 12 years in the NFL with the Buccaneers and Raiders. His brother David also played for the Tide, winning a national championship in 1978.

Hannah was always a big fan favorite, pretty unusual for an offensive lineman. He was listed as 6'2", 265, which even for that era was not huge. But the combination of strength and agility made him a terror on the line, whether hitting head-on or getting the legs moving as he pulled in front of his running back. And there was the durability resulting in this astounding stat: Hannah missed five games due to injury in his entire 13-year career.

"I never met a more intense athlete, he would actually get upset when opponents wouldn't confront him," says Donaldson. He recalled watching Hannah hitting the blocking sled in training camp one year, with a crowd of fans looking on from a safe distance behind a fence. "He just kept going, hitting the sled harder and harder. You saw the crowd starting to get nervous and then back off, even though they were behind the fence," he says with a laugh. Basically, watching John Hannah hitting the sled at camp from behind the fence was like watching a tiger roar at the zoo from outside the pen. You pretty much know you're safe, yet you're still not quite sure.

When *The Sporting News* ranked its hundred greatest NFL players of all time in 1999, Hannah was rated the second-highest offensive lineman after Anthony Munoz and the 20th greatest player overall.

And so the Pats got set to open the 1985 season with a pretty good blend of youth and experience. The question still to be answered following the 4–4 run to finish out 1984 was whether Berry was indeed the guy to make it come together. The players and the front office liked his chances mainly for two reasons: (1) his straightforward approach and (2) his attention to detail. Defensive players in particular were suddenly being coached on going for the ball on tackles to create turnovers. Practices typically began with drills on the proper way to fall on the ball to recover fumbles. Says Garin Veris: "His belief was that if you do the small things, or things that seem small, big things will happen." Everyone knew that Berry's detail-oriented approach as a player had worked. His countless hours spent perfecting his pass routes had earned him a bust in the Hall of Fame ("as a player he literally ironed his own uniform" says Donaldson). So why not assume his approach will work until proven otherwise?

"You could see people coming together. Raymond said if we're not pulling together, we aren't going anywhere. You could see the players buying in," says Sullivan. As much as players hear that kind of rhetoric all the time and might sometimes be inclined to dismiss it as corny, the feeling was that Berry oozed a sincerity that made them actually feel it.

The Patriots' biggest strength, the defense, was not only talented but blessed with good health during the 1985 season. Every defensive starter played in at least 13 games. All four of the regular defensive backs—Marion, Roland James, Clayborn, and Lippett—started all 16. Linebacker Johnny Rembert and defensive back Rod McSwain, both from Clemson, added the key depth.

With Berry and Rust at the controls all season for the first time, the Pats would finish sixth in NFL in fewest points allowed in 1985 (290) after finishing 18th (352) the previous year. And pretty much the same with turnovers: seventh in the league in turnover ratio in 1985 after ranking 18th in 1984. With a pass rush led by Tippett, Blackmon, and Veris, the defense would average just over three sacks per game and outsack their opponents 51–39.

The ball control offense wouldn't change much from 1984 aside from Craig James increasing his workload as the clear featured back. Tony Collins, a former 1,000-yard rusher, would be utilized more as a receiver out of the backfield, his 52 catches leading the club by a wide margin. The offensive depth came from receivers Cedric Jones and Stephen Starring and running backs Robert Weathers and Mosi Tatupu, a short yardage power runner who was also a demon on special teams. Big Derrick Ramsey, acquired from the Raiders the previous year, would spell Lin Dawson at tight end.

And the biggest decision of all—it would be Tony Eason at quarterback to open the season. Steve Grogan and his supporters—and he had many—were not particularly happy about it, but Eason had done well after stepping in for Grogan during the early part of the '84 season, completing 60% of his passes with 23 touchdowns the rest of the way. His downside was taking a lot of sacks, but as a first-round investment with a lot of perceived upside, the brain trust seemed to be intent on giving Eason every chance to capture the job as he entered his third season. An NFL season is a tough grind, though. Before this one was over, the Patriots would need both of their QBs.

***

On Thursday night, August 29, 1985, as the Patriots prepared to fly to the West Coast for their final preseason games against the Los Angeles Rams (they'd lose 14–13), Boston Red Sox left-hander Bruce Hurst took the mound on a muggy night in Cleveland. Roughly six thousand fans were scattered throughout Municipal Stadium to take in the play-out-the-string matchup between the fifth-place Red Sox and seventh (and last)-place Indians. The season was shaping up as a big disappointment in Boston, a promising first half wiped out by a brutal August slump. But for Hurst it was just the opposite; during the club's early hot streak he was little help, now during the tough dog days he was a rare bright spot. In his last outing against the Twins at Fenway Park, the 27-year-old had tossed nine innings of five-hit ball in a tough 1–0 loss. On this night against Cleveland, Hurst allowed a first inning base runner but then struck out middle-of-the-order threats Julio Franco and Andre Thornton to leave him stranded. After the Sox scored a run in the top of the second, Hurst gave up a base hit to Pat Tabler and then a homer to Cleveland's impressive young power hitter Brook Jacoby in the bottom half that gave the Indians a 2–1 lead. Carmelo Castillo followed with a double, but Hurst got the next two outs to end the inning.

The next Indians hit came when Thornton led off the bottom of the ninth with a single, by which time the Red Sox had put 17 runs on the board. Hurst finished with a six-hitter and 11 strikeouts in the 17–2 blowout, his seventh win in his last 10 decisions and sixth complete game in his last 12 starts. In his next outing in Texas, Hurst would strike out 10 pitching into the eighth inning and win again.

Hurst's second-half roll was a startling contrast with his early struggles when opponents were teeing off on his mostly two-pitch arsenal (fastball, curve) as he hesitated to get aggressive against right-handed hitters. In mid-June with his ERA over 6.00 he was demoted to the bullpen and forced to face the boo birds whenever he made an appearance. On Sunday, June 16, at Fenway with the Sox going for a four-game sweep over Toronto, Roger Clemens's troublesome right shoulder had flared up in the sixth inning, prompting manager John McNamara to replace him with Hurst (Clemens would miss most of the second half). The boos rained down over the slumping Hurst, the word "bum" tossed out by more than a few people. It only got worse as he gave up three hits and three runs as the Jays took a 5–3 lead. The Red Sox would rally late for an exciting 7–6 win to get the sweep, but Hurst couldn't have been feeling very good.

He'd always had his share of ups and downs since debuting with the Red Sox in 1980 and essentially becoming a regular starter in 1983. He was proving to be durable, making his 30-odd starts and pitching his 200-plus innings each year. When he was putting the fastball and curve where he wanted to, Hurst could be one of the toughest lefties in the league. But he couldn't do that in every game, and throughout the season he was giving up a lot of hits—well over 200 each year from 1983 to 1985.

Hurst's catcher Rich Gedman explained that expanding the repertoire, which Hurst finally did with the help of pitching coach Bill Fischer, was the key to sealing the deal as a consistent pitcher.

"He had a good fastball that he could locate and a really good curve but he needed that third pitch," says Gedman. "He developed not really a forkball [as some described it], but a little split-change. It allowed him to really get in on right-handed hitters which he hadn't been comfortable with. I always looked at Bruce as a very good pitcher; it was just a matter of time before he started executing consistently." When a left-hander pitching in the shadow of Fenway's Green Monster suddenly has a pitch he's comfortable throwing inside to righty hitters, his overall confidence tends to rise. "He got more aggressive, started attacking the zone," says Steve Krasner, the Red Sox beat man at the *Providence Journal*.

HURST'S TALE OF TWO SEASONS IN 1985:

Through June 23: 2–7, 6.66 ERA

After June 23: 9–6, 3.51 ERA

He would make it into at least the seventh inning in 19 of his last 20 starts in 1985, with seven complete games. His 189 strikeouts ranked fourth in the American League.

Bruce Hurst's turnaround wasn't enough to save the 1985 Red Sox from sinking out of the race as the season went along. Things had been exciting to start under new manager John McNamara, a veteran of four previous major league managing jobs in Oakland, San Diego, Cincinnati, and California. The Sox had opened the season with a three-game sweep of the Yankees at Fenway. Then after plodding along for the next month or so, they took off on a scorching run from late May into June, winning 17 of 19 including the four-game sweep of first-place Toronto. They trailed by just 2½ in the American League East.

But it didn't last. They gave up some ground over the next month and a half and then watched the bottom fall out when they lost 15 of 17 in August, including seven of seven to the Yankees. By the time September rolled around, the Sox were 60–68 and playing out the string. They did have a strong final month to finish 81–81, but a .500 season was nothing to sing about. To the fans it was just another tease, a promising start followed by "same old Sox." The season's key lowlights:

- Clemens, the young burgeoning ace, got hurt and made only 15 starts.
- Jim Rice was productive but didn't have one of his big years.

- Outfielder Tony Armas dealt with some injuries and saw his homer total drop from 43 to 23.
- Second baseman Marty Barrett disappointed in his second full season, his average dropping from .303 to .266.
- Designated hitter Mike Easler was subpar, hitting .262 with a 98 OPS-plus (below 100 league average).
- The shortstop tandem of Jackie Guitierrez and Glenn Hoffman was mostly awful on both sides of the ball.
- The bullpen was mediocre at best aside from solid right-hander Bob Stanley (87 innings, 2.87 ERA).

On the plus side:

- Wade Boggs tore the cover off the ball as usual.
- The underrated Dwight Evans had another strong year.
- Gedman did well in his second season as the full-time starting catcher.
- Flamboyant right-hander Dennis "Oil Can" Boyd had a very good year on the mound in his second full season in the rotation; a workhorse who tossed 272 innings with 15 wins.

Also on the plus side, of course, was the turnaround of Bruce Hurst. No one was particularly looking at his improvement as a key piece of a possible upcoming championship, because no one was thinking about the Sox in those terms just yet. The club's regression during the first half of the 1980s had been a big letdown from the good teams of the mid-to-late 70s that had contended strongly a few times even if they'd come up short of a title. The team finished no better than third between 1980 and 1985, and finished fifth three times. The Red Sox were a lot like the Patriots, running in place for the past half-dozen years, winning a few more games than they were losing but not scaring anyone.

The worst part was that the Red Sox didn't have that look of a team on the rise. It's one thing to finish .500 with a young club that figures to get better. But at the close of the 1985 season, five of the seven most productive players in Boston's lineup—Rice, Evans, Easler, Armas, and first baseman Bill Buckner—were 31 or older. Clemens, their 23-year-old pitching phenom, was facing arthroscopic surgery for his sore shoulder. It was becoming a familiar look: a slow team of veteran hitters that could be fun to watch when they got the bats going at Fenway but without the athleticism and pitching depth to hang with the top teams all season. For most people, 1986 could wait. It was football season.

***

September wasn't as good a month for the Patriots as it was for the Red Sox. Fortunately for the Pats they weren't playing out the string of a humdrum season, they were just getting warmed up. The most encouraging part was that the A-list talent was very much on display during the early season, making the big plays they were brought in to make as the club split its first four games. Blackmon and Tippett sacked Green Bay quarterback Lynn Dickey three times apiece in a season opening win, one of Blackmon's coming in the end zone for a safety. Blackmon added another sack the following week in a loss at Chicago (a game with shades of things to come with the Bears' stifling defense having its way all afternoon), and Tippett provided a defensive touchdown with a 25-yard scoop-and-run fumble recovery in a home loss to the Raiders.

Meantime Fryar showcased his explosiveness with a 40-yard TD reception in the Raider game one week after returning a punt 85 yards for the decisive touchdown in a 17–14 win over the Buffalo Bills.

And Craig James was doing a little bit of everything, running for a 65-yard touchdown to put away the Green Bay game, breaking a 90-yard catch-and-run touchdown on a short pass from Eason for the team's only score in the 20–7 loss to Chicago, and tossing a five-yard TD to Tony Collins on an option pass against the Bills. With each passing week he was looking like that elite back the team had signed him to be.

Craig James was a Texas boy who grew up in the Houston area where he starred in football and baseball at Stratford High School, about six miles down the road from Spring Woods High School where Roger Clemens was working his way up to the Texas Longhorns and beyond. James says he once faced Clemens in an advanced league for high school–aged players. So how did that go? "I hit a foul home run off him that went about a mile and then struck out," he remembers.

Clemens doesn't recall that encounter, but as a former defensive end at Spring Woods he does have some tough memories of trying to stop James on the football field. "He was a man amongst boys out there, trying to tackle him was no fun."

James turned down a contract offer from the Yankee organization to pursue a football scholarship at SMU just as that program was being built into a power by Ron Meyer.[1] He wound up in a pretty unusual situation in which he split time at tailback with future Hall of Famer Eric Dickerson as part of the "Pony Express" Mustang backfield of the early 1980s. The coaching staff alternated Dickerson and James by series—not the type of thing you would see very often. As much as it could be a strange feeling to be one of the best backs in the country and still just the second best on your own team, James believes the system worked well, not only for the Mustangs but for the way it helped keep both backs healthy.

"It allowed us to be fresher entering the NFL," says James. "Eric and I had grown up 30 minutes apart but we didn't know each other. You had to work hard every Monday to Thursday to earn the playing time. They monitored each drive. He would wind up averaging about 19 carries and I would average about 17."

The job share may have cost Dickerson the Heisman Trophy in 1982, when he ran for over 1,600 yards and 17 touchdowns and finished third in the voting behind Hershel Walker and John Elway. But the fact that the coaches found a way to give James significant playing time despite Dickerson's presence showed what they thought of his ability. He wound up complementing Dickerson with over 900 yards and almost five yards a carry in 1982.

After his short stint in the USFL, James joined the Patriots at the beginning of the 1984 season. But his reunion with Meyer, his first college coach, didn't go as smoothly as he'd hoped. James found himself back in a job share all over again, one that he didn't think he deserved this time. Incumbent Tony Collins was a solid pro, but he wasn't Eric Dickerson. "Tony Collins was the back but I had beaten him out, everybody knew it. I would have had 1,800 yards," he says. "Ron was a good coach, he knew talent, but playing me more would have looked like he was favoring his college player."

But that all ended after Meyer was let go at midseason. "Raymond Berry told me before his first game, 'you're starting,'" James says.

The result over the next season and a half was the best pure runner the Patriots probably ever had. At a solid 6 feet and 215 pounds, James was a cutback runner who had good speed but just as importantly had that feel for the flow of the play—an instinctive runner who could change speeds, slowing down to wait for a hole to develop and then accelerating. He'd wind up with 1,227 yards on the ground in 1985, exactly seven fewer than Dickerson had with the Rams (on 29 fewer carries). And he was a legitimate dual threat—27 catches out of the backfield for another 360 yards. Being the featured runner on a running team was a nice gig, and James particularly remembers the way the backs and the offensive linemen constantly pushed each other.

"Unless you're Barry Sanders you need an offensive line. If we didn't run hard behind them, they would let us know; if they missed blocks, we would let them know."

As they headed to Cleveland for Week Five, the Patriots had plenty of reason to believe they were headed in the right direction despite the ordinary 2–2 start. A road loss in Chicago against a top defense wasn't a surprise. The 35–20 loss to the Raiders at Foxborough was the frustrating one. The defense had turned in a big effort—Los Angeles punted 10 times—but a few key mistakes led to three defensive touchdowns by the Raiders on a pair of pick-six interception returns and a fumble recovery in the end zone. Disappointing, but nothing that a few adjustments and a bit more luck couldn't cure.

Of course an inconsistent start is only acceptable for so long before some frustration starts to set in, before you leave the field angry and vowing to pick it up a notch. That's what happened to the Patriots in Cleveland against a pretty ordinary Browns team they expected to beat. In a close but sloppy game that featured eight turnovers (five by Cleveland), the Pats defense had its hands full all day with the Browns' first-year running back Kevin Mack, a bruiser out of Clemson who had spent a year in the USFL and who was already on his way to becoming one of the NFL's best backs. With Mack running for 115 yards on 20 carries and catching 5 passes for another 85 yards, Cleveland churned out 28 first downs and 447 total yards, the most yardage the Patriot defense would allow all season.

The game was tight all the way. The Browns led 14–13 at halftime, thanks in part to some razzle dazzle when receiver Brian Brennan, the former Boston College Eagle two years removed from catching passes from Doug Flutie, took a swing pass behind the line of scrimmage from quarterback Gary Danielson and tossed a 33-yard strike to tight end Ozzie Newsome for a second-quarter touchdown.

With the Pats trailing 17–13 in the third quarter, Eason, who threw for over 300 yards on the day, hit Stanley Morgan for a 22-yard touchdown and a 20–17 lead. Danielson, meanwhile, had been forced from the game with a bum shoulder after he'd been intercepted by Raymond Clayborn and was forced to make the tackle after Clayborn had returned the pick 38 yards. Danielson's third-quarter injury brought the NFL debut of Bernie Kosar, the Browns' quarterback of the future who the team had grabbed with a supplemental pick in the 1985 draft following Kosar's decision to leave the University of Miami with two years of eligibility remaining.

Kosar was intercepted once by Fred Marion but otherwise did okay, completing 9-of-15 for 104 yards. Most importantly, he coolly engineered the fourth-quarter drive that culminated in Mack's 10-yard TD run for a 24–20 lead. The game ended in dramatic fashion when the Browns defense stuffed the Patriots on a goal line stand to pull out the win.

The players in red were not happy.

"Clayborn had a confrontation with [Browns coach] Marty Schottenheimer at the end of the game," says Garin Veris, though he doesn't recall exactly how the argument started. "They were about to go at it on the field. There was a little scrum."

But the real show took place a few minutes later inside the New England locker room starring Andre Tippett as the leading man. Chairs as flying objects were reportedly involved. "We got to the locker room and everyone was really upset. Tippett destroyed that locker room. Later we had a meeting and then got started on a roll," Veris says.

Craig James remembers: "We knew we were good. There was a fear of a missed opportunity. We locked in more; we had a feeling we weren't going to miss our chance."

And from Steve Grogan: "Andre Tippett went berserk after the Cleveland game. He just lit up the defense." Jim Donaldson, covering the game for the *Providence Journal*, concurs with the others but also remembers this little nugget from Tippett: "We're too good for this s--."

Apparently Tippett got his point across. It would be seven weeks before the Patriot defense would give up 24 or more points again.

A nice gift came their way the following week when offensively challenged Buffalo Bills came to Foxborough. The 0–5 Bills were the league's lowest scoring team—quarterbacks Vince Ferragamo and Bruce Mathison would combine to throw nine touchdown passes for the entire season against 31 interceptions. Coach Kay Stephenson had just been sacked the previous week and replaced by defensive coordinator Hank Bullough. Predictably, the New England defense shut things down all day, sacking Ferragamo four times, intercepting him twice, and forcing a pair of fumbles while allowing just 162 total yards.

But the most significant development of the Buffalo game happened in the second quarter, when Tony Eason took a hard sack and went out with a separated left shoulder. Even though it was his nonthrowing shoulder, Eason would be lost for a few weeks. Steve Grogan, who hadn't started a game in a year, was back in there. The Patriots were in a tough game because for all of the Bills offensive woes, their own offense wasn't doing much better. Trailing 3–0 at halftime, Grogan engineered a third-quarter drive that culminated with an 18-yard touchdown pass to Fryar for a 7–3 lead. They added one more score in the fourth quarter when Clayborn picked off Ferragamo and returned it 27 yards for a TD. Luckily that's all they would need as the Bills rarely threatened. The good part was that the game ultimately was not as close as the 14–3 final score; the Pats outgained the Bills by more than a two-to-one margin with Grogan connecting on 15-of-19 passes for 282 yards. So his ability to move the team was there even as they came up short of the end zone more times than they'd have liked.

For Grogan, being back in the saddle was rejuvenating. Still just 32, he'd been starting to think that people were seeing him as an old man while the team seemed committed to the transition to Eason, who was clearly the better pure passer if not the assertive leader and all-around threat Grogan was. It was early in the previous season that Eason had replaced a struggling Grogan in the first half of a game against Seattle with the Patriots trailing 23–0. Eason led a furious comeback to a 38–23 victory, and the job was his for the rest of 1984 and into 1985. Grogan wasn't happy, but he didn't make waves.

"It bothered me but I had a contract with the Patriots and I was there to help however I could," he says now. "I like Tony Eason and I wanted to help him as much as I could and as much as the team would let me."

Grogan had arrived in New England in 1975 as a fifth-round pick out of Kansas State, a Texas native with a fearless style and a rare ability as a threat both running and throwing. Grogan started seven games and appeared in six others as a rookie as he took playing time from Jim Plunkett, the former Heisman Trophy winner and number one overall draft pick who was still struggling with inconsistency and lack of protection in his fifth season. When the Pats traded Plunkett to San Francisco after the season, Grogan had the job.

As the starter for the next four years, he did well as a dual threat, leading the league with 28 TD passes in 1979 and rushing for over 300 yards each season including a quarterback record 539 yards in 1978. The downside: He threw more than 20 interceptions each year. Some injuries by the early 1980s had him splitting time with Matt Cavanaugh, a second rounder out of the University of Pittsburgh who never broke through as a full-time NFL starter but gave the Pats a hedge against the injury risks taken on by the full throttle Grogan. Then came the 1983 drafting of Eason, soon to be groomed as Grogan's successor. For most of the fans, though, there was no rush. They loved Grogan, and the mild-mannered rookie whose college profile didn't match those of Dan Marino or John Elway was going to have a tough time swaying them.

Remembers Bob Lobel: "The fans wanted no part of Tony Eason." And from Lesley Visser: "I always thought that Tony Eason suffered from what he was not," referring to the inevitable comparisons to Marino, Elway, and Jim Kelly from the same draft, which didn't do much for his confidence.

Mention Steve Grogan's name to anyone who saw him play and the word that always jumps out is "tough." Fan Richard Chaiton of Medway, west of Boston, recalls: "I remember not liking Tony Eason; he wasn't a tough quarterback. Grogan was tough, I always liked him." John Molori, just as he was transitioning from fan to reporter, says: "I always loved Grogan for his toughness, Eason wasn't that tough. Grogan told me that one time when he was in the locker room taking off all the padding he wore that Eason came over and asked him why he played so hard—didn't he want to be able to play golf, etc.?" Another point Molori makes, though, does give some credence to the perception of Grogan as an old 32 in 1985. "Grogan was fearless, he could really run with the ball. At 32 he seemed like 38 because of all the hits."

The players generally keep things diplomatic. Craig James: "Some of the veterans like Hannah may have talked about it more, but they both wanted to win and we all had a job to do." Garin Veris: "Grogan by that point was kind of Mr. Patriot. Tony hadn't been there as long. Hey, we were winning. Steve, when he wasn't playing, was like a starting QB on the sidelines." Veris then adds the inevitable kicker: "Steve was the toughest player I ever played with."

Jim Donaldson, though, believes that defining Grogan vs. Eason as hard-nosed Texan vs. laid-back California dude, as tough guy vs. wimp, is to oversimplify things way too much. "Hannah said after the Super Bowl that Tony should have played with a skirt on [but] Tony got a bad rap. If Tony looked downfield and didn't see anyone open, he would take the sack. Grogan would hang in there until the last second and let a pass go even if no one was open." In other words, Grogan's fearlessness had a downside: a tendency to get a bit helter-skelter, which led to turnovers. Concludes Donaldson: "Grogan was tough. If you were casting a Western he would be the sheriff. Tony was more like, hey, I like football but it's not everything."

Eason's injury meant there wouldn't be any controversy over Grogan's upcoming start at home in a big division game against the Jets. But there would be one big change in Berry's approach. The 11-year veteran would take charge of the play calling in the huddle, which the younger Eason wasn't permitted to do. "A key to my success was that Raymond Berry had played with Johnny Unitas [when he was a veteran QB calling the shots]. He said, 'I think our best chance is for you to call your own plays.'"

Grogan's first start against the Jets in Foxborough on October 20 didn't exactly kick-start the offense, at least not for most of the game. The Pats found themselves in a defensive struggle, a 6–6 game into the fourth quarter, all on field goals. The defense sacked Jets QB Ken O'Brien five times, three of them by Tippett, and forced two fumbles. Grogan didn't do much statistically, completing just 11-of-32 for 171 yards with a pair of sacks. But there were the key plays in the fourth quarter as the pace picked up. His 36-yard touchdown strike to Fryar put New England ahead 13–6. After the Jets drove for a touchdown to tie the score, Grogan engineered another drive and finished the job himself with a three-yard bootleg to the left for the go-ahead touchdown.

O'Brien led the Jets down the field one last time before the New England defense sealed the win deep in their own territory in the closing seconds. With the crowd imploring the home defense as the Jets knocked on the door, strong safety Roland James popped Jets fullback Tony Paige after a catch inside the five-yard line to knock the ball loose. Garin Veris fell on the fumble to end the Jets' final drive. The Patriots had a big divisional win, 20–13.

It made for a big day for Veris, a 22-year-old fresh out of Stanford who had never so much as visited the East Coast before his first Patriot training camp. The game-saving recovery in which he tilted his body as he went down so as to position himself between the ball and the nearest opponent was at least partly a product of Berry's hammering away at the details right down to the proper way to recover fumbles. Veris didn't know it, but he was about to become the star of the team film room. "Coach Berry kept showing it on film and talking about it. He'd say 'Here's our fumble drill,'" Veris says.

He's quick to credit coaches and veterans for fast-tracking his path to a bigger role with the defense as he reached the midpoint of his rookie season. "I had a decent training camp, going against Hannah, Brock, Holloway, which really helped me in my pass rush and then helped me become an every-down player. And on the line Julius Adams was my mentor; he taught me to get off the snap quickly. I also learned from [D-Line coach] Ed Khayat, who was an excellent coach. He taught me to be quick to the ball."

The best part for Veris and others on the defensive unit was carrying out Rod Rust's philosophy, which called for a lot of moving pieces and relied on having players who were athletic enough to run to the ball quickly. Not the easiest system to pick up, but a lot of fun once it started clicking. Veris explains: "We did a thing called 'run a game' where people on the line moved a lot. For example, the nose tackle would hit the center then go around to the end and the defensive end came to the middle. The offense didn't know where we were going. It really messes with the mind. It made it hard for the offense to know who to hit."

With seven takeaways and just one touchdown allowed over the previous two games, the defensive scheme seemed to be coming together. The Patriots, now 4–3, would get a relative breather in Tampa Bay the following week before returning home for another big AFC East battle against the Dolphins.

***

On October 25, 1985, Bill Walton took his cue from head coach K. C. Jones and peeled off his warmups as he rose from the visitors' bench during the first quarter at Brendan Byrne Arena and checked into the game against the New Jersey Nets. It was opening night, and so it was real. The big redhead was a Boston Celtic.

This was the big experiment, a roll of the dice by team president Red Auerbach and general manager Jan Volk in trying to make their perennial powerhouse even better: to take that step from major contender to clear-cut favorite to capture the 1985/86 NBA title. The trade that had brought Walton from the Los Angeles Clippers for forward Cedric Maxwell, a Celtic mainstay for eight seasons, was generally seen as intriguing but risky.

Everyone pretty much knew the basic Walton story—an all-time talent and former league MVP whose career had been besieged by injuries. Countless operations to correct stress fractures in his feet had enabled his career to continue on but never to the point of playing full seasons. During his first 10 years with the Trail Blazers and Clippers Walton had never played more than 65 games in a season. During the stretch of 1978/79 through 1981/82 he seemed to be as good as retired, playing 14 games *total* over those four years. Eventually the latest medical procedures and all that rest allowed him to continue again—gradually. "The doctors kept telling me, Bill you gotta stop playing. But I'm an optimistic guy. I always thought I could get through it. I had stopped playing on doctor's orders. Then one day I'm playing with my children in the street and discovered I could run again. They said, 'Dad, we never saw you run before.' I went back to playing basketball, I started playing once a week. Then it became two per week, then three."

He ramped it up enough to play in 55 games and 67 games respectively in the two years before he got to Boston. Celtic brass figured that bringing in Walton as a part-timer to rotate in for Robert Parish and Kevin McHale could work—fewer minutes meant a better chance of staying healthy.

The plan was logical but carried no assurances. And it wasn't as if the club got him for nothing. Cedric Maxwell had been a very valuable piece for the 1980s Celtics, an underrated star playing in Larry Bird's shadow who averaged double digit points every year and always shot a high percentage (55% for his career and leading the league twice). His assortment of twists, turns, and moves made him one of the NBA's most dangerous players when he got the ball in decent position inside. Walton himself says that Maxell "wasn't just good, he was one of the best I ever played against in terms of defending him while he had the ball in the paint. The way he could get that shot off."

It was Maxwell who had been MVP of the 1981 NBA Finals when the Celtics took out Moses Malone and the Houston Rockets in six games for the first championship of the Bird era. And it was Maxwell who had come out smoking in Game Seven of the memorable 1984 Finals against the Lakers with 24 points, eight rebounds, and eight assists to lead the Celtics to a 111–102 win in the first Bird-Magic Finals clash.

But sometimes circumstances come up that can cause even the best of relationships to sour. That's what happened with Cedric Maxwell and the Celtics in 1985. A bad knee that year had limited him to 57 games, the first time he'd ever missed any significant time in his eight NBA seasons. Injuries can happen, but more important was the front office view of how he was handling it. *Boston Globe* columnist Bob Ryan, who covered many of the Celtic teams of that era, remembers: "Maxwell was unhappy. He had a knee injury and it was thought he hadn't worked hard enough to get back." One day in the summer of 1985 Ryan was at Larry Bird's house to do a story on Bird's brother Eddie. At one point Bird momentarily excused himself to take a phone call. When he returned, he filled Ryan in on the news that would eventually set the wheels in motion for a big trade. "Larry said, 'It looks like Max doesn't want to play for us anymore,'" Ryan says.

And so the Celtics' esteemed front line would get a makeover. The Bird-Parish-Maxwell starting trio backed up by Kevin McHale in the super-sub role, a winning formula for five years and two championships, was ditched. Walton would now be the supersub as McHale moved into the starting lineup in place of Maxwell. It all looked good, as long as Walton's health held out. Even he knew that would remain a question mark all year. "All my injuries had come from playing too much basketball. There was always a level of uncertainty. Red took a chance on me," Walton says.

The deal took some time to complete as salary cap issues were sorted out. Walton wound up forfeiting a chunk of his Clipper salary to play for the Celtics for $450,000, with the Celtics also paying a chunk of Maxwell's Los Angeles salary. "Walton had to buy his way out from Donald Sterling. He really wanted to be here," says Jan Volk.

It didn't all go as planned on opening night. Larry Bird shot just 5-for-15 while Nets forward Buck Williams powered his way to 23 points and 15 rebounds as New Jersey rallied from 12 points down in the fourth quarter to win in overtime 113–109. Walton saw the floor for 19 minutes—what would be his average for the season—contributing four points and five rebounds. He also committed five fouls and a ghastly seven turnovers. "Yet another date that I was a disgrace to basketball," Walton muses now in his typical over-the-top, sort of half-serious self-criticism.

Not to worry. After their opening night stumble, the Celtics won their next eight games, including a couple against those clubs that would prove to be two of their toughest challengers in the East (or at least what passed for tough challengers for the 1985/86 Celtics). McHale, Bird, Parish, and Dennis Johnson all went for more than 20 points in a win over Milwaukee on October 30. Two nights later, in the season's fourth game, Walton had his first real vintage supersub outing at home against the Atlanta Hawks. Playing half the game, Walton shot 5-for-6 for 14 points and grabbed eight rebounds. Exactly what he was there to do, and then some. The effort helped the Celtics overcome 40 points by Dominique Wilkins and pull out a 109–105 win.

The early season cruise was on. Losses were rare—the next one after opening night came in the team's 10th game and third in four nights, a two-point decision at Indiana in which Bird went for 33 points and Walton for 16 in 22 minutes. The pattern was developing—the occasional Celtics loss was almost always close, virtually always away from home, and often during a rough spot on the schedule when the guys were tired. The Celtics had the best starting five in the NBA, Walton was seizing the moment as the sixth man, and the rest of the bench was deep. As young as the season was, you were already getting the feeling that it might be a cruise to the finals—as long as Bill Walton's health held out.

Chapter 2

Late 1985

The Patriots needed a quarter to adjust to the tropical Florida weather on October 27 (almost 80 degrees and humid at game time), spotting the Tampa Bay Bucs two early touchdowns before getting things going and pulling away for a 32–14 win. James threw an 11-yard TD pass to Collins on a second-quarter option pass and later ran for two fourth-quarter scores. The defense contained James Wilder, one of the league's top rushers, holding him to 62 yards on 21 carries, and sacked quarterback Steve DeBerg three times, including one by Blackmon in the end zone for his second safety-sack of the season.

And so, the Pats rode a three-game winning streak back home as they got set to square off against Dan Marino and the Dolphins. In what was shaping up as a three-team race in the AFC East, both teams came into the game 5–3 and a game behind the Jets for the division lead.

On a rainy afternoon in Foxborough, Grogan and the offense got little going in the first half. Miami put together one first-quarter drive that ended in a 3-yard touchdown run by rookie power runner Ron Davenport, then added a 26-yard Fuad Reveiz field goal in the second quarter for a 10–0 lead. Tony Franklin's 38-yard field goal got the Pats on the board, trailing 10–3 at halftime.

But in what was shaping up to be their trademark, the Patriots saved their best for the fourth quarter. Trailing 13–3 they drove to the Miami 28 where they faced a fourth down and one. Berry, seeing his team's failure to get close to the end zone all day and undoubtedly sensing that this would be his best chance, decided to go for it. That is, really "go for it" with the gutsiest call of the 1985 season. In the short yardage situation, Grogan handed off to Tatupu straight ahead. But instead of plowing forward as the Dolphins expected, Tatupu turned and tossed the ball back to Grogan—it was a flea flicker. Grogan arched his pass over the middle for Greg Hawthorne, who had beaten Dolphin cornerback William Judson on a post pattern. Touchdown. The Miami lead was now 13–10, and Sullivan Stadium was getting loud.

The Dolphins' next drive reached the New England 44 when Marino went long down the right side for his top receiver, Mark Clayton, who almost corralled what would have been a sure touchdown but for Ronnie Lippett hustling right to the end of the play to just get his hand in there enough to deflect the ball from Clayton's grasp (Don Shula's decision to kick Lippett out of that Dolphin practice a few years earlier was really looking bad now).

After the Patriots held the Dolphins from there, the offense pounded the ball on the ground to move crisply down the field. Strong running by Collins and James got the Pats to the 13-yard line with a first down. Tatupu then got a great block from Hannah to bust one up the middle to the 2. Two plays later, Grogan took the snap and rolled right, pumping his arm as he looked to throw to Derrick Ramsey. Dolphin linebacker Bob Brudzinski reacted by dropping back to cover Ramsey, leaving Grogan a clear path into the end zone. The Patriots had their first lead of the day with three minutes left. Grogan and the Patriot sideline celebrated along with the fans, still out there in full force despite the weather.

Miami's last chance ended when a Marino pass intended for Clayton was deflected by Rod McSwain and intercepted by Roland James. Your final, 17–13. For the Pats it was their fourth straight win and the biggest yet, pushing them past Miami into second place and still a game behind the Jets.

Hear someone use the term "Big Three" in the context of Boston sports, and what comes to mind? Probably the Celtics of the recent past, when Paul Pierce, Ray Allen, and Kevin Garnett came together to lead the team to an NBA title in 2008. In fact, the term has become almost the exclusive property of the NBA, a product of the salary cap era where teams are generally built around three highly paid stars surrounded by role players.

But the original Boston Big Three might have been the three guys who spearheaded the Patriot pass rush attack in 1985: Andre Tippett, Garin Veris, and Don Blackmon. The trio that had already been getting after opposing quarterbacks since the start of the year took it to another level as the season wore on. In consecutive wins over Indianapolis and Seattle that moved the Patriots to 8–3, Tippett, Veris, and Blackmon combined to sack the quarterback 12 times. Their quickness was what allowed Rod Rust's aggressive approach to work. Teams were just finding it too difficult to block quick, athletic defenders rushing from the outside. The Pats broke open their defensive struggle with the Colts with 27 second-half points highlighted by a Fryar 77-yard punt return TD for a 34–15 win. In Seattle the following week, Blackmon played hero again when, with the score 13–13 in the fourth quarter and the Seahawks inside the New England 10, he tipped a pass by quarterback Dave Krieg that Fred Marion intercepted right in front of the goal line. Marion got an opening and raced 85 yards the other way to the Seattle 14, setting up Grogan's touchdown throw to Fryar that held up for a 20–13 win.

The winning streak was at six as the Patriots headed some 200 miles south to East Rutherford, New Jersey, for a November 24 showdown with the New York Jets. The teams came in tied for the AFC lead at 8–3 with Miami a game behind. Unfortunately the day ended in a thud of the worst kind—not only was the winning streak snapped, but the quarterback who had engineered it went out with a major leg injury.

On a sunny, crisp day at the Meadowlands and the Jets leading 6–0 in the second quarter, Grogan led a drive that brought the Pats to a key third-and-one at the Jets' 22. Grogan pitched out to the right to Tatupu, who was denied the first down when Jets' linebacker Kyle Clifton stacked him up for a two-yard loss. But more important was what happened away from the play. Jets' defensive tackle Ben Rudolph rolled along the ground until he collided with Grogan from behind. The unsuspecting Grogan fell backward over Rudolph and then came up limping. He walked off under his own power, but the leg just hurt too much. The prognosis would come shortly: broken tibia. Grogan was done for at least the rest of the regular season. Tony Eason, who hadn't played in six weeks, was back in at quarterback. And just to complete the bummer sequence, Franklin missed the 41-yard field goal try.

It was a strange play. NBC commentator Merlin Olsen didn't seem to think there was any intent on Rudolph's part, describing Rudolph as being "knocked into Grogan." But the replay didn't show any additional red jerseys around Rudolph. Even assuming he had been knocked down a bit earlier in the play, there was no clear reason for the extent of his rolling around that brought the collision with Grogan, who, for his part, believes he knows perfectly well what the reason was. "In my opinion he was trying to take me out," he says now. Based on the replay, it's tough to argue the point.

As for the game, the streak was bound to end sometime. The stats played out about as close as the team's equal records: The Jets gained 401 yards, the Patriots 399. Both teams lost two fumbles and were penalized five times. The Jets sacked the quarterback six times, the Patriots five times.

A couple of big plays wound up deciding this one for the Jets. The first one came with the Jets up 6–3 in the third quarter after a steady Pats drive inside the Jets 10 imploded when they tried some trickery with a reverse to Fryar, who coughed up the ball on a hit by safety Johnny Lynn. On the second play after the turnover, quarterback Ken O'Brien went over the top to speedy receiver Wesley Walker who caught the pass on his own 35 and then outraced everyone to the end zone to complete an 88-yard touchdown for a 13–3 lead.

With Grogan feeding the play calls to Eason from the sideline, the Pats showed their resilience with a pair of impressive fourth-quarter drives. The first ended with a 29-yard TD pass from Eason to Cedric Jones and the second with Franklin's 28-yard field goal to tie the game with 16 seconds left.

The Jets got the win in overtime thanks to a big punt return by Kurt Sohn, who broke free down the sideline for 45 yards to the New England 15 to set up Pat Leahy's game-winning field goal, 16–13.

Losing both a game and a quarterback makes for a tough Sunday. The good news was that the Pats were still in solid shape at 8–4 and that Eason had looked strong in his return to the field, completing 23 of 34 for 221 yards without an interception. Crunch time had arrived: four games left and a tight playoff race. Grogan would be around to help but not to play. It was Eason's team the rest of the way. Says James: "We recognized that the year before we had blown a chance to make the playoffs. We knew we could make the playoffs."

***

Right after the Celtics' eight-game winning streak went down in the two-point loss at Indiana, they went out and won their next nine in a row. At this point they were 17–2 and within a few bounces of being 19–0. They continued to beat up on some of their key eastern rivals, defeating the Sixers twice and the Pistons and Bucks once each. In the 110–103 home win over Philadelphia on November 22, Kevin McHale torched Charles Barkley for 32 while Robert Parish took it to Moses Malone for 20 points and 12 rebounds. Bird, meantime, showed why he had the ability to be the about the best player on the floor even on those nights when his shot wasn't falling. He finished with 11 points on just 5-of-16 from the floor but still carved up the Sixers with nine assists and nine rebounds. A few days later in Philly, the Celtics won again by holding the Sixers to 15 fourth-quarter points in a 98–91 win. Dennis Johnson scored 20 on 9-of-14 from the floor and played his usual tenacious defense, holding his counterpart Maurice Cheeks to 5-of-15 shooting.

Johnson was in many ways the wild card of the great Celtics teams of the '80s—a true star in the backcourt, another Hall of Fame player to go with the four they already had on the front line. At the time he never seemed to quite get the recognition he deserved, probably because he never fit neatly into the role of a classic point guard or classic shooting guard. He was a streaky shooter and not a flashy passer. He had a quick first step but not a ton of speed. What Johnson had was the all-around game. He was a dogged defender who always seemed to be in synch with the others offensively. He had that subtle ability to deliver the ball to the big men in the post in perfect position. He consistently showed good judgment when deciding whether to shoot or give it up. And his physical strength made him effective at posting up opposing guards near the baseline and hitting that little turnaround jumper. And just for fun there was this little quirk: Whenever Johnson went to the foul line, the number of dribbles he would take before shooting a free throw always equaled the number of years he'd been in the league. Check any clip of Johnson at the line in 1985/86 and you'll see 10 dribbles.

"Nothing fazed him," says Bob Ryan. "He was a destructive defender who was always up for big games. Larry Bird would say that when DJ went to the basket you knew he was up for the game."

The Celtics were gifted Dennis Johnson from the Phoenix Suns before the 1983/84 season in a trade for Rick Robey, a husky backup center out of Kentucky who could rebound and clog the middle when he was in the game to spell Robert Parish. But how do you compare a decent backup center to an All-Star guard, a guy who had been an NBA Finals MVP with the Seattle Supersonics and had once been traded for Paul Westphal, one of the premier guards of his time?

Ryan believes that Johnson wasn't clicking well with his Phoenix running mate Walter Davis and that the Suns were intent on breaking up that back-court. Also, "the Suns thought Robey would blossom in a bigger role but it didn't happen, he basically ate himself out of the league." While Johnson was winning a ring in Boston during the first year after the trade, Robey was averaging six points and three rebounds a game for a Phoenix team whose win total dropped by 12 from the previous year. Johnson was known to be feisty and temperamental at times, a guy who sometimes clashed with coaches. The Celtics, in clear need of backcourt defense, took the risk. "They generally thought you could bring a guy into the Celtics atmosphere and he'd respond," says Ryan. The theory worked with DJ, who would go on to average 15 points and six assists per game in 1985/86 while being named to the NBA All-Defensive team for the eighth straight year. Of all the feathers in Red Auerbach's cap, this was one of the bigger ones.

"Johnson understood individual defense, he understood team defense, he was physical and he anticipated exceptionally well," says Rick Weitzman, who broadcast Celtics games on radio alongside Johnny Most for two years before becoming a scout with the team. "Very quick hands. He took a lot of pressure off the inside guys by not letting his man get to the basket."

As the early season hummed along, the Celtics' handling of the 76ers pretty much showcased the way they were asserting their dominance in the Eastern Conference. Remember, before Celtics-Lakers truly took hold as the memorable grudge match that would go on to define the era and join Larry Bird and Magic Johnson at the hip for eternity, the Boston-Philly battles for eastern supremacy made up the defining NBA rivalry of the early 1980s. The edge back then tilted toward the Sixers. Three times in the four years from 1980 to 1983, Bird's first four seasons, it was Philadelphia advancing out of the East to play in the NBA Finals, where they lost to the Lakers twice and beat them once. The one year the Sixers didn't make it they'd held a three-games-to-one lead over the Celtics in the 1981 Eastern Conference

Finals only to see Boston rally back to win in seven games and then go on to beat Houston in the Finals.

But as the 1980s gradually aged, so did the Sixers. Key players like Malone, Julius Erving, and Bobby Jones, while still strong, were moving past their peaks. Shooting guard Andrew Toney, who torched the Celtics so often during the early '80s that he was tagged "The Boston Strangler," was hobbling on a bum ankle. The Sixers still had a solid club, and they did infuse some youth by drafting Barkley in 1984, but they didn't have enough to hang with a Celtics team that by the mid-80s was better and deeper than ever, especially as former NBA starters like Scott Wedman and Jetty Sichting had arrived to bolster the bench along with Walton. The peak Boston clubs of 1984–1987 would pretty much leave Philadelphia in the dust to become the clear Beasts of the East on their way to four straight NBA Finals.

The one-sided trade for Dennis Johnson two years earlier wasn't a rare thing for Auerbach; it was pretty much par for the course. He had nabbed each and every member of the league's best starting five in a way that could be called unorthodox, either as a trade that turned into a robbery or by using the draft in an unusual way.

Auerbach had used his first-round pick in 1978 to select Bird a year before he was set to leave Indiana State University to turn pro and then waited to sign him before the next year's draft. Rules at the time allowed an NBA team to draft a college player the year his class graduated (how quaint does that sound now?) even if the player had another year of college eligibility remaining. The stipulation applied to Bird, who had sat out a season after his transfer from Indiana to Indiana State and wound up a fifth-year senior. So Auerbach passed on a chance to improve the Celtics immediately by waiting a year on Bird, watched his team go 29–53 in 1978/79, then watched Bird take the league by storm in 1979/80 as the team shot all the way to 61–21 and to a trip to the conference finals. With patience came a franchise player for the ages.

A year later the Celtics pulled off a draft-day heist of the Golden State Warriors. Boston owned the top overall pick of the 1980 draft thanks to an earlier trade with Detroit. Auerbach initially wanted to use the pick to take University of Virginia big man Ralph Sampson, who had just completed his freshman year with the Cavaliers and who some speculated might come out for the draft. Auerbach offered Sampson big money to forgo his last three years of college eligibility to join the Celtics and seemed truly miffed when Sampson decided he wasn't ready for the NBA and turned him down. Sampson wound up staying at Virginia for four years before the Houston Rockets took him number one overall in 1983.

With Sampson staying in school in 1980, the projected first pick was Joe Barry Carroll, a seven-foot senior center who had just led Purdue to the NCAA Final Four. So high were many scouts on Carroll that they saw him as a rare big man who could change a franchise in the mold of Kareem Abdul-Jabbar or Bill Walton. Like Ralph Sampson but with more experience and polish. The Warriors, who held the third pick, wanted him.

But clearly Auerbach and the Celtics people had not hopped onto the Carroll bandwagon. They agreed to send the top pick, along with the No. 13 pick they also owned, to Golden State in exchange for the third pick and incumbent center Robert Parish, the four-year veteran that Carroll would figure to replace with the Warriors. After the Warriors took Carroll with the first pick and the Utah Jazz grabbed explosive guard Darrell Griffith of Louisville with the second, the Celtics used the third pick to take Kevin McHale, the spry 6'10" forward-center from Minnesota. Later with pick No. 13, Golden State took a forward from Mississippi State named Rickey Brown. Carroll would go on to a decent 11-year career with five teams but never won much and never dominated to the degree that the Warriors expected. Brown lasted five years in the NBA as a fringe player before heading overseas. McHale and Parish would wind up in the Hall of Fame. But none of it would have happened had Sampson taken up Auerbach on his offer.

"We were a little bit lucky there," says Jan Volk. "It turned out to be a turning point in my career. Ralph Sampson was a player of huge potential. Sometimes you get it right, sometimes you don't."

Kevin McHale brought that combination of size and footwork that was just too much for opposing forwards. The endless supply of moves he could throw at you in the low post made him nearly unstoppable. The pump fakes, the up and under, or the little fake toward the hoop and then the step back; he was almost automatic for two points or a trip to the foul line. Around the NBA only Hakeem Olajuwon, he of the thousand and one post moves himself, would eventually rival McHale in that part of the game. Charles Barkley has called McHale the toughest opponent he ever faced, a list that presumably includes Bird.[1] Teammates called McHale "the black hole," because when the ball went into him in the low post it rarely came back out. Of course there was a good reason for that: McHale averaged 21.3 points and 8.3 rebounds in 1985/86, shooting 57% from the floor in his first year as a starter.

McHale's fellow twin tower, Robert Parish, came to Boston without a real high profile. He had played his college ball at Centenary in his native Louisiana and then in relative NBA obscurity with mostly mediocre teams in Golden State (not a lot of nationally televised games back then). He was quite good during his time with the Warriors, averaging 17 points and 10 rebounds during his final two years there, but the team was intent on Joe Barry Carroll.

Nicknamed "Chief" for the way his running gait resembled the chief character in the basketball scene in the movie *One Flew Over the Cuckoo's Nest*, Parish wasn't flashy, he didn't have the million post moves like McHale, he didn't talk much. He just went out and put up a workmanlike performance every night. You could watch the game and not take much notice of him, then check the box score in the next day's paper and see that he'd finished with 18 points and 11 rebounds. Parish could rebound, score inside, and despite an awkward-looking shot, could drain those 10-to-15 footers from the baseline. The kicker was his constant hustle. Parish was consistently one of the best centers in the league at running the floor, for which he was rewarded with easy baskets on the fast break. Bob Ryan calls him "a top ten center of all time," and it's tough to argue the point. Parish not only had the stats—30th leading scorer and 8th leading rebounder in NBA history—his durability was truly on another level. He wound up playing 21 seasons in the NBA, appearing in at least 74 games in all but the last one. Who does that?

Entering his 10th NBA season in 1985/86, Parish saw his minutes drop a bit with the arrival of Walton, undoubtedly a good thing that kept him fresher at age 32. Still playing more than 30 minutes a night, he averaged 16 points and nine rebounds a game, shooting 55% from the field. Quiet and stoic on the court, Parish was in many ways the heartbeat of the team, often laughing and hamming it up on the team bus and in the clubhouse. "Robert was a quiet guy from the South but he could also be very funny," says Lesley Visser. "Together he and Bill were a force." Remembers Walton: "On the bus he was the guy holding court, reciting the events of the day, needling everyone. He was like a late-night talk show host."

Walton recounts that his first order of business upon arriving in Boston was to go and talk to Parish, literally before anything else. "I knew Chief from Golden State, he never got a fair shot there. M. L. Carr [just retired from the 1984/85 Celtics] picked me up at the airport and I say, 'We're going to Chief's house.' He says, 'Why?' I say, 'I want to talk to Chief.' I told him I was there not to take anything away from him. I'm there to help make him even better. Chief was the foundation, the pillar who allowed Larry and Kevin to do the things they did." What the Celtics wound up with was probably the best one-two punch at center in NBA history. Walton likens entering a game for Parish to "following a Brinks truck down a bumpy road and they forgot to close the back doors."

The last bit of Auerbach's deft touch in putting together the 1985/86 club came in the 1981 draft when he used his second-round pick on Danny Ainge, a great college guard from Brigham Young who happened to be such a good athlete that he was already playing major league baseball with the Toronto Blue Jays. His Boston pro sports debut had come not at Boston Garden but at Fenway Park in June 1979, when he went 0-for-4 against Chuck Rainey and Tom Burgmeier in a loss to the Red Sox. Ainge had made national waves in the early spring of 1981 when he led BYU to back-to-back NCAA Tournament wins over UCLA and Notre Dame in the Cougars' run to the Elite Eight. Yet he had already announced his intention to pursue baseball full time out of college, which dropped him from the first round of the NBA draft as teams shied away from him. The Celtics went ahead and took him in the second round on the chance his baseball career didn't work out. It didn't take long. Ainge's .187 batting average near the end of the 1981 season spurred a change of heart. By December he was a Boston Celtic.

So there's your great starting five for the 1985/86 Celtics. Larry Bird drafted a year early. Infielder Danny Ainge drafted a round late. Robert Parish, Kevin McHale, and Dennis Johnson acquired for Joe Barry Carroll, Rickey Brown, and Rick Robey. That's pretty good work.

The unheralded guy in all this was Jan Volk, who served under Auerbach in a variety of roles, including assistant general manager from 1980 to 1984, and then assumed the GM role himself when Auerbach decided to kick himself upstairs as president and give up the GM title. Fans at the time figured Volk as a general manager in name only, a guy who, as a lawyer by training probably handled things like contract details while Red no doubt called the shots on personnel. While it was true that Auerbach always had the last word on a player, Volk had become a solid basketball man after more than a decade with the club. His player evaluation skills were well respected, even if mostly behind the scenes. "A real GM, not a bean counter," says Bob Ryan. "Red was available for consultation but Jan was involved in all the key decisions."

Volk looks back at his Celtics tenure, which lasted until 1997, this way: "No matter how successful you were, Red was going to get the credit. If you accepted that, then it was a great place to work. He was a quotable guy, passionate, aggressive. But for all the success he had, he recognized he always had holes he needed to fill. That's what I did."

So Volk did his diligent best to get the most from the scouting staff, evaluate players the best he could, all without losing his sense of humor over Auerbach's pull. He recounts the time that Bob Lobel came to his office one June day to do a TV interview on an upcoming draft. "He asked if we were ready for the draft. I said, 'Everyone will weigh in with their opinions to form a consensus, and that's who we'll go with—unless Red wants to draft someone else.'"

Rick Weitzman, a college star at Northeastern and a bit player with the Bill Russell Celtics of the late 1960s before his broadcasting and scouting days, says that Auerbach's management style was to welcome input from the staff but making sure it stood up to his challenges. "Red was very good at playing Devil's advocate," Weitzman says. "If you liked a player, he would try to get you to back off your opinion. If you held your ground, he appreciated it. It didn't bother me if he didn't go with my opinion, he had the final say."

The Celtics' latest winning streak came to a halt on December 6 at Boston Garden, courtesy of the Portland Trail Blazers. A game that would normally have gone down as just another night in December destined to be forgotten instead became memorable for one reason: It was the only one that the Celtics would lose at home all year, regular season and playoffs combined. It would be a pretty remarkable run even though the NBA was very much a home cooking league generally—only a few of the elite teams would manage winning road records. A top team like the Celtics would figure to do even better at home than most, and they almost always limited the number of home losses to single digits during the Bird era. But one loss the whole year? That's a freakish stat which showed that the team was on another level in 1985/86. The question was whether the historic building was truly a factor or whether it was simply too tough to guard Larry Bird, Kevin McHale, and company in a hostile road environment without your own fans to draw energy from. Do professional athletes really get intimidated by history, ghosts, and championship banners?

Jeff Twiss believes they did a little bit when you add it all up. "When coming in for a game, first you think about it being the same floor where Russell, Cousy, and Havlicek played. Then you look up and see the championship banners and all the retired numbers. Then you look and see that Tommy Heinsohn, who was one of those players, is broadcasting. Then finally you see Red Auerbach sitting in Loge 1, center court across from the bench. Red liked to see the interaction on the bench, see how a player reacted when he came out."

It is a lot to soak in. Even though the players make the arena more than the arena makes the players, you can see why Boston Garden was as tough an environment as there was in the NBA. Just as interesting: Twiss's revelation of Auerbach's seating choice and why. Another example of no detail left to chance by the team patriarch.

On this night against Portland, it was just a rare case of things not quite clicking. The Blazers were something of a Jekyll and Hyde team around this time, inconsistent but stocked with a lot of athletic players who could run you out of the gym on a given night. With Clyde Drexler going for 19 points and Jerome Kersey coming off the bench for 22 points in 22 minutes, they pushed the pace and pulled away in the fourth quarter for a 121–103 win.

For the Celtics, the loss wouldn't just be their only one on the Parquet Floor, it would be the only one they would drop by more than 10 points for the entire year. A quick side note: Portland also got a big game from their young big man Sam Bowie, who finished with 18 points and 13 boards in 30 minutes playing mainly against Parish and Walton. Bowie was a guy you had to feel bad for—big and talented but just too injury prone dating back to his college days at Kentucky to play many full seasons or to live up to being the No. 2 overall pick in the 1984 draft. He would go on to be remembered as the guy drafted one spot ahead of Michael Jordan, for which the Blazers were subject to a lot of ridicule. But to watch a 24-year-old Bowie score, rebound, and run the floor at Boston Garden in December 1985 is to watch a snapshot of what the Blazers could have had if their gamble on his health had turned out differently. He still wasn't going to be Jordan, but he had the makings of a top NBA big man.

The loss to Portland kicked off what would be the one mini slump that Boston would endure in 1985/86, losing five of nine games in a run that culminated in a nationally televised Christmas Day loss in New York in double overtime, a brutal ending to a game that the Celtics had led by 25 points in the third quarter. The NBA's first-ever lottery pick from the 1985 draft, Patrick Ewing, went for 32 points and 11 rebounds to counter Parish's 24 points with 18 boards and McHale's 29 points that included 15 from the foul line.

The Celtics were still 21–7 despite some December doldrums. And the stretch did have its bright spots. The brightest had to be the December 18 track meet–type game at the Garden against the Dallas Mavericks, an offensively talented team with Mark Aguirre, Rolando Blackman, and Detlef Schrempf. Boston took the up-tempo game 137–117, showcasing the motion and ball movement that was their trademark.

If you ever played basketball as a youth, then you may have attended one or two of those local clinics that many towns offer, the kind put on by a local high school coach who would bring along a few of his players on a Saturday morning and demonstrate proper techniques for passing, moving without the ball, running the pick and roll, defensive positioning, and other various fundamentals. But if you happened to live in the greater Boston area, you could get the same lesson by simply turning on a Celtics game. You would almost call the Boston Celtics a serious version of the Harlem Globetrotters, a traveling band of players that substituted ball movement, pinpoint passing, and boxing out for trick shots and hijinks. They were a traveling clinic, showcasing nightly demonstrations of fundamental basketball.

For all the individual stars lining the roster, the Celtics truly played the team game. In Bird and Walton they had the best passing forward and best passing center in the game, and maybe ever. Any player would pass up an open shot to hit a teammate who was closer. They rebounded and threw strong, accurate outlet passes; they ran the floor; they cut to the basket; and they found the open man in the half court. The big men—Parish, McHale, and Walton—were adept at sealing off defenders inside and catching passes in traffic and then finishing around the basket.

Watching them, it was hard not to think about Bill Walton's previous championship team, the 1977 Portland Trail Blazers. The Finals victory by that fundamentally sound Blazer squad over a Philadelphia team stacked with scorers Julius Erving, George McGinnis, Doug Collins, and Lloyd Free (later to be known as World B. Free) was touted as a victory for the team game over individual talent. By the time the 1985/86 Celtics came along, it was as if someone had found the magic formula for combining the two to create almost the perfect basketball team. Find a group of All-Stars willing to constantly move and share the ball. Use the individual talent when you need it—when the shot clock is running down, you can always get the ball to Bird to do his thing or throw it into McHale in the post. As Walton puts it: "Everybody played to win. We were completely committed to the team game. We liked and respected each other. And we had Larry Bird and Kevin McHale and no one else did."

Use any cliché you'd like—clinic, poetry in motion, artistry—when the Celtics were clicking, it was just a thing of beauty to watch. They would average 29 assists per game for the season, virtually tying with the Lakers for the league lead. And that's without a virtuoso point guard like Magic Johnson to average more than 12 by himself. In Boston everyone got in on the fun.

In the game against Dallas, the Celtics dished out an almost absurd 46 assists on 59 field goals. A sampling, from a YouTube clip from an account called Larry Legend:

- Bird hitting a cutting DJ for a basket and one
- Bird hitting McHale in the low post for a jump hook over Aguirre
- DJ passing from three-quarter court ahead to McHale running the floor for an easy two
- Ainge leading Bird from across the lane for a short bank shot
- Ainge threading one to Bird in a crowded lane for an easy chance underneath
- Bird from the perimeter finding Walton on a backdoor cut
- Ainge from just across midcourt hitting a running Bird for a left-handed layup
- Bird bouncing a pass between the legs of defender Uwe Blab to a cutting DJ, who gets the hoop on a goaltending call
- Ainge bullet from the perimeter to an open Bird underneath
- Bird lob over the defense to DJ underneath for an easy two

Bird would finish the night with 35 points and 10 assists, McHale with 28 and 10 rebounds. And Danny Ainge, drilling jumpers and finding open men all night, would wind up with 20 points and 13 assists. It was one of those nights in which Ainge was able to showcase the entire portfolio of skills. A guard whose outside jumper was as pure as that of any player on the team, including Bird, Ainge tended to get stereotyped as a "shooter" at the expense of his all-around game, which could be exceptional. This was a premium athlete who had once been named All-American in football, basketball, and baseball during his high school days in Eugene, Oregon.[2] Ainge could pass, handle the ball, and push the fast break as well as plenty of NBA guards.

Defensively he was fearless, never backing down from the likes of Michael Jordan or Isaiah Thomas.

To Celtic haters of the time, Ainge was the franchise face, IDed as the guy who whined and complained too much when something didn't go his way ("ugh, I hate Ainge" was a common phrase when watching a game with a non-Bostonian). His facial expressions did have that whiny look sometimes, but the image mainly served to distract people from noticing what a hard-nosed competitor he was. In his fifth season at 26, Ainge seemed to have found his groove with the team after some stops and starts earlier in his career, particularly during Bill Fitch's coaching days. His backup Jerry Sichting observes that "Danny Ainge really grew into his role. He had been a backup when Gerald Henderson was there, and Fitch had a quick hook. He was really hard on Danny." Along with McHale becoming a first-time starter following the Maxwell-Walton trade, the team had the tools to take things to a new level, Sichting figures. "Those two guys really became entrenched in the starting lineup."

Ainge averaged 10.7 points and 5.1 assists a game in 1985/86, shooting better than 50% from the floor and better than 90% from the foul line. There's little doubt that he could have scored more on a lesser team, but his game blended perfectly with the All-Stars he was playing with. And remember, this was all before the dawn of what we would call the NBA's three-point era. Even though the league had introduced the three in 1979/80, it would take years for teams to integrate it into the offense as a regular weapon. For most of the 1980s the trifecta was little more than a desperation, late-game comeback tool. Even sharpshooters like Ainge and Bird would typically take no more than a couple of threes per game, often fewer. But as Jeff Twiss points out, Ainge ultimately proved to be one the early pioneers who normalized the three-point shot as part of the normal offensive flow. By the late '80s he'd be putting up four to five per game. "Danny was one of the first in the NBA to test the waters with three pointers. Teammates would get on him, but then lay off when he made them," Twiss says.

The Boston machine may have slowed down a bit around the holidays, but no one was worrying. After blowing the Christmas Day game in New York, the Celtics would lose exactly once over the next month and a half.

***

The Patriots figured to have a pretty easy time getting back on the winning track against the 3–9 Indianapolis Colts at the Hoosier Dome. But a subpar game by the defense and some general sloppiness that led to 14 penalties totaling over 100 yards allowed Indianapolis to hang around.

Eason, in his first start in six weeks, mostly had his way against the porous Colts defense, throwing for 293 yards on 20-for-28 passing and three touchdowns. But Colts' running backs Randy McMillian and George Wonsley ran well all afternoon to sustain several drives and pick up 23 first downs. After Eason's 14-yard TD pass to Stanley Morgan put the Pats up 17–7 in the second quarter, two subsequent Colts drives resulted in a field goal and a McMillian 6-yard touchdown run to tie the game.

With the score still tied in the fourth quarter, the Pats struck twice on a four-yard run by James and Eason's second TD strike to Morgan, this one for 25 yards. But another touchdown run by McMillian got the Colts to within 31–24 before a New England drive and a one-yard plunge by Tatupu essentially iced it. The final was 38–31.

The defense came back with a big effort the following week, shutting down the Detroit Lions in a 23–6 victory in Foxborough for the Patriots' eighth win in nine games. They held quarterback Eric Hipple to 144 passing yards and sacked him twice. Eason came out with his best Steve Grogan impersonation by running 16 yards for the game's first score and then tossed a touchdown pass to Derrick Ramsey in the second quarter. The Pats controlled the game all the way as they ran up 216 yards on the ground with James going for 115 and Tony Collins for 61 on just 10 carries.

A big Monday night game in Miami beckoned the next week. The Patriots were going in as winners of eight of nine, the Dolphins as winners of five straight. Something would have to give. With two weeks to go, the Patriots, Dolphins, and Jets sat in a three-way tie atop the AFC East. Everyone knew that the Monday night matchup could well decide the division, especially with the Jets facing the Bears the following week.

And so it came on December 16, 1985. Early in the evening in New York, mafia boss Paul Castellano was gunned down on a crowded Manhattan street, paving the way for John Gotti to take control of the Gambino family. But a little bit further north the main event of the night came at 9 p.m. Monday Night Football. New England at Miami, both teams 10–4. The Jets had indeed lost to the Bears over the weekend to drop to 10–5. For all practical purposes, this was for the AFC East title. It was a rainy night with a muddy field at the Orange Bowl, where the Pats hadn't won since the Johnson administration. A spirited Monday night crowd was out to see it stayed that way.

The Patriots plugged and plugged, trying to pull out the win. They played from behind all night; they came back. As usual they saved their best for the fourth quarter. And they could well have won. In the end they just didn't.

The rain and mud made for some sloppiness—both teams turned the ball over four times. Dan Marino threw just one touchdown pass, but the Dolphins got three field goals by rookie placekicker Fuad Reveiz from plus-40 yards and a pair of 1-yard TD plunges from Ron Davenport, their tough power back out of Louisville.

The Pats trailed 17–7 at halftime, 20–10 entering the fourth quarter, and 27–13 with about nine minutes left. But their physical and mental toughness persisted to the end. Eason led an impressive drive on which he hit two key passes to Ramsey and Morgan and then got to the 1-yard line on a Dolphin pass interference in the end zone. Tatupu took it in on the next play to make the score 27–20. Then came the omen for what the Patriots had to look forward to in January: some special teams magic. On the kickoff, Rod McSwain stripped return man Joe Carter on the 15-yard line. Cedric Jones scooped up the ball and strolled right into the end zone. Just like that, the game was tied.

Marino responded with a workmanlike drive, blending runs and short passes to reach the Patriot 31 before Nelson and McGrew stuffed Davenport on a third-down run. Reveiz came in and drilled a field goal try from 47 yards right down the middle. Miami led 30–27 with just under five minutes left.

On their final drive, the Pats moved the ball on the ground to midfield, converting a fourth-and-inches just after the two-minute warning on Tatupu's 5-yard run behind Holloway. Two plays later Eason threw a perfect touch pass near the right sideline to Collins curling out of the backfield to give the Pats a first down at the Dolphin 34. With just over a minute on the clock, they were just about in Franklin's range for a tying field goal and within striking distance of a go-ahead touchdown.

Then on second down, the disappointing ending. Eason overthrew Ramsey down the middle and watched the ball sail right into the arms of Miami safety Glenn Blackwood. It was Eason's third interception, which marred an otherwise strong night throwing the ball. The comeback had come up just short.

And so the Pats came home to face the task of shaking off a tough loss after a short week. New England had to beat the 7–8 Cincinnati Bengals in the regular season finale to clinch a wild card and reach its first non-strike year playoff since 1978. And they could still win the division if a win were accompanied by an unlikely Miami loss against 2–13 Buffalo.

A chilly December day in Foxborough—game time temperature 24 degrees—didn't seem to bother the fans, who turned out in full force and full voice to urge their club into the playoffs.

It wouldn't be easy. Coached by the innovative Sam Wyche and led by young, talented skill position players, Cincinnati boasted the third-highest scoring offense in the league. Lefty quarterback and future All Pro Boomer Esiason was in his second year and on his way to 3,400 passing yards with 27 TDs against 12 interceptions. His main targets were wide receivers Eddie Brown, the former Miami Hurricane nabbed by the Bengals in the first round of the 1985 draft, and five-year veteran Cris Collinsworth, who at age 26 had already seen three Pro Bowls. The pair would rack up more than 2,000 receiving yards and 13 touchdowns in 1985. Most observers thought that the Bengals had the best wide receiver tandem in the NFL.

The good news for the Pats was that the Bengals ranked near the bottom of the NFL in scoring defense, yielding about 27 points a game.

Berry put together a conservative game plan that limited Eason to 15 passes as the Pats pounded the ball on the ground for 281 rushing yards while averaging a hefty 6 yards per carry. James set the tone early with a 35-yard dash to the Cincinnati 9 that led to a Franklin field goal and a 3–0 lead. After a Jim Breech field goal tied the score on the next drive, Collins ripped off a 27-yard run to midfield and then Eason, off play action, launched a perfect bomb downfield to Morgan, who had gotten a step on the defense and reeled the ball in on the 3-yard line on his way into the end zone. It was a rare treat for the fans braving the chill in Foxborough—just the fourth time in the previous 12 games that the Pats' usual slow starting offense had mustered a first-quarter touchdown.

Before the quarter ended, Fryar exploded for a 35-yard punt return to the Cincinnati 20, although Franklin missed the eventual field goal try.

A second-quarter Cincinnati drive featuring some strong inside running by big fullback Larry Kinnebrew moved the ball inside the Patriot 10 and led to a Breech field goal that made the score 10–6. The running game wouldn't last for the Bengals, though. The New England defense would handle the Cincinnati rushing game most of the way, daring a young quarterback, albeit a talented one, to beat them. Tippett and Blackmon contained the outside with dogged pursuit while Veris, Nelson, and McGrew consistently clogged the inside. Kinnebrew and speedy outside threat James Brooks would combine for a manageable 86 yards on 25 carries.

The pace picked up when James coughed up the ball on a hit by Reggie Williams and watched Cincinnati rookie linebacker Carl Zander scoop up the ball and take it inside the Patriot 15. The Bengals looked to be in business, but on their first play from scrimmage Ronnie Lippett stepped in front of Esiason's pass looking for Collinsworth in the left flat for an interception at the 10-yard line and ran it all the way to the Cincinnati 30. The Pats ran the ball right at the Bengals, staying on the ground in five of six plays until Collins plowed ahead on a misdirection and broke a couple of tackles for a 9-yard touchdown run and a 17–6 lead.

They held the Bengals to a three and out on the next drive as Nelson made a nice open field tackle of Brooks on an underneath pass to keep him short of the first down marker. Then Cincinnati punter Pat McInally, in his haste to keep his kick away from Fryar, shanked one off the side of his foot for an embarrassing 13-yarder. The Patriots had it on the Cincinnati 35. They again pounded the ball on the ground, this time as far as the 13 until the drive fizzled. Franklin kicked a 30-yard field goal to make the score 20–6 just before the half ended.

The crowd was giddy and the vibes couldn't have been better inside Sullivan Stadium as the Patriots faced the final 30 minutes of their regular season, the playoffs right in their grasp. But it took just one play for the tone to change. Bengals' backup receiver and return man, Mike Martin, ran back the second-half kickoff 44 yards into New England territory with Franklin, the last line of defense, shoving him out of bounds. Four plays later Esiason found Brown on a quick slant over the middle and then watched him explode past everyone to the end zone for a 33-yard TD catch. Suddenly it was 20–13.

A few possessions later Cincinnati drove to the New England 13 as Esiason hit Brown and Collinsworth with a couple of key passes to carry the drive. After the Patriots' defense stiffened, Breech booted a 30-yard field goal to get the Bengals within 20–16 early in the fourth quarter.

Things were getting tense. But at the same time, the Patriots were in their element. This was a club that had owned the fourth quarter all season, outscoring their opponents 135–82. Sure enough, on their second play from scrimmage on the next drive, Eason aired one out down the middle of the field to Morgan for 45 yards all the way to the Cincinnati 17. Morgan was undoubtedly feeling it as the big play man on this day—he'd now piled up 129 receiving yards on just three catches. Three plays later James caught a little swing pass from Eason just inside the 20 and then outran everyone down the right sideline for a big touchdown to bump the Pats' lead to 11 points with just over eight minutes left.

As the Patriots got set to kick off, Fryar jumped up onto the team bench and implored the crowd to get loud and help the team close out the game that would get them to the playoffs. The crowd did get loud, but the Bengals still weren't finished. After a penalty and a couple of incompletions had them backed up with a third and 20 on their own 35, Esiason threw long down the right sideline for Brown, who was well covered by McSwain and Marion but used great concentration to pull in the pass and stay inbounds at the New England 22. Esiason then hit Collinsworth at the 8-yard line and, two plays later, hit him again in the end zone. It was a 27–23 game with nearly six minutes left.

But the fourth-quarter team didn't wilt. Keeping the ball on the ground, James busted a long run to midfield. Three plays later at the two-minute warning came the biggest play of the game and probably of the season, at least since the flea flicker against Miami. Facing fourth down and inches on the Bengal 42, Berry decided to go for it rather than punt the ball away to a potent offense that still had all three of its timeouts left. The call was an inside handoff to little used Robert Weathers for just his third carry of the game. Running right, Weathers bounced outside and picked up great blocks from

Lin Dawson and Greg Hawthorne, who sealed off the whole side as Weathers blew through. Almost immediately he was in the clear, running 42 yards for a touchdown and a celebration with the end zone fans. It was Weathers' first touchdown of the entire season.

Cincinnati's last drive reached midfield before Esiason threw incomplete on 4th down with under a minute to go. It was over, 34–23. The Patriots were playoff bound.

James finished his 1,200-yard regular season with 142 yards on 25 carries to lead the ground assault, with Collins and Weathers combining for more than another 100 yards on just 13 carries.

On the final day of the regular season, the Patriots, Dolphins, and Jets all won, leaving Miami alone atop the AFC East at 12–4 with the Jets and Patriots both qualifying as wild cards at 11–5. The Pats would open the playoffs at the Jets, whose advantage in the tiebreaker formula (conference record) allowed them to host the game.

After their 2–3 start, New England had closed the season with nine wins in 11 games—both losses being three-point nail biters on the road against New York and Miami. That meant that with a few more fortuitous bounces of the football, the Patriots could have easily been riding an 11-game winning streak. Aside from the Chicago Bears stomping on opponents in historic fashion over in the NFC, New England was playing as well as any team in the NFL.

The Patriots-Jets December 28 wild card game looked like an even match on paper—both teams 11–5 and splitting the two regular season games with each team winning a close one at home. Yet around town there was a calmness and a sense of inevitability that the Pats would win. The hot streak to close out the season gave the Patriots that look of a team peaking at the right time, so who cared about a couple of losses in September?

You could hear it from fans during the week. Most seemed little worried about the team's second foray into the Meadowlands, the place where Steve Grogan had gone down in a tough loss a month earlier. In the bars and around the office during the days leading up to the game it was: "There's no question in my mind they're going to win this one," and "The tough one is the Raiders next week," and other such sentiments.

The fans' hunches were on the mark, as it turned out. New England controlled the game most of the way, forcing four turnovers and holding the Jets to 58 rushing yards. After a Ken O'Brien to Johnny Hector 11-yard touchdown pass gave the Jets a 7–3 lead in the first quarter, the Patriots scored the game's next 20 points, controlling the ball and avoiding any turnovers.

Eason passed for a modest 179 yards, but he was an efficient 12-for-16 including a 36-yard touchdown strike to Morgan in the second quarter.

The Pats essentially put the game away midway through the third quarter with 10 quick points. After Franklin finished up a drive by booting his third field goal of the day, the New England special teams struck again. Johnny Rembert stripped Hector on the kickoff and then grabbed the ball as he sat on the ground. With the Jets players lamenting the turnover and seeming to think that the play was over, Rembert, realizing he'd yet to be touched, alertly got up with the ball and ran 15 yards into the end zone for a 23–7 lead. The final would be 26–14. It was off to Los Angeles for the game that would prove the Patriots' hot streak was no fluke.

Chapter 3

January 1986

On Friday night, January 3, some 45 hours before the Patriots and Raiders would kick off in Los Angeles, the Celtics ran their record to 25–7 with a 129–117 home win over New Jersey. Dennis Johnson, who had scored 29 the previous night in a win at Indiana, stayed hot with 24 and eight assists. Bird jumped in and out of passing lanes all night to torture the Nets with eight steals to go with his 29 points and 10 rebounds. Boston played the game without Danny Ainge, who had rolled an ankle in Indiana the night before. Starting in his place was Jerry Sichting, who in 36 minutes knocked down eight of nine shots for 17 points to go with six assists. Guard Sam Vincent, the first-round draft choice from Michigan State whose rookie minutes were very much limited by the acquisition of Sichting, stepped up in the primary backup role with 9 points in 14 minutes.

The Celtics had dealt for Sichting (pronounced "see-sting") shortly before the season started to shore up their backcourt depth, which had been an issue since the trade of Gerald Henderson after the 1984 championship season and the decline of veteran Quinn Buckner, who was clearly slowing down at age 31. So in September '85 the Celtics dealt Buckner to Indiana for a second-round draft pick, then turned around and traded the pick back to Indiana along with a future second rounder for Sichting, a solid five-year veteran who had lost his starting job the prior year after the Pacers drafted point guard Vern Fleming out of Georgia in the first round. Buckner would only make it to the middle of the season before retiring from the Pacers; Sichting had pretty much hit the lottery by landing in Boston.

Jerry Sichting's NBA story is one of the more interesting and inspiring ones you'll find. The Martinsville, Indiana, native was a very good college player at Purdue, where he'd played with Joe Barry Carroll and led the Boilermakers to the Big Ten co-championship with Magic Johnson's Michigan State squad—the one that would go on to the national title—in 1979. But at 6'1", he was a borderline NBA prospect. The Golden State Warriors took him in the fourth round of the '79 draft and gave him a good look, but they cut him near the end of camp.

"I had never thought that much about playing pro ball. At Purdue I never had visions of the NBA," Sichting says now. "By senior year when we tied Michigan State for the Big Ten title, I started to think I might have a chance. There were ten rounds, so I thought I might get drafted somewhere, but it wasn't like I was sitting in front of the TV watching. There were no cell phones. I was out that day working a camp. I didn't even know I was drafted until three or four hours later. I wound up being one of the last one or two players they cut."

Sichting considered the Continental Basketball Association, even reporting to the Maine Lumberjacks. But he found the atmosphere repellant and shelved the plan after two days. "I saw all the clowns they had there. I could smell dope in the hallways, the floor was too slick, just so disorganized." He went home to Indiana, took a job at a sporting goods store, and played ball on the side with an AAU team. "It was a good fit for me," he says of his bosses. "They were good guys; they'd let me take days off to play tournaments."

At the same time, Sichting's hometown Indiana Pacers were going through a coaching change, bringing in former Laker coach Jack McKinney to replace Slick Leonard for the 1980/81 season. The new regime decided to hold an open tryout, one of those cattle calls where a team might find a long-shot, under-the-radar player. Sichting was in shape, and he wanted to go. "I knew a guy in their front office and I asked him, 'Can I come to this?' He said absolutely, and it was the start of the process to get back." He did well enough to score an invite to the Pacers' upcoming rookie camp, and then to the team's regular training camp. By October he had a spot on the roster.

He backed up for two seasons with underwhelming numbers, but a bigger role awaited. "The team was in financial trouble, and no one was coming to the games. They started to get rid of some of the starters," says Sichting. "The owner Sam Nassi looked like he wanted to cut costs and sell and make a little profit for himself [Nassi did sell the Pacers in April 1983]. That's how I got to play. That's usually the best way, to get thrown into the fire. I got better." Sichting could handle the ball and bury an open jumper as well as many guards around the league. He wound up as the primary starter at point guard for the next two years until the drafting of Fleming bumped him back into a reserve role. Even then he was getting decent minutes and averaging 11 points a game. But he knew he didn't fit into the Pacers' long-term plans, especially with Fleming in the fold. His five-year run had been stitched together through a series of one-year contracts. It was time to move on.

The way Sichting saw it, "I wasn't good enough to take the Pacers to the playoffs but I wanted to play in the playoffs and make some of that playoff money. I was better than most backups so I figured I can back up on a better team."

His arrival in Boston didn't overwhelm him, exactly. Sichting was a five-year NBA veteran, after all. But it was certainly different. "With the Pacers I had five rookies on my team. Now I'm going to a team that had about five All-Stars. I was confident in myself, but I was nervous. I knew what I was walking into." What the Celtics got was a guard with a hard-nosed, no-nonsense style who could handle the ball and shoot. Rotating in for Ainge and Johnson, he'd connect on 57% from the field and better than 90% from the foul line in his 20 minutes a game in 1985/86. In a period of six years Sichting had gone from borderline NBA prospect cut from his first team to an integral bench piece for what may have been the best NBA team of all time.

"Very tenacious, fearless, and a good shooter," says Volk. "He defended really well. Isaiah Thomas hated playing against him. I remember the following year in the playoffs Danny was hurt for part of the Detroit series and Sichting started three games. Isaiah threw the ball at him."

Asked whether he was one of those guys who often stayed after practice to fire up 50 or 100 jumpers, Sichting doesn't quite answer directly, but offers this: "I kept at it, but mainly I shot a good percentage because I didn't take many bad shots. I had a pretty good pull up jumper where you can get the guy going back, but mostly I took a lot of open shots."

Sichting was part of what the Celtics called the "Green Team," the backups in coach K. C. Jones's rotation, so named for the green practice jerseys they wore when taking on the starters, who wore white. Walton and Wedman, also former NBA starters, were the other charter members. Filling out the squad were center Greg Kite, forward David Thirdkill, and guards Vincent and Rick Carlisle. Five of the seven Green Teamers—all but Sichting and Carlisle— had been first-round NBA draft picks. The deals that the Celtics made to bring in Sichting and Walton obviously pushed some of the other bench players further down in the rotation, particularly Kite and Vincent. You look at a guy like Sam Vincent, who probably had visions of being that first guard off the bench upon being drafted in the first round in 1985 only to see that role disappear when the team acquired Sichting just before training camp, and you figure he can't be very happy. Yet you'd be hard pressed to find anyone who remembers him or anyone else complaining. "That's K. C.," says Jeff Twiss. "He'd had to wait his turn behind Bill Sharman. He could tell Sam to bide his time." More than most NBA clubs, the Celtics still lived by the tradition that rookies were to mostly sit and learn more than play. Super rookies like Larry Bird and Kevin McHale were exceptions when they were drafted, but otherwise the younger guys were expected to wait their turn.

In practice, drills were taken seriously and scrimmages *very* seriously. Wedman describes the fast break drill where the ball never touched the floor as a display "that could have been a video set to music. We'd say 'this would be great on ESPN.'"

The white vs. green scrimmages that ended practice almost became the stuff of legend, probably about the best basketball there was that hardly anyone saw. "For us the scrimmage was like a playoff game," says Wedman. "We'd have loved to be starters but we were ready when the time came."

Of course starters carry heavier workloads than the subs do during the season, so it's generally not that unusual to see the second unit bring more energy in practice. But Walton says that rule didn't apply too strongly to the '86 Celtics. "The white team was playing huge minutes, I called them the stat team. They didn't need to practice as much, but these were competitive dudes. I remember Carlisle once wanted to fight DJ after they were scrapping." From Sichting: "Yeah, it got pretty intense. We started keeping track on a chalk board in the practice locker room, tracking who won the scrimmages. We beat them our share. We really pushed each other."

Coach K. C. Jones took notice of how hard the players pushed. For him it was great, because it meant that he didn't have to. Jones was generally a cool customer, quiet and even-keeled on the bench. Entering his third season, Jones was gunning for his third straight trip to the finals, having won in 1984 and then just missing in '85. He was pretty much already Celtic royalty, earning eight championship rings as a defensive-oriented guard on the Bill Russell teams of 1959–1966, which had followed two NCAA crowns with Russell at the University of San Francisco. And don't forget his two titles as an NBA assistant, with the 1972 Lakers and 1981 Celtics.

Jones could be quietly intense but he wasn't a screamer or a control freak. Basically a made-to-order coach for a veteran team that, led by Larry Bird, didn't lack for self-motivation.

"The best motivation you can have is from your peers. K. C. saw the level of intensity we had and loved it," says Wedman. "He had been around long enough and let that happen. He knew the chemistry we had. It was the best chemistry I'd ever had on a team."

Sichting, something of a hard-nosed point guard in the Jones mold himself and later an NBA assistant coach for many years, says that Jones "didn't yell a lot but you could tell when he was upset. We had a lot of leaders—he knew he didn't have to motivate us. If we had a bad game, pity the team that played us next. When we were rolling, he let us roll. The biggest flaw in a coach is over-coaching."

Bob Ryan at the *Boston Globe* never thought that Jones had the whole package as a pro coach, calling him "the least knowledgeable person ever of NBA personnel. He was about appealing to jocks to win games." Of course when you're coaching talented, highly motivated veterans, that approach tends to work. Ryan agrees that Jones was the perfect coach for the Celtic teams of the mid-'80s, especially after the four-year reign of Bill Fitch, an old-school taskmaster who, despite a .738 winning percentage and a championship, had worn out his welcome.

"Fitch was a drill sergeant; he paid attention to detail. After games he'd call his buddy [and fellow NBA coach] Cotton Fitzsimmons and talk late into the night. Everyone had quit on Fitch except for Larry. K. C. was the perfect antidote after Fitch left," says Ryan.

Most generally felt that Jones represented the franchise well on and off the court. Polite and reserved, with the occasional hankering to unwind as a man about town. Remembers Lesley Visser: "Dick Stockton [the CBS Sports broadcaster who was her husband at the time] and I used to go see K. C. sing at the Parker House." Red Sox right fielder Dwight Evans, who paid visits to the Celtics locker room on a few occasions says that "K. C. Jones was one of the finest people in sports, a gentleman."

And even if he wasn't the most detail-oriented coach, the players he had in 1986 wouldn't change anything. "We would do anything for K. C. Jones," says Walton. "He was classy, he had perspective, and he had patience. He was perfect for our team."

The Celtics continued to pile up wins in January, routing the Denver Nuggets at home and then taking road games on back-to-back nights in Indiana and Atlanta to run their record to 30–8. McHale and Parish hammered away inside against the Pacers for 28 and 20 points respectively, while Wedman hit six of seven shots of the bench for 13. The next night in Atlanta, the Celtics rallied from a 22-point halftime deficit to win a wild one in overtime 125–122. Bird lit it up for 41 points to outduel Atlanta's third-year star Dominque Wilkins, who went for 36 (Bird-Wilkins was becoming something of a budding rivalry), while Wedman was again hot off the bench with 21 points on 10-of-16 shooting.

The Celtics had three days to rest up before the Lakers invaded Boston Garden for the teams' first meeting of the year.

***

Garin Veris recalls the mood of the Patriots' players as they headed to Los Angeles for the AFC Division–round playoff game. "We were full of confidence. Berry was very good at taking things one week at a time. We felt like we could beat the Raiders, in Los Angeles, Las Vegas, or Oakland."

John Molori remembers the big moments and the emotional aftermath. "When Bowman recovered the fumble in the end zone, I remember thinking they're going to beat the Raiders. After the game there was the sight of Brian Holloway coming into the locker room crying like a baby."

The satisfying victory in Los Angeles was the team's second straight road playoff win, and one that was all the sweeter coming against the Silver and Black. There was some tough history between the clubs that was still fresh in the memories of many fans: the 1976 Ben Dreith playoff game and of course the 1978 preseason game in which Pats' receiver Darryl Stingley had been paralyzed on a viscous hit by Raider defensive back Jack Tatum. More recently, relations had been frosty between Billy Sullivan and Raiders' owner Al Davis going back a few years when Sullivan was among the owners to vote against Davis's quest to move his team from Oakland to Los Angeles.[1]

Patrick Sullivan's little fracas with Matt Millen and Howie Long at the end of the game just added to the drama. Molori was pretty much incredulous at the time: "He must have been drinking. I remember thinking, he's getting in the faces of the Raiders. And real Raiders, not today's Raiders. Matt Millen, Penn State linebacker? Howie Long? It's like, are you kidding me?" He adds that "Sullivan then called [*Boston Globe* columnist] Will McDonough a shill for Al Davis. McDonough was not that supportive of the Patriots; he was never a fan of the Sullivans."

Patrick Sullivan, for his part, has a pretty simple explanation: Sometimes that competitive spirit just gets to you a little too much. "I let my emotions get away from me. It took attention away from our team, especially our offensive line. What a job they did." All these years later, Long and Sullivan can actually laugh about it once in a while. "The funny thing is I bump into Howie all the time doing what I do now," he says, referring to his position as founder and president of New Hampshire-based Game Creek Video, a company that provides production trucks and other equipment for televised sporting events. The business often intersects with Fox Sports, where Long works as an NFL analyst.

But much more important than the post-Raider game drama was the fact that the team was headed to its first AFC Championship Game in, of all places, Miami. Back to the Orange Bowl, the site of 18 consecutive losses including the heartbreaking Monday nighter just 27 days earlier that had cost the Pats the division title.

Despite the Orange Bowl history, the Patriots went in to Miami on January 12, 1986, feeling good. Two road playoff wins, including the comeback in Los Angeles, and 11 wins in 13 games overall will do that. The rallying cry in Boston during the days leading up to the game, seen in bars and billboards and heard on local radio: "Squish the Fish." Clearly, the fans were ready to blow past the Orange Bowl jinx for good. The players felt ready too, even if the infamous losing streak played with the mind a little bit. Garin Veris: "That was all I heard. It's hard not to notice it. But once you're on the field, get that first hit, it's just football."

Still, Pete Axthelm wasn't a believer, even after the Patriots had proven him wrong in the Raider game the previous week. He told Bob Costas pre-game he was going with Miami minus six points. Even some of the guys on the Raider squad the Patriots had just vanquished weren't believers. Says Veris: "I can still hear Lester Hayes telling us we were going to get our butts beat in Miami."

The Dolphins did come into the game as hot as the Patriots, winners of eight straight. They were the defending conference champs, having lost the previous year's Super Bowl to San Francisco. Although they did have some trouble the previous week in the Divisional round against Cleveland, a heavy underdog that shot out to a 21–3 lead in the third quarter before Miami rallied back with three straight touchdowns to pull it out 24–21.

The Dolphins were a passing team. Young stud quarterback Dan Marino had just finished his third season with 30 touchdown passes and over 4,000 yards. His big targets were speedy receivers Mark Clayton and Mark Duper, with veteran Nat Moore rotating in and tight end Bruce Hardy contributing 39 catches and four TDs. The running game was a job share similar to the kind that the Patriots had employed before landing Craig James. Leading rusher Tony Nathan had finished the season with 667 yards. Miami averaged 27 points a game in 1985, fourth most in the NFL.

The Dolphins were average defensively, although they got a boost when three-time All Pro linebacker Hugh Green, unhappy with all the losing in Tampa Bay, bought his way out of his Bucs contract earlier in the season to join the Dolphins.

And perhaps no NFL coach carried more pedigree than Don Shula, who in 16 years with Miami had turned in exactly one losing season while winning a pair of Super Bowls. Before Miami, Shula's NFL head coaching career went back to 1963, when he took over the Baltimore Colts at age 33 and went 71–23 in seven seasons. One of his best players in Baltimore: Raymond Berry, who played the last five years of his career under Shula and who was now a virtual novice head coach trying to outwit Shula in a conference cham-pionship game.

The Pats also had some sad and bizarre adversity to deal with. They would be without Irving Fryar, who was sent home with a cut finger that he originally said was a self-inflicted accident with a kitchen knife but which later reports indicated was the result of a domestic dispute with his wife, Jacqueline. Either way, the Pats would have to win the conference without him.[2]

Jim Donaldson sums up life with Irving Fryar in the 1980s: "Irving was a blithe spirit. You couldn't *not* like Irving," he says. "He was charming, out and about, he got around. Of course his wife didn't like it."

It was a damp Orange Bowl once again, similar to the Pats' previous trip in December. The crowd of seventy-five thousand included a pretty decent

New England contingent that had made the trip south, a bunch of whom had brought their "Squish the Fish" signs. Bob Lobel remembers finding a penny as he walked around near the field before the game, which he treated as a lucky sign. "I still have that penny," he says. Steve Grogan was healthy and in uniform, but Eason, who had been in there for seven weeks, was clearly the starter at this point.

It didn't take New England long to set the tone. On the Dolphins' very first play from scrimmage, Steve Nelson knocked the ball loose from running back Tony Nathan. Garin Veris recovered the fumble on the Miami 20. The Dolphins ultimately stopped the Pats on a third and goal, and a short field goal by Franklin gave New England a 3–0 lead.

Miami went ahead 7–3 early in the second quarter when Marino marched them down the field and then hit backup tight end Dan Johnson with a 10-yard touchdown pass. But an early deficit wasn't going to throw the Patriots off their plan to run at the Dolphins, believing they could win the battles in the trenches. So they ran and ran, and ran some more.

On the next drive Robert Weathers found daylight on the left side and then broke several tackles for a 45-yard run to the Miami eight. On third down from the four, Eason hit Tony Collins in the end zone for a 10–7 lead. On the second play of Miami's next drive, Marino fumbled the snap and the Patriots recovered on the Dolphin 36. James ran twice for 20 yards and then Eason hit Morgan for a first down on the 2. On the next play Eason rolled right and found Derrick Ramsey for a touchdown. New England led 17–7.

Miami drove to the Patriot 15 late in the half but Reveiz, the super-footed rookie place kicker who had missed just five field goal attempts all year, sent one wide right from 32 yards. The Pats led by 10 at halftime. The conservative game plan was working like a charm—New England had outrushed Miami 123 to 24 during the half while avoiding a single turnover and holding the ball for more than 18 minutes.

You could only shake your head and laugh at the way the second half opened. Franklin kicked off for New England. Dolphins' deep man Lorenzo Hampton fielded the ball on the 9. As he ran across the 25, Mosi Tatupu did what Mosi Tatupu did: delivered a big hit from the side to separate Hampton from the ball. Greg Hawthorne recovered the fumble. The Patriots takeaway meter now stood at *13* across two-plus postseason games. The giveaway meter remained at 2.

James and Collins alternated runs to bring the Pats to the cusp of the goal line with a fourth and inches inside the 2. Berry decided to go for it. With Miami expecting a run, Eason faked a handoff to Tatupu and threw to his left to a wide-open Weathers in the end zone. New England had capitalized on yet another turnover and led 24–7.

The Dolphins briefly turned the tables when Roland James, subbing for Fryar on punt returns, fumbled a Reggie Roby punt that was recovered by the Dolphins on the New England 43. But after the Dolphins had moved the ball to the 17, Marino's throw over the middle was picked off by Fred Marion inside the 5. In turning Miami away yet again, Marion had competed the hat trick, as NBC announcer Dick Enberg put it, with an interception in all three postseason games.

And so it went. On their next drive the Pats took to the ground and ran the ball straight into the gut of the Miami defense to chew up seven minutes of clock. The drive ended with Franklin missing a 41-yard field goal try, but the third quarter was almost over.

Miami had one bit of fight left. Roland James's tough day on special teams continued when he fumbled his second punt, this one on his own 15. Marino hit Nathan for a touchdown on the next play to bring Miami within 24–14 early in the fourth quarter.

The crowd came to life as the Dolphins held New England on the next series and got the ball back on their own 37. But on just the second play, yes, another fumble. Tippett and Nelson made the hit on ball carrier Joe Carter, and Julius Adams made the recovery.

Keeping the ball on the ground, the Patriots picked up two first downs against a tiring Dolphin defense to the Miami 20. On the next play James picked up a great lead block from Weathers on Hugh Green and sprang outside for a big run to the 1-yard line. Tatupu took a pitchout on the next play and ran left into the end zone. It was 31–14 with under eight minutes left. Not even Dan Marino was going to pull this one out.

Marino did lead a drive downfield with a series of underneath passes as the Patriot defense began playing it loose. But the drive that got inside the 10-yard line ended in frustrating fashion when Miami receiver Mark Duper got flagged for unsportsmanlike conduct for ripping off his helmet and throwing it to the ground after he didn't get a borderline pass interference call against Clayborn in the end zone. Duper's frustration backed the Dolphins up to the 28-yard line with a fourth and goal. From there Marino tried Duper in the end zone again. This time Clayborn intercepted. The Dolphins' sixth turnover of the day.

The last four minutes were uneventful. It was essentially a beat down, 31–14. The Patriots hadn't just squished the fish, they had fileted them, fried them over a hot flame, and eaten them for dinner. The Orange Bowl losing streak was history. The Super Bowl drought was history. A roar went up as Berry was carried off the field, one you could hear loud and clear as the New England fans turned up the volume after many Dolphin fans had ducked out early.

How complete was this win? The Dolphins scored just once in the second half, keeping with a pattern that saw the Patriots' defense yield a total of 14 second-half points across all three playoff games. The offensive line manhandled their opponents to the tune of a 255–68 advantage in rushing yards as the Pats held the ball for just about 40 minutes. Eason threw for a paltry 78 yards, but the run-oriented offense kept him efficient. Three of his ten completions went for short touchdowns and, as always, no picks. Eason made it through all three conference playoff games without a single interception.

Marino threw for 248 yards but needed to put the ball up 48 times to get them. The Patriots contained his passing attack all day—only one Marino completion went for more than 20 yards—and picked him off twice.

The Pats had probably screwed up the Super Bowl matchup that most neutral fans around the country wanted. As Molori points out: "Remember the Dolphins were the only team to beat the Bears that year. The whole country wanted to see the Dolphins-Bears rematch. They wanted to see Marino against that Bears defense."

Not that the Patriots could have cared any less about messing that up.

"As a kid you never dreamed you would go to a Super Bowl to watch it—now I was going to play in one," says Craig James. Recent Stanford grad Garin Veris had his own unique perspective coming off the previous year's Dolphins-49ers matchup at Stanford Stadium. "I had been the security guard for the Dolphins bench in the last Super Bowl, and now I was going to be on the field playing. It was surreal. But really I was most happy for guys like Hannah, Adams, and the other veterans."

And from Pat Sullivan: "I just felt really great for my dad. He took some shots and he finally made it."

***

Boston Garden filled up quickly on Wednesday night, January 22, 1986. The yuppies in their suits and power ties (pink and yellow were in) coming straight from their downtown offices, the kids and their parents from the surrounding neighborhoods. It was one loud, green melting pot. There was nothing like a playoff-like game in the middle of the season to warm up a cold January night. With the fans still giddy over the Patriots' rout of the Dolphins ten days earlier and gearing up for the Super Bowl, the Los Angeles Lakers were in town for their first game at the Garden since they ended the Celtics' season in Game Six of last year's finals, the only time a Celtic opponent ever celebrated a title on the Parquet Floor.

The Celtics-Lakers rivalry was in full bloom at this point, the teams having split the last two NBA Finals against each other. With the 1980s Celtics peaking to the point of moving convincingly past Philadelphia and anyone else in the East, they were now as dominant as Magic, Kareem, Worthy, and Co. were in the West, which they had taken five times in six years. The collision course to a third straight NBA Finals clash seemed inevitable as both teams toyed with the competition—Boston came into the game 30–8, Los Angeles 32–7.

Maybe it was the energy from the jacked-up crowd, maybe it was the Lakers being a bit tired playing their third road game in four nights, or maybe it was simply that first confirmation that the Celtics were the superior team this year, but it wasn't too much of a contest. Boston maintained a steady lead throughout, led by eight at halftime, and then cruised to a 110–95 win. Not everyone believes in "statement games," those midseason matchups against potential playoff opponents that may or may not have a psychological effect later on. But for anyone who is a believer in statements, Boston had certainly made one. Six Celtics scored in double figures. Dennis Johnson, clearly up for this big game, outplayed his namesake, Earvin (Magic) Johnson, with 22 points, six assists, and seven rebounds. Bird and Parish both put up double-doubles, Bird with 21 points and 12 rebounds and Parish, 16 with 11 rebounds.

But make no mistake, it was the big sixth man who stole the show. Bill Walton was everywhere, running the floor, playing both ends, and making things happen. He and the crowd seemed to feed off each other's energy as he took it to the Lakers with 11 points, eight rebounds, and *seven blocked shots* in just 16 minutes on the court.

Twice he blocked Kareem, once from the front and once from behind. He blocked Michael Cooper driving down the lane. He drove on Kareem and scored on a lefty runner. Later he sealed off Kareem inside, took a rifle pass from Ainge from the corner and dunked. He took a pass in the post, turned on Mitch Kupchak, and drained one of his old-school bank shots. Then he grabbed an offensive rebound off a McHale miss, gathered himself as three purple jerseys surrounded him, and went up strong for a slam. When Jones took him out of the game during the second half, Walton pumped his arms and fists as the crowd gave him a rousing ovation. The fans were watching vintage Walton, the UCLA and Portland Trail Blazer Walton. Not for as many minutes of course, but vintage all the same. Yeah, this marriage was working out. Worries about his ability to hold up physically were waning. With the season only halfway done you couldn't know for sure, but you didn't get the feeling that Walton's health was going to be a big issue the rest of the way.

Walton always enjoyed the challenge of going up against Kareem Abdul-Jabbar, the guy who had preceded him as John Wooden's dominant big man at UCLA and who Walton has always called his toughest NBA opponent. On this night a 38-year-old Kareem wasn't much of a match for the Parish-Walton tag team, shooting 6-for-20. The Lakers shot 38.6% as a team.

Maybe the best way to describe Bill Walton is that he isn't a guy who does anything halfway. If he's in, he's in. Basketball, music, cycling—he attacks it all with boundless energy. He doesn't just listen to music, he absorbs himself in it and takes life lessons from the lyrics of Bob Dylan, the Grateful Dead, and others (you may know that Walton is a devout Deadhead who has been to more than 800 shows of the Dead and its offshoot groups, sometimes even sitting in on drums). The bike isn't for leisurely rides through the neighborhood, it's for serious workouts. He attacked the stuttering problem he suffered with as a youth with enough vigor to score a long career as a television color analyst after his playing days ended, a gig he still holds today.

"I like speed and constant motion, riding my bike, playing drums, playing basketball," he says.

Growing up in San Diego with parents who held no interest in sports ("just wasn't their bag, my parents were about music and education," he says), Walton was playing basketball with professionals at the local gym when he was 14, a growing ninth grader who the big guys would invite into the games during their summer off-season workouts. Pat Riley, Jim Barnett, and John Block ran with him, and later Calvin Murphy and Elvin Hayes.

While his path took him to UCLA, Portland, and the San Diego/Los Angeles Clippers, Walton says he had already become a big fan of the Celtics as a kid in the 1960s. "Bill Russell, Sam Jones, K.C. Jones, Satch Sanders, and then [John] Havlicek," he says. He took to Laker radio broadcaster Chick Hearn and the way he painted the picture of the Celtics' motion and ball movement. Hearn, the longtime Laker guy, had unwittingly created a Celtics fan and, eventually, a Celtic.

As he began to get past the worst of his injuries by the mid-'80s, Walton figured he wanted to keep playing, but not for the dysfunctional Clippers. "Eventually I came to realize that life with [owner] Donald Sterling was a dead-end street," he says. The Lakers were a possibility, but their GM Jerry West, who knew Walton well—part of West's run as a Laker star in the early '70s overlapped with Walton's UCLA days—nixed the idea when he saw Walton's medical records. But Red Auerbach and Jan Volk were ready to roll the dice on him. If he harbored any doubts at all, the writer David Halberstam, who Walton describes as a longtime friend and mentor, helped dispel them. "David told me, 'Bill, the Celtics are for you,'" Walton says.

He knew Halberstam was right. "I love the team game, the fast break game. I loved the cultural identity of the Celtics. I thought I knew how good the basketball would be but I actually underestimated it," he says. "Everything good can always be traced back to leadership. Red was superb and Larry was superb."

So as usual Walton was all in. On the court he brought an infectious enthusiasm, as if deep down he knew the season figured to be one last run at glory.

To Walton, the arduous 82-game NBA season wasn't a grind at all. "The season is only long when you're injured. It's only long when it hurts to play. When you've got it going it's a dream," he says.

Off the court, Boston was a new city to call home for a while, and he was going to soak it all in. Walton lived in Cambridge and rode the T to the Garden on game nights ("red line to the green line" he remembers). Fans would spot him riding his bike through Cambridge and playing chess with the locals in Harvard Square.

Not that he was above indulging in the good life once in a while too. "I had a friend named Roman who was in the entertainment business. He knew every restaurant in town. We would go to these high-end, over-the-top restaurants after hours, like after a game. They'd open up for us." Yes, it was good to be a young man and a Boston Celtic in 1986. In a way it was a team made for the times. The 1980s yuppie era when people spent long hours at the office and long hours at the bar. Work hard and play hard. The Celtic players' office happened to be a basketball court, but it's the same idea. Says John Molori: "The team played hard and drank beers after the game, focused and fun loving," he says.

Molori remembers the Walton phenomenon. "I thought the '86 team was epitomized by Walton. He loved being a Celtic, loved the environment, riding his bike, you'd see him out there. The face of that team was Walton." Relaying this observation to Walton brings a quick rebuke: "Make no mistake, Larry Bird was the face of the Boston Celtics." Of course Walton is right that Bird, the top star, was the leader and "face of the franchise" in the traditional sense. But you also see Molori's point. Walton was the new guy and the key difference maker, playing with all that enthusiasm, visible in public. In a sense he was a franchise face too.

The sixth-man role was made to order for Walton and the Celtics. He'd play a career high 80 games in 1985/86 and average 7.6 points and 6.8 rebounds in 19.3 minutes a game. Not big headline numbers, but his season was filled with big-time performances as he often put up double-doubles or near double-doubles playing about half the game. At 33 he did it in shorter bursts, but that's all the team needed. "No question the trump card was Bill Walton," says Bob Ryan of the Celtics turning it up a notch from the earlier '80s teams. "He was blessed with good health. He comes in and has this symbiosis with Bird that was almost unfair." Many probably remember that classic Walton dish out of the post to a cutting Bird along the baseline as a common sight.

A look at some of the underlying advanced stats tells the story. For instance, the best way to measure a player's rebounding isn't just the number of boards he averages per game, but the number he gets compared to the number he could conceivably get when he's playing. Faster-paced games with more shots going up will produce more opportunities for things like rebounds and assists than a slower-paced game would, so you adjust each player's stats accordingly.

In 1985/86, Walton ranked 2nd in the league in defensive rebound percentage and 4th in overall rebound percentage, based on the percentage of available rebounds he grabbed when he was in the game. In blocked shot percentage he ranked 11th, all while shooting 56.2% from the floor. A stat called Win Shares per 48 Minutes attempts to assess a player's overall value by rolling up these numbers along with others that contribute positively or negatively to wins—assists, turnovers, free-throw percentage—and multiplying them out over a 48-minute game, the idea being to estimate how effective a player is within the context of the game and his minutes. On that basis, Walton ranked No. 18 in the NBA in 1985/86. (These things are never perfect, but for perspective Bird ranked No. 1, McHale No. 4, and Parish No. 13, so figure the formula is probably pretty accurate.)

What all these advanced stats mean is that Walton was one of the NBA's top players when he was on the floor. Ryan still marvels over his rebounding skills. "Like sweeping crumbs off the table," he says. "Just incredible timing on the defensive boards—you'd say almost flirting with goaltending the way he'd grab the ball just out of the cylinder."

Was the rebounding technique natural or learned? "Both," Walton says. "I loved to practice rebounding. I was happy to rebound when our shooters were shooting—Ainge, Wedman, Sichting, Bird. Watching the ball, moving toward the rim, then the calculation. . . ."

The Celtics won two more games to finish out Super Bowl week. With McHale sidelined with a bad Achilles, Wedman started against Golden State on Friday night and poured in 21 points with 13 rebounds in a 135–114 win. The rest of the bench kicked it in as well. Sichting hit all five of his field goal attempts to finish with 12 points and six assists in 18 minutes. And David Thirdkill, the young journeyman out of Bradley University who was now playing for his fifth team in his fourth NBA season after not working out as a first-round pick for Phoenix in 1982, caught fire off the bench for 20 points in 22 minutes. Joe Barry Carroll, incidentally, shot 2-for-14 for 6 points for the Warriors.

On Super Bowl Sunday, the Celtics and the Philadelphia 76ers gave the fans a very entertaining opening act in which Boston rallied in the second half for a 105–103 win at the Garden. Wedman had another good start in place of McHale, shooting 8-for-13 for 16 points. Bird's shot was off (9-for-25) but as usual that didn't matter so much with him since he connected for three three-pointers including one from half court at the third-quarter horn, and made all seven of his free throws to finish with 28 points to go along with 14 rebounds. Walton was Walton once again, attacking Philly centers

Moses Malone and Clemon Johnson for 19 points and 13 rebounds in just 25 minutes.

With the season at the halfway point, the Celtics were 33–8 and had the next three days off. Time to go home and watch the Super Bowl. Unfortunately for the fans, Walton, Wedman, and Bird would be the three best Boston players they would see that day.

***

There probably isn't much need to go through too many details of the Patriots' anticlimactic dud of a trip to New Orleans for Super Bowl XX. Better to take heart in the fact that in getting there the way they did, the victory was already realized. It was then their bad luck to go head-to-head in the big game against what might have been the best NFL team of all time. The swaggering 15–1 Chicago Bears, they of defensive coordinator Buddy Ryan's famous 46 defense that had allowed barely over 10 points a game during the season and then shut out both the Giants and Rams in the NFC playoffs. So vaunted was Chicago's smothering defense that it was hard to notice that their less-heralded offense averaged 28 points a game, second-best in the league.

These were the Bears of Dent and Singletary and Hampton, of loudmouth head coach Mike Ditka and loudmouth, renegade quarterback Jim McMahon. And the Bears of respected veteran running back Walter Payton, getting to his first Super Bowl at age 32 (remember the Bears were in their first Super Bowl too), and the commercially celebrated, overrated defensive tackle and part-time fullback William (Refrigerator) Perry.

Still the fans in Boston were hopeful, and for good reason. Their team had been on a major roll. They were fundamentally sound under Raymond Berry and didn't beat themselves. Sure, everyone knew the kind of season the Bears were having, but we're talking about one game. If we catch them on less than their best day, why not?

A perfectly logical thought, but it just didn't happen. The Pats' mostly smash-mouth, run-right-at-'em style just didn't match up well against Chicago's defense, which emphasized stacking the box with eight players near the line of scrimmage to stop the run and pressure the quarterback.

The game seemed to be settled in the first minute or so, even as it was the Patriots who took a 3–0 lead. Things started with the Pats picking up right where they left off in the AFC playoffs, forcing a Payton fumble on the game's second play to get the ball on the Chicago 19. Here we go? Not this time.

Eason missed on three straight passes, two of which he threw off of his back foot under big pressure. Franklin kicked the 36-yard field goal for the game's first points, but the Chicago defense seemed to be the biggest winner of the series. You just sensed how difficult it was going to be to move the ball on them.

And settling for the field goal wasn't nearly the most damaging part of New England's first series. On the very first play, tight end Lin Dawson blew out his knee on a noncontact play as he cut toward the sideline on a pass pattern. For the Pats, losing a tight end that early messed with their game plan, which called for using both Dawson and Ramsey to counter Chicago's defensive pressure with quick, short passes that the quarterback could get off after a short drop. According to Steve Grogan, "We had spent two weeks preparing a two–tight end offense to offset the 46 defense. Then suddenly we had to change the game plan." The competitor in Grogan can't help but mull the what-ifs; in addition to the Dawson injury he recalls a potential interception that Don Blackmon could have run back for a touchdown "but it went right through his hands." By and large, though, the Bears' dominance was thorough enough that it's hard to say that a couple of plays would have changed much.

That first minute of the game was the Patriots' highwater mark. By the end of the quarter, the Bears led 13–3. By halftime it was 23–3. Eason did not complete a single pass in the first half, going 0-for-6. "When Tony took the snap he saw Mike Singletary," says Lesley Visser of the relentless Chicago pressure.

"At halftime we knew it was over," says James. "It was disappointing to get to the pinnacle and fall short. When we got behind it became a passing game and that's not who we were."

Grogan came in—nice that he could see action in a Super Bowl in his 11th season—but it didn't make any notable difference. By the time he connected with Fryar for an 8-yard touchdown pass in the fourth quarter, the Bears had 44 points, their last touchdown coming almost as an insult when Perry lined up at fullback and plunged in from the 1.

The running game couldn't get anything going at all. The Patriots' rushing total: 11 carries, 7 yards. Yes, for the game. Overall, they were outgained 401–123. What had to make the outcome even more disappointing was that the Patriots had mostly sworn off any fun in New Orleans' French Quarter to concentrate on preparing for the game. "No one was out on Bourbon Street. We were all in by 10 p.m. You heard McMahon and others from the Bears would be out all night. So much for discipline," says James with a laugh.

The Bears defense forced six turnovers and sacked Eason and Grogan seven times, including Grogan in the end zone late in the game for the last two points in a 46–10 final. It's called running into a buzz saw. It happens, even to conference champions.

"The focus now is that we had a great season, [but] at the time it was disappointment," says Pat Sullivan.

And from Garin Veris: "They hit us hard that day. We [the defense] were on the field a lot. Hey, we had a great run. We were part of that Boston sports history and proud of that."

PART II

February to June, 1986

Chapter 4

February 1986

February, the dullest month on the sports calendar, many say. The Super Bowl and the NFL season have just ended (at least they did back then, before the steady creep toward a February Super Bowl). March Madness and baseball are still a little way off, as are the NBA and NHL playoffs. That leaves the dog days of winter, that mundane part of the pro basketball and hockey seasons when the individual games don't seem to mean a whole lot—there's only so much drama in following your team's chase for "playoff positioning."

The Boston Bruins were in the midst of an average year, their second straight after a long run of strong seasons, on their way to a 37-31-12 record and a first-round playoff exit at the hands of the hated Montreal Canadiens. Their Garden mates, the Celtics, just continued to win, which was almost dull in its own way, as in, we know how the season is going to play out, can we just skip ahead already?

But since that wasn't going to happen, it was best to think of a trip to the Garden to see the Celtics, as Bob Ryan once put it, as the sports equivalent of a night out at the theater or the opera. Or settling in for a TV broadcast knowing it was the best reality programming you would find that night (sports was truly the first reality television, right?). The Celtics were live entertainment at its best—the game of basketball played about as well as it was played anywhere in the world, performed by the most skilled professionals in the business. Just appreciate and enjoy. The playoffs would arrive soon enough.

After wrapping up January with back-to-back wins in Chicago and Washington, the Celtics hit February having lost just once since the Christmas Day meltdown in New York. Then they seemed to sleepwalk through the early part of their February 2 game as they watched the Seattle SuperSonics run by them for a 37–20 lead after one quarter in a game in which old friend Gerald Henderson would hit them with 20 points and seven assists. But the Celtics woke up in time to shave the deficit to 12 by halftime and then blitz the Sonics in the second half for a 114–101 win, a 30-point swing from the end of the first quarter.

Kevin McHale took a shot at getting back from his injured Achilles in the next game at Milwaukee, which figured as a reasonably tough road test. The Bucks were a strong team led by a genuine superstar in Sidney Moncrief and his top wingmen, Terry Cummings, Ricky Pierce, and Paul Pressey. Coming into the game at 32–17, they were good enough to at least harbor thoughts of being the team that could potentially knock off the Celtics in the Eastern Conference playoffs in the spring. Again, the significance of "statement games" is debatable, but a win here certainly wouldn't hurt Milwaukee's confidence.

The game turned into a mixed blessing for McHale. Coming off the bench, he gave his team a lift by hitting all six of his shots to score 13 points in 12 minutes. Nice, but not worth the price: He also aggravated the injury and would be out for the next three weeks. But even playing on the road with limited minutes from McHale, the Celtics were just too much for the Bucks. They broke open a tight game with a 37–24 third quarter on their way to a 19-point win, 112–93. And again, contributions came from everywhere as the ball kept moving, evidenced by the Celtics' 33 assists on 45 field goals. Dennis Johnson dished out eight of them while his smothering defense helped hold Moncrief to 4-of-13 shooting. Parish went for 20 points and seven rebounds while Bird showed his usual brilliance with 24 points, nine rebounds, and six assists. Wedman added 17 points on 8-of-13 from the floor while Sichting passed for five assists and made both of his shots from the floor in 19 minutes.

The Celtics may have been a bit tired when they returned home the next night to face Washington, a team with average talent but also with perhaps the NBA's biggest curiosity (or at least the tallest) in Manute Bol, the 7'7" project from Sudan who had come to the league via the University of Bridgeport. Bol swatted five Boston shots on the night as the Bullets kept it close for a half. But Bird's 26 points and 16 rebounds and Parish's 25 points helped the Celtics pull away in the second half for a 103–88 victory. Walton controlled the boards along with Bird, pulling down 17 rebounds in 28 minutes to go with 13 points.

The win was the Celtics' 13th in a row. With the season just a little more than halfway over, they already owned separate winning streaks of 8, 9, and 13 games. The record was 38–8 as they got set for a long road trip out West.

Cross-country road trips are tough in the NBA, and, yes, the Celtics did lose a few times on this one. Three out of seven to be exact. Playing without McHale, the Celtics began the trip with a tight loss in Sacramento and ended it with a tight loss in Denver, a game that Walton missed with a minor ankle injury. In between they took four of five including the trip's signature game, the Sunday afternoon CBS special against the Lakers for a two-game regular season sweep of their NBA co-power. Most any eastern team would take a 4–3 West Coast trip in a heartbeat. For the '86 Celtics it could practically be called a slump, except in the way the games showcased some of the qualities—flexibility, depth—that would help propel them the rest of the way. With Wedman starting in McHale's absence, Bird began mixing it up inside and crashing the boards even more than usual, essentially filling the power-forward vacuum while McHale rested his sore Achilles. Bird would grab double-digit rebounds in six of the trip's seven games, putting up triple-doubles in three of them.

Friday night, February 14, in Portland would become somewhat famous as the "Bird playing lefty game," after Larry Bird decided, apparently to help break up the monotony of the long trip, that he would play the game left-handed. The memory is a bit overdone—Bird did score left-handed from in close a few times, mostly early in the game. But anything medium to long range came with the natural right hand, and then once the tight game progressed into the second half, he mostly ditched the left-handed thing altogether. Once again the Blazers, the only road team to win a game at Boston Garden this season, were proving to be a thorn in the Celtics' side. Leading scorer Kike Vandeweghe, who had missed the game in Boston, lit it up for 38 points with Clyde Drexler adding 20 and nine assists. The game was close all the way and wound up in overtime, where a Bird leaner in the lane in the final seconds pulled out a wild 120–119 win. Bird's left and right hands were good for his biggest triple-double of the season: 47 points, 14 rebounds, and 11 assists. Johnson went for 29 on 11-of-18 shooting, while Ainge, the "shooter," put the ball up only three times as he passed off for 12 assists.

Two days later came the marquee game of the trip. The Lakers at The Forum, Sunday afternoon, national TV. Bird hit the boards hard all afternoon to the tune of 18 rebounds to go with his 22 points and seven assists. Dennis Johnson again outplayed Magic Johnson, finishing with 23 while Magic, almost implausibly, did not hit a field goal (0-for-4) in his 38 minutes. James Worthy went off for 35 points to keep the Lakers close all the way through, but the Celtics held on to their small lead through the fourth quarter to pull it out, 105–99. Jones used 10 players in the game, with Walton and Sichting chipping in their usual solid numbers off the bench and even Rick Carlisle getting in on the fun with 10 points on 5-for-7 shooting.

Things got a little bit chippy in the second half when Sichting and Byron Scott exchanged shoves and then Kite hacked both Kareem and Mike McGee with tough (well, let's be honest, dirty) fouls to prevent layups. The hard foul on McGee set off a minor brouhaha of words and shoves. When Magic and Michael Cooper came up close to Kite, he kept a blank stare as he used each hand to shove both of them away at once. You could almost read his mind: *You're Magic Johnson and I'm just Greg Kite? What do I care? Get out of my face.* It was almost like a statement within a statement for the Celtics—not only are we beating you this year, but our 10th man isn't impressed with your star.

The team still didn't see Boston Garden right away upon its return from out West, playing the first home game in 18 days at the Hartford Civic Center against the Indiana Pacers. The Celtics played three games in Hartford every year, a custom that helped the club stay engaged with that part of the fan base. So the Pacers didn't have to face any banners or ghosts, which was maybe why they kept it close most of the way. But the Celtics ultimately swatted them away with a big fourth quarter to pull away, 113–98. Parish had a huge night with 27 points and 15 rebounds while Bird put up yet another triple-double. And Scott Wedman again had the shooting touch going, sinking 8-of-11 for 19 points.

Wedman was making the most of his time in the starting lineup even though he knew he'd be giving it up upon McHale's return. And he was fine with that. He had come to Boston midway through the 1982/83 season in a trade with Cleveland, prepared for a reduced role at age 30. "It was a great time for me to come there, under the circumstances. I wanted to win a championship. What made it easy was the talent of Larry Bird. That made it real simple."

As a Celtic he became best known for sinking all 11 of his shot attempts in the team's 148–114 thrashing of the Lakers in Game One of the 1985 NBA Finals, a game dubbed "The Memorial Day Massacre." It was a beatdown that remains memorable in team history despite the Lakers coming back to take the series in six games that year.

A quiet sort who grew up in Kansas and Colorado, Wedman was drafted out of the University of Colorado by the Kansas City-Omaha Kings with the sixth overall pick in 1974, five spots behind Bill Walton. He was a svelte 6'7" and he could shoot the basketball. Wedman was one of the NBA's better players from the mid-1970s into the early '80s, averaging at least 15 points a game for six straight years and earning two All-Star Game nods while playing for some pretty decent Kansas City teams with Nate Archibald, Sam Lacey, and Otis Birdsong. He went to Cleveland as a free agent in 1981 and then to Boston a year and a half later in a trade for young big man Darren Tillis, the Celtics' first-round draft pick in 1982 who wasn't getting much playing time.

The veteran reserve role suited Wedman. After eight seasons, he was happy to trade minutes for rings. He got one of those in 1984 and now he was gunning for a second. Not that it was easy right away, even for a veteran of Wedman's stature. Matched up against Bird in practice, he wasn't cut any breaks. Bird went at him hard. "Larry tested everyone who came through that door, everyone had a bit of a hazing period." He was passionate about his health, doing aerobics and even bringing his own water to practice. He took some ribbing, but he's pretty sure the approach benefited him: "Yes, I was little bit ahead of my time. I'd bring my own water. I wasn't the most physically gifted player but I would be ready to play. I never pulled a hammy or anything like that, any injuries I got were from contact."

Wedman maintained his Kansas City home during the offseason, where he had a real estate business that he still runs today. But he soaked up as much of New England as he could. "We lived in Natick," he says. "My wife and I thoroughly enjoyed Boston. I'd usually take a week or two off right after the season and we'd see the Cape, Newport, and some other places. Then it was back to Kansas City to start working out."

Chapter 5

March–April 1986

As February droned on, the highlight of the month was the gradual return of Kevin McHale. He first gave it a whirl in a win at New York but the rust was still heavy—five turnovers and no points in seven minutes. But it didn't take very long. He began shaking it off at home the next night with 14 points and eight boards in 17 minutes in a win over San Antonio and then dropped 26 on the Clippers and old friend Cedric Maxwell in a 124–108 win on February 28.

It all led up to a March 2 matchup against the Detroit Pistons, a rising team in the East that had given the Celtics a pretty tough second-round playoff series in 1985 before bowing out in six games.

For Boston and other teams around the league, the Pistons weren't quite the hated antagonists they would become about a year later, but they were getting there in a hurry. Their big guys, Bill Laimbeer and Rick Mahorn, were called the "Bruise Brothers" and generally detested as dirty players, Laimbeer in particular. Boston's homer radio play-by-play man Johnny Most, who never seemed to meet an opponent he liked or respected, would refer to the pair as "McFilthy" and "McNasty." He first came up with the monikers for Mahorn and fellow tough guy Jeff Ruland when they played together with the Washington Bullets and later transferred them to Mahorn and Laimbeer when they teamed up in Detroit. It was hard to tell which guy was which, though it didn't much matter as they were interchangeable. You would hear statements occasionally from Celtic brass that showed some respect to Mahorn as a guy who, while sometimes dirty, was at least genuinely tough. As for Laimbeer, forget it. He was sneaky-dirty, a cheap-shot artist who would throw elbows at players who weren't looking and sometimes even get down on all fours behind an opposing player who, should he happen to take an unsuspecting step back, could fall right over Laimbeer and seriously hurt himself, à la Steve Grogan–Ben Rudolph (if no one was ever badly hurt by this little technique it wasn't for Laimbeer's lack of trying).

The Pistons' other big antagonist you probably remember from the era, Dennis Rodman, was still a year away from being drafted. But it was best to not let yourself get distracted by Detroit's physical style, because the team could play. They had the dynamite backcourt of Isaiah Thomas and Joe Dumars, backed up by Vinnie (Microwave) Johnson, so named for his knack for entering a game and heating up in a hurry. Laimbeer (unlike Mahorn) did have some skills to go along with his villainous tricks—he was a good rebounder and shooter who could hit that "pick and pop" open jumper. Laimbeer's former Notre Dame teammate Kelly Tripucka was a scorer at the small forward spot, averaging 20 a game.

The Pistons had one more bad guy, not so much in a general sense but a player who fueled the fire for Larry Bird. Detroit's center–power forward Kent Benson had been a college star at Indiana a decade earlier. As a veteran Hoosier he had reportedly not been very nice to Bird during Bird's brief freshman tenure at IU, a mistake of lasting consequence that continued to motivate Bird whenever the Celtics played a Benson team.

In this latest Sunday afternoon CBS game, Detroit came out with good energy to match the Celtics during a first half of numerous lead changes. Riding Thomas (25 points, 14 assists) and Tripucka (20 points), the Pistons led by three at the break. But then it was McHale, in his last game coming off the bench, who would power Boston past Detroit in the second half. Scoring from inside, hitting open shots from outside, and running on the break, McHale scored 14 of the Celtics' 36 third-quarter points to drive them to a 9-point lead.

The onslaught continued in the fourth quarter as the Celtics pulled away for a 20-point win, 129–109. McHale finished the afternoon 10-for-10 from the floor and 5-for-5 from the line for 25 points in just 23 minutes. It was pretty safe to say that he'd shaken off all the rust. Bird's sweet game against Kent Benson brought 35 points, including 11-of-11 free throws, and Ainge went off for a career high 27 on 11-of-18 shooting. Competition was officially becoming scarce. The Celtics had now won 14 of 16 against their four tough-est Eastern Conference rivals, Philadelphia, Detroit, Milwaukee, and Atlanta, not to mention their 2-for-2 against the Lakers. Overall, they were 47–11. The biggest challenge the rest of the way, it seemed, would be staying interested and staying sharp.

Few fans in Boston knew much about Kevin McHale when the Celtics drafted him with the No. 3 overall pick out of Minnesota in 1980 as part of what would become the renowned "McHale and Parish for Joe Barry Carroll trade." He wasn't a high-profile college player, at least not outside of Minnesota and perhaps other parts of Big Ten country. In an era before myr-iad cable networks were broadcasting college games all over the place, most fans knew what they were spoon fed from a limited TV schedule that centered on the top college programs and the March NCAA tournament. All-American honors went to players like North Carolina's Mike O'Koren, Duke's Mike Gminski, DePaul's Mark Aguirre, and Notre Dame's Kelly Tripucka.

Minnesota and McHale ran mostly under the radar. The Golden Gophers were never a tournament team during McHale's four years, partly because of prior recruiting violations resulting in a postseason ban from the NCAA for part of that time. The typical fan in Boston hadn't seen McHale on television and had little idea of who he was beyond the vague knowledge that he was considered a good prospect in the 1980 draft.

But while the name Kevin McHale didn't particularly register with the average fan, it registered with those who were paid to know about him: NBA scouts and general managers. Obviously there was a reason he went so high in the draft. The size, the wingspan spawned by those long arms, the footwork, and the shooting touch—the only surprise to Jan Volk was McHale not being picked even higher.

"We would have taken McHale with the number-one pick," he says, an assertion that if true makes it all the more galling to a Warriors fan that the Celtics managed to pry Robert Parish away from Golden State to switch picks in a deal that landed them the guy they wanted anyway. Those countless post moves you saw from McHale weren't particularly learned over time while he was wearing Celtic green, they were there from day one, according to Volk. "He came factory installed, he had all the bells and whistles," he says.

McHale's low-post game naturally got him to the free-throw line a lot, where he took advantage by shooting 80% for his career. And there was the defense. Big enough to guard a center or power forward and quick enough to guard some small forwards, McHale would block a couple of shots a game and alter enough others to make the NBA All-Defensive team (either first or second team) six times. Says Rick Weitzman: "He had unique skills, an unstoppable low-post player and a *terrific* defensive player. He could cover, really defend."

With a breezy personality and a penchant for jokes, McHale was the guy who kept things loose on the '80s Celtics. And he'd yak it up with pretty much anyone who would listen. "He could talk to anyone in a coffee shop at 2 a.m.," says Jeff Twiss. McHale once told Scott Wedman that he'd emptied the special water Wedman brought to practice and refilled the bottle with tap water (Wedman still isn't sure if McHale actually did this or was just messing with him by telling him he did). Twiss remembers the time McHale pranked Johnny Most, the team's heavy smoking, raspy-voiced radio man. "Kevin put one of those exploding cigarettes into Johnny's pack. Johnny yelled out in panic," Twiss says.

His easygoing manner came through in media interviews, such as when he'd ask a morning drive radio host on the air to see that the station play something that afternoon by his fellow Hibbing, Minnesota, native Bob

Dylan. "I'll be heading into town about three, how about a double shot of Bob for me?"

Through it all, he seemed to have a knack for remembering where he came from and accepting his role of Robin to Bird's Batman on the Celtics. Once, after playing 50 minutes or so in a double overtime game, a reporter understandably mentioned his workload and that he must be exhausted. "Kevin stopped for a minute and talked about his dad working 14-hour days in the iron mines in Minnesota. He didn't complain about minutes. He had a knack for putting things into perspective," Twiss says.

On the court, few doubt that his big numbers could have been even bigger in a different situation, one where the offense flowed through him more often. "Kevin McHale could have been a historically great scorer, but he recognized that wasn't the best recipe for the team. He recognized that Larry was the centerpiece. His ego didn't require him to be the top dog," says Volk. It was a template that others followed. "Dennis also went that way, and Robert went that way." And from Weitzman: "He was the kind of guy who went with the flow, he saw the success the organization was having and he didn't want to rock the boat."

The wins continued to pile up. After the Detroit game the Celtics took both ends of a home and home against the Chicago Bulls and then defeated the Ewing-less Knicks team at Boston Garden 115–108 with McHale's 20 points leading six players in double figures (New York's strong fourth quarter made the final score closer than the game was). It was the Celtics' 8th win in a row, their second 8-game winning streak to go along with separate streaks of 9 and 13 games. The record was 50–11.

The latest streak ended the following night in Washington when the Bullets rallied from a 10-point halftime deficit to force overtime and then pull it out 110–108. Manute Bol again played the intimidator by blocking eight shots to help his club overcome huge games from Boston's big men: McHale poured in 33, and Parish grabbed *25 rebounds* to go with 16 points.

Two nights later in Dallas a two-game losing streak ensued, despite a game-long highlight show from Larry Bird. Driving the lane, hitting the offensive glass for rebounds and putbacks, and bombing away from the outside (4-for-7 from three), Bird went for 50 points on 18-of-33 shooting and 10-of-11 from the line. Just for kicks he added 11 boards and five assists. Unfortunately it wasn't quite enough as the Mavericks, boosted by 32 from Rolando Blackman, 24 from Sam Perkins, and 18 with 10 assists from their solid, underrated point guard Brad Davis, reeled off 35 fourth-quarter points to pull out the game 116–115.

But nothing in the 1985/86 script was changing for the Celtics. Win a bunch of games, lose a couple of tight ones, and then win a whole bunch more. They took the next two games of the Texas trip, in Houston, in San

Antonio, and then went to Atlanta and won there by shooting 58% with six players again in double figures to offset 42 points from Dominique Wilkins (Sichting and Walton combined to sink 9-of-11 off the bench). Then it was back home on Sunday, March 16, for a 118–101 spanking of the Sixers as Bird went for 36 with 14 rebounds.

The win over Philly kicked off a long eight-game homestand to close out the month of March. The Celtics won every one of them, including a 30-point blowout of Cleveland in Hartford in which Bird connected on 5-of-6 threes and scored 43 points in 29 minutes, and a 19-point win over Washington on March 28 when Walton started for an injured Parish and put up 20 points and 12 rebounds in 26 minutes (Manute Bol blocked only three shots in this one). It was Boston's 60th win of the season against 13 losses, marking the sixth time in Larry Bird's seven seasons they had reached the 60-win plateau. And this time they'd done it with nine games to spare. Getting set to play out the last bit of the regular season, the Celtics had already clinched the best record in the Eastern Conference and were 4½ up on the Lakers for top record over-all and home court advantage throughout the playoffs, a perch they would wrap up shortly.

***

Down in Winter Haven, Florida, just a few hours before the Celtics col-lected win No. 60, the Boston Red Sox edged the New York Mets in an exhibition game 6–5 in 10 innings. There was some of the usual minor news as spring training wound down—pitcher Mike Trujillo and outfielder Kevin Romine were being optioned to Triple-A Pawtucket. And one piece of news that was a bit more significant: GM Lou Gorman announced that he had swapped his designated hitter Mike Easler to the Yankees for their DH, Don Baylor. Well, okay, thought most people, including the local press. One veteran bat dealt for another, the lefty going to Yankee Stadium to take aim at the short right filed porch and the righty coming to Fenway Park to take aim at the Green Monster. Makes sense. The only real surprise was any deal with the Yankees as trades between fierce division rivals were rare. The last time the Sox had dealt with the Yankees was back in 1972 when they were hosed into giving up future relief ace Sparky Lyle for a forgettable infielder named Danny Cater.[1] That one had smarted—Lyle would win the American League Cy Young Award for a 1977 Yankee club that edged the Red Sox by 2½ games in the A.L. East.

Baylor had taken George Steinbrenner's money three years earlier when he signed in New York as a free agent but then found that playing for Steinbrenner wasn't much fun. He wanted out of there but he also wanted the right situation. Armed with a no-trade clause, he had reportedly vetoed an earlier deal that would have sent him to the White Sox for Carlton Fisk when the White Sox declined to guarantee his option for another year.[2] Baylor was 36 and, like Easler, coming off a pretty modest 1985 season, so expectations weren't grand. The trade wasn't viewed as anything earth shattering, just as a good fit from a righty-lefty standpoint, one that figured to add some power to the DH spot.

But no matter who was DHing, no one was picking the 1986 Boston Red Sox to win the American League East. In fact, few were picking them to finish as high as third, or even fourth. Local columnist Mike Barnicle of the *Boston Globe*, mainly a metro and politics guy who delved into sports here and there, couldn't resist a classic rip job just a couple of days after the Baylor trade in his March 31 column. Don't get too excited about this upcoming season, Barnicle warned his readers.

In his biting, sarcastic season preview, Barnicle described the 1986 roster as "a collection of misfits, crybabies and overpaid no-talents." Manager John McNamara was a "house boy" and "so close to Haywood Sullivan that he often resembles a boil on Sully's neck. That's why he's there." Reliever Bob Stanley, who'd had some good seasons in Boston but wasn't, shall we say, the perfect picture of a physical specimen "must have an incentive clause in his contract that provides him with doughnuts instead of money." As for Wade Boggs, who cared that he could rake with the best of them, he was basically a selfish singles hitter who would never lead a team to a World Series: "Wade Boggs has never shared a cab, had a drink or eaten a meal with anyone other than his bat." There was a bit more, concluding with: "They stink, they are pathetic, they are at best a .500 club."

Okay then.

Most fans in Boston weren't as down on the Sox as Mike Barnicle was, but they weren't expecting a whole lot either. Why would they after the mediocrity they'd been witnessing for the past few years? The nice run of the mid-to-late 1970s, when the Red Sox contended strongly a few times even as they'd come up short of a championship had given way to a lot of average teams in the 1980s. Fred Lynn, Carlton Fisk, Rick Burleson, Luis Tiant, and longtime leader Carl Yastrzemski were gone, leaving Rice, Evans, and Stanley as the only holdovers from better days.

The pitching staff had lacked anything resembling an ace in the starting rotation or a lights-out reliever in the bullpen during the first half of the 1980s. Their last true stud pitcher was Dennis Eckersley during his first two Boston seasons in 1978 and '79. But the early '80s brought Eck's decline (long before he would reverse course as a relief pitcher in Oakland), and the likes of Mike Torrez and John Tudor, while solid at times, weren't going to fill the hole at the top.

The Sox had tried out players like catcher Gary Allenson and shortstop Glenn Hoffman without much success. Veteran stopgaps like outfielder Rick Miller and first baseman–designated hitter Tony Perez came and went. The team did score a good trade when they acquired third baseman Carney Lansford from the Angels in 1981 and watched him win a batting title. In 1982 Lansford missed a month with an injury which gave a young Wade Boggs an opening at third base. Lansford returned but Boggs had shown that he clearly ought to play every day. The Sox were able to parlay Lansford into a deal with Oakland for power-hitting outfielder Tony Armas, who would pop 36 homers in his first year with Boston in 1983 and then lead the league with 43 in 1984. But Armas's success wouldn't last as injuries cut into his production shortly after he turned 30. After 1984 he'd hit just another 61 homers over his last five seasons.

Just as few people had expected anything different from the Patriots in the fall of 1985, why would they expect anything different from the Red Sox in the spring of 1986?

The phenom, Roger Clemens, was fresh off minor surgery on his pitching shoulder. He was not having a good spring, and McNamara was not going to pitch him during the opening series in Detroit. Bruce Hurst would get the opening day nod, followed by Oil Can Boyd and Al Nipper. Clemens wouldn't go until the second series of the year in Chicago.

At that point, who knew what kind of season lay in store for Clemens? His young career was already at something of a crossroads. Since debuting in the big leagues in May 1984, he'd shown potential greatness, once striking out 15 Kansas City Royals in his rookie year. But the troublesome right shoulder kept nagging at him. A classic power pitcher (fastball, slider), his early career had been a series of stops and starts. Clemens started 35 games across 1984 and '85, about the equivalent of one full season. Persistent shoulder pain is always a big concern for a pitcher, enough to wonder if his career will ever really get going.

Clemens recalls the frustration that was his 1985 season. "In some games the velocity was there early but by the fourth inning I couldn't break a pane of glass. With the team not going anywhere in '85 they shut me down and my agent recommended this doctor down in Georgia, not well known then, Dr. James Andrews. Doc and I put together a pitching plan. He'd say that some days you'll feel like you can throw 90—don't." After the arthroscopic procedure, Clemens stuck with the plan to ramp up gradually. "He said, 'You're always going to have the shoulder of a 35-year-old.' Some days I felt like I could pitch in a big-league game, some days it was hard to play catch from 30 feet."

Dr. Andrews, of course, wouldn't remain under the radar much longer. In a long career as the sports industry's most successful orthopedic surgeon, he's saved more athletic careers than he could ever count. Says Clemens: "Someone, it may have been Bo Jackson, once said that if Doc had a quarter for every athlete he's put back on the field, Bill Gates would be cutting his lawn."

Clemens was feeling stronger by the time spring training 1986 came around. The question was whether it would all hold up as the season got going and if he'd be able to put together a big full year for the first time. "Back then arm surgery was a coin flip," says Bill Ballou, a reporter with the *Worcester Telegram & Gazette* who would pick up the full-time Red Sox beat the following year.

Elsewhere, much of the roster would be familiar. Bill Buckner and Wade Boggs manning the corner infield spots. Jim Rice, Tony Armas, and Dwight Evan patrolling the outfield. Marty Barrett, a decent contact hitter with so-so range in the field was back for this third full year as the starting second baseman. Rich Gedman was a solid young catcher who could hit, that spot looked fine. The bench wasn't a strong suit. Steve Lyons, a good athlete who could chase the ball down in the outfield but was not much of a hitter, was the fourth outfielder. Team CEO Haywood Sullivan's son Marc, in the middle of a 137-game big league career in which he'd hit .186, was the backup catcher. Utility men Dave Stapleton and Ed Romero, whom Gorman had picked up in a trade with Milwaukee for relief pitcher Mark Clear, backed up in the infield (quite amazing how often Dave Stapleton's name would later come up in '86 Red Sox lore for a guy who would get on the field in just 39 games and bat .128).

The Easler-for-Baylor swap looked to be a potential minor upgrade at DH, nothing more. Before he brought in Baylor, the other big deal that Lou Gorman had made during the winter was his swap of starter Bobby Ojeda to the Mets for young pitchers Calvin Schiraldi and Wes Gardner (along with a few lesser prospects tossed in on both sides). At the moment, that big deal was seen as, well, not that big of a deal. Who knew what Schiraldi or Gardner would turn out to be? Ojeda had had his ups and downs at Fenway the previous few years, but the thinking was that the lefty junk baller figured to be more consistent in a spacious National League park like Shea Stadium.

Schiraldi, the key man from Gorman's perspective, was a young guy with a big arm who hadn't yet tapped his potential. Gorman was familiar with Calvin Schiraldi. A former teammate of Clemens at the University of Texas, Schiraldi had been drafted by the Mets when Gorman was there as a top lieutenant to general manager Frank Cashen. Schiraldi had been part of the big group of young pitchers the Mets were assembling in the minors during the early '80s along with Dwight Gooden, Ron Darling, Walt Terrell, and some others. But his occasional call-ups to the big club in 1984 and '85 hadn't gone well. The Mets, fully ready to contend for a title after 98 wins in

1985, preferred a young veteran like Ojeda to round out their starting rotation. For now, Sox fans couldn't know how much to expect from Schiraldi, who was still a work in progress. He'd open the season at Pawtucket where he'd be converted to a relief pitcher. Power arms like Schiraldi's were known to sometimes flourish in the bullpen; maybe that spot would be the right one for him.

The position that remained in a seemingly constant state of flux was shortstop, a weak link since the departure of Rick Burleson after the 1980 season. For the past five years the spot had been manned by a combination of Glenn Hoffman and Jackie Gutierrez, neither of whom managed to distinguish himself with either the bat or the glove. Before the start of the '86 season, Gorman found some salvage value for Gutierrez by swapping him to Baltimore for reliever Sammy Stewart. Hoffman would open the season at short but wound up suffering from a concerning condition involving his heart valve. He would recover physically, but he wouldn't see any more major league action until a few token appearances near the end of the season. By May the club would replace him with young call-up Rey Quinones, who never got going offensively or defensively.

As usual it would come down to the pitching, which was littered with question marks. Certainly Boyd looked solid. Everyone knew that Clemens could be a lot more than solid, but would he be healthy? And what to make of Hurst, he of mediocre career numbers but who at last sight looked like a guy turning the corner? Was his big second half in '85 for real? The bullpen looked thin, with Stanley the biggest name out there among Joe Sambito, Steve Crawford, and Sammy Stewart. Would these guys they got for Ojeda, Schiraldi, and Gardner bring much help?

Overseeing all of it was John McNamara, a veteran manager who was generally respected for knowing the game but not thought to be much of a difference maker. A Californian and a career minor league catcher during his playing days, McNamara's big-league clubs tended to play to their talent level—winning records with the A's and Reds, losing records with the Padres and Angels. He was a safe, noncontroversial pick to replace the retiring Ralph Houk in Boston in 1985. Fans saw a .500-type manager running a .500-type team. He had no real use for the press, showing little patience for those who might second guess him.

"Taciturn" is Steve Krasner's best one-word term to describe McNamara. According to the Oxford dictionary, the word means "reserved or uncommunicative in speech; saying little." That was McNamara, a reserved sort who was guarded with the media. "If he got a question from a reporter he didn't know he'd turn his head, look down his nose, and say, 'Where are you from?' He wasn't the type to sit in the dugout during batting practice and tell war stories," Krasner says. But, he adds, "The veterans liked him because it was 'just go play.'"

Krasner is a lot more diplomatic than Bill Ballou, who picked up the Red Sox beat in 1987. "John McNamara was the single most difficult person I ever dealt with in sports," Ballou says flat out. "He was uncomfortable in the spotlight. I think he was a problem drinker. He'd snap, roll his eyes." Ballou's observations, to be clear, came a little bit after 1986, by which time McNamara may have been tired of answering the constant swirl of questions about the World Series and had even less patience with the press. And sometimes he didn't trust their motives. Once, according to Ballou, McNamara "stared right at [*Boston Globe* writer] Dan Shaughnessy while telling reporters, 'Some people pick us to win just so I can get fired if we don't.'"

With opening day in Detroit around the corner, the Sox looked much like the .500 group from the year before. A lot would have to go right to change that. But sometimes that's just what happens. After all this was Boston, and it was 1986.

***

The Celtics didn't stop after victory No. 60 against Washington. Wins over New Jersey, Cleveland, Detroit, and New York ran their latest unbeaten streak to 14 games. And so they owned winning streaks of 8, 9, 13, 8 again, and now 14. The streak was finally snapped in the next game at Philadelphia in a crazy ending when Julius Erving grabbed possession off a jump ball in the foul circle and sank a three-pointer at the buzzer for a dramatic 95–94 Sixers win. So to sum up what the Celtics did over about six weeks: win eight straight, lose by two, lose by one, win 14 straight, lose by one. If roughly three more shots fall they're riding a 25-game winning streak. The response to the buzzer-beating loss in Philly wasn't exactly panic—Jones toyed with the lineup by starting the Green Team in Milwaukee two nights later and watched them roll to a 126–114 win over the 55–24 Bucks behind 22 points and 12 rebounds from Walton, 15 points from Sichting, and 26 with 14 rebounds from Bird off the bench.

No doubt the most impressive win during the tail end of the streak was the 122–106 victory over the Pistons at the Garden on April 2, when the vaunted front line had its way with Bill Laimbeer and Kent Benson. Parish put up a monster game with 30 points and 18 rebounds, McHale went for 24 and 8 rebounds on 12-of-18 from the floor, and Bird registered yet another triple-double with 29 points, 11 rebounds, and 13 assists. If you're keeping count, that's 83 points and 37 rebounds from the starting frontcourt alone. For Bird, the triple-double was his ninth of the season; he'd finish with a league-leading 10. He would wind up the year 4th in the NBA in scoring (25.8), 7th in rebounding (9.8—the highest among non-centers or power forwards), 14th in assists (6.8—the highest among non-guards unless we count Milwaukee's Paul Pressey who slid back and forth between small forward and guard), 1st in free-throw percentage (89.6%), 1st in three-pointers made (82), and 4th in three-point shooting percentage (42.3%). The advanced stats—efficiency rating, win shares—rated him at the top of the league. At the end of the regular season he would be voted NBA Most Valuable Player for the third year in a row.

There are only so many ways to capture the career of Larry Bird with anything that you haven't likely seen or heard countless times. The talent, the confidence, the legendary blue-collar work ethic. Though he ostensibly played at small forward most of the time and at power forward some of the time, he never particularly fit either spot in the traditional sense. Rather, he was just Bird; he could do it all. Play the tough game and play the finesse game. Battle fearlessly in the paint where he could score and rebound, and launch rainbows from the outside. Run the floor and push the break. And of course the passing ability. He was the main scorer and main facilitator at once. Defensively he wasn't quick enough to guard some opposing small forwards one on one, but he had the instinct for anticipating passes and getting steals. "There was no part of the game he couldn't do," says Rick Weitzman. "At some point you would take it for granted but it was a rare attribute."

Put simply, Bird just always seemed to make the right play. He'd have a shot lined up but then give it up at the last instant if he spotted a cutting teammate. "He just saw the court so well, and he had that innate confidence," says Bob Lobel.

He could be tough and demanding with his teammates, but they didn't seem to mind. The familiar line comes from Jan Volk: "Larry Bird made everyone else better." That notion that the mark of a great player is one who makes his teammates better has become a bit of a cliché, but that doesn't make it any less true. When your top player is clearly a team guy who puts winning above everything else, how does anyone dare play for himself? And when you find that moving without the ball brings the reward of a pass for a layup or open jumper, you're motivated to move without the ball. Fundamentals beget fundamentals. And it usually seemed to start with number 33.

Remembers Jeff Twiss, "You never wanted to turn your eyes away from him because you might miss one of those quick strikes or tip passes."

Bird could be described as a flashy player, but you never got the feeling that he was trying to be flashy. The entertaining stuff was just a natural by-product of his fundamentals and instincts. The quick no-look pass was effective because it allowed him to zip the ball past a defender before the defender was ready—that it looked flashy and made the fans say "whoa!" was just an unintended bonus. Same for when Bird would bounce a pass between a defender's legs: simply the best way to get the ball from point A to point B. It's almost impossible for a defender to get to a ball that's on a downward trajectory coming toward him and then hits the ground right by his feet. It's a more effective pass than trying to slip it past the defender to the side or over the top, where it's easier to deflect. So again, it's a pure fundamental play that happens to look flashy.

Most of what you hear about Bird these days concerns a different part of his game: trash talking. Hop on YouTube and you could spend half the day perusing videos of Larry Bird trash talking stories, mostly from humiliated former opponents who have apparently decided that enough time has passed to look back and laugh now. It's as if the on-court cockiness has now over-shadowed his game when it comes to shaping the Bird legend. It's all pretty surprising to those who saw him play, because the trash talking really wasn't apparent at the time. Bird rarely looked animated on the court, so you didn't particularly notice it on television, or even if you were at the game. Bird came across more like a silent assassin than a big gum flapper, yet he was subtly getting into his opponents' heads. From Scott Wedman: "Larry's trash talking wasn't that boisterous. He'd get in your ear and tell you what he was going to do."

There's little doubt that Bird's play and his arrogance toward his opponents went hand in hand, each feeding off the other. There's rarely greatness with-out confidence, and vice versa. "He had a cockiness that great players *have* to have," Weitzman says. "He was as competitive an individual as I've ever met. His desire for success set him above anyone else, except maybe Magic. When McHale scored 56 one game [in March 1985], you knew Bird would have to beat that, and he did." And when that intensity and focus really set in, forget it. Remembers Walton: "Sometimes K.C. would send Scotty Wedman in for Larry, and Larry would just say, 'I'm not coming out, find someone else.' Scotty would look back at K.C. like . . . ?"

Weitzman and others who were around Bird at the time also remember his modest and humorous sides off the court. Sometimes he'd challenge report-ers to free-throw shooting contests before practice. "His teammates didn't want to play him," Weitzman says. Once when the Celtics' team bus passed by a Home Depot ad on the side of the road that included the catchphrase 'Need a bench? Call Home Depot' Bird blurted out, "I guess I need to call Home Depot."

He was good with the local press, dutifully rehashing the games night after night, though he didn't particularly like attention. Says Jeff Twiss: "What he'd say postgame was usually spot on, he could break down the game very well. But Larry didn't want the spotlight, his theory was 'I'm not the Boston Celtics,' yet everyone wanted to talk to Larry." Bird generally reserved the national telecasts as a time for spreading the wealth around. "Larry wouldn't do the walk-off interview with CBS, not because he didn't like them but because it was 'McHale had a great game, talk to him.' It was just Larry being Larry. He'd say, 'Jeff, I get paid to play basketball, not to do interviews.' "

Bill Walton recounts one of the ways Bird would take care of his teammates off the court. "There was a place a couple of blocks from the Garden called the Scotch and Sirloin. The owner was Harry and he was always trying to get Larry to endorse the place. Larry didn't want to do it but Harry kept pestering him. Finally Larry says okay, but he tells Harry don't pay me a dime, just make sure my teammates can come in anytime and eat for free. If they don't tip enough let me know. Often when Larry was ready to leave, but only when he thought no one was watching, he would walk around and sprinkle hundred-dollar bills on the tables. Larry always carried a huge wad of cash."

On the court, the Larry Bird of the mid-1980s was an all-time player at the height of his power. Not just part of an exclusive group but the undisputed king. That roughly three-year window when Kareem, Dr. J, and Moses Malone were moving past their peaks and Michael Jordan hadn't yet reached his. When Magic was nearly as great but not quite; when Isaiah Thomas, Charles Barkley, Dominique Wilkins, and a few others were great but not quite as great as Magic. From 1984 to 1986 the NBA was Larry Bird's league. Three straight MVPs, three conference titles, two championship rings, and averaging close to a triple-double (26 points, 10 rebounds, and seven assists a game over the three seasons). And all with John Hannah-like durability: Bird missed exactly five games in three years.

Where to rank Larry Bird among the all-time greats? It's a tough question that could be debated ad nauseam. But consider that in remembering the Celtics shooting from 29 wins to 61 wins the year Bird joined them, it's essentially impossible to find a player who had a bigger impact on a team after being drafted. Wilt Chamberlain led the Philadelphia Warriors to 49 wins in 1959 from 32 the previous year. Bill Russell in 1956 nudged the Celtics win total up by just five, from 39 to 44. Michael Jordan's Bulls went from 27 wins to 38 in 1984. Oscar Robertson bumped the Cincinnati Royals from 19 wins to 33 in 1960. Both Rick Barry (1965 Warriors) and LeBron James (2003 Cavs) more than doubled their clubs' win totals from 17 to 35 but still wind up in arrears of Larry Bird. Kareem Abdul-Jabbar comes closest, immediately pushing the Milwaukee Bucks from 27 wins to 56 wins in 1969. He'd win a title the following year, just as Bird would in his second season.

None of this is to suggest that some of these players may not rate higher than Bird on the all-time list—again, you could debate the pecking order of this group of players forever. But the fact that none could match him in the immediate turnaround department says a lot. Especially when you consider that the only other player of any significance the Celtics added in Bird's rookie year was M.L. Carr, a decent player at the time but no All-Star.

Otherwise, Bird was playing with the same group that had sputtered to a 29–53 mark a year earlier.

As for Magic Johnson, he joined a 1979 Laker team that was a lot better than the Celtic team Bird inherited, one that went 47–35 the prior year with the likes of Kareem, Norm Nixon, and Jamaal Wilkes. Adding Magic pushed that squad over the top to 60 wins and a championship in 1979/80, but he wasn't quite the top dog in L.A. right off the bat the way Bird was in Boston. Sure, their individual rivalry was great for the league, and it's been well documented that they pushed each other year after year, each drawing motivation from a desire to outdo the other. Ultimately Magic would win five championship rings to Bird's three during the Lakers' extended run of excellence that lasted a few years longer than Boston's. And with Bird being three years older (remember he came out of Indiana State as a fifth-year senior as Magic exited Michigan State as a sophomore), he eventually hit that downside of the slope a bit sooner. But as far as their first several years in the league together up through at least 1986—check the stats and watch the clips—Bird was the man.

Bear in mind that all of this was happening at a time when the NBA was hitting its peak with Larry Bird and Magic Johnson as the leading men. The league was flourishing in popularity after a rough stretch in the late 1970s, that early post-merger period with the ABA when marquee franchises like the Celtics and Knicks were down, the pre-Magic Lakers were solid but not making it out of the Western Conference playoffs, and CBS was airing Sonics-Bullets NBA Finals games in 1978 and '79 on late-night tape delay. But the 1980s felt like a whole new era. Bird and Magic entered the league, then Isaiah, then Dominique, then Barkley and Michael. By 1984 new commissioner David Stern was pushing the league to market around its new stars, and it was working. Attendance and ratings were rising. The Celtics were reborn and the Lakers took the big step from contender to powerhouse. Eventually Patrick Ewing pushed the Knicks back into the national consciousness, too, although they never got a title.

All this marketing and commercialism around the new generation of stars was beyond anything the NBA had ever had before. Even Bird, who never particularly craved the limelight and who turned down more than his share of commercial offers, was out there in his memorable Converse ads with Dr. J and Magic. Eventually Michael Jordan would take the player endorsement game to a new level altogether—he and Bo Jackson becoming the first athletes to essentially become their own brands—but it was Bird and Magic who first made the '80s the '80s.

The Celtics closed the 1985/86 regular season by winning two of their last three to finish 67–15, 10 games better than any team in the East and 5 better than the Lakers, the top seed in the West. The win total was the highest of the

Bird era and one short of the franchise record set in 1972/73, when a John Havlicek injury hurt them in a conference finals loss to the Knicks. Against the NBA's next five best teams—Los Angeles, Milwaukee, Philadelphia, Houston, and Atlanta—the Celtics went 19–2. They would open the playoffs on April 17 against the Chicago Bulls, who had managed to squeak into eighth seed in the Eastern Conference with a 30–52 record. A big mismatch perhaps, but there was a caveat. The Bulls had played the bulk of the season without Michael Jordan, who had suffered a broken foot back in the third game of the year. But Jordan had made his way back for the final 15 games and would be ready for the playoffs.

***

April 7, 1986, was a crisp but sunny day in Detroit, opening day for the Red Sox and Tigers. After the opening ceremonies, Detroit right-hander Jack Morris wound up and threw the first pitch of the season to Dwight Evans, who swung and launched the ball more than 400 feet over the left-centerfield fence. One pitch, one homer in the books. That should have been quite the omen for the 1986 Red Sox, and perhaps it was, but they lost the game 6–5 despite three more homers from Rice, Baylor, and Gedman. Kirk Gibson hit a pair of two-run shots for the Tigers, one off Hurst in the fifth and another off Sammy Stewart in the seventh for the deciding runs. The Tigers beat the Sox by the same 6–5 score again in the next game by rallying for two in the bottom of the 10th against Bob Stanley and Steve Crawford after Wade Boggs's fourth hit of the day had knocked in a run in the top half to give Boston a 5–4 lead. The Sox salvaged the finale of the Detroit series behind a strong outing from right-hander Al Nipper, who allowed just four hits pitching into the ninth in a 4–2 win.

The Sox followed by taking two of three in Chicago with Roger Clemens winning his first start despite five walks and just two strikeouts. But the last game there shrunk the bullpen just six games into the season when Wes Gardner hurt his shoulder while mopping up in a 12–2 victory. He'd wind up having arthroscopic surgery and missing the season. Half the Gardner-Schiraldi duo that the club had parted with Bob Ojeda for was already done for 1986.

The Red Sox opened at home on April 14 against the defending world champion Kansas City Royals. More than thirty-four thousand people crammed every corner of Fenway on a Monday afternoon to see Oil Can Boyd pitch well most of the way against Kansas City's veteran lefty Charlie Leibrandt in a game that stood 2–2 after seven innings. Were this 21st century baseball, there's little doubt that John McNamara would have removed his starter after the solid seven innings, particularly in April. But in 1986 it rarely worked that way. Boyd was a front-line starter, and he still looked strong after retiring the Royals in order in the seventh. No need to take him out, the thinking went. So Boyd began the eighth, allowed three hits and two runs before getting an out, and walked off the mound, trailing 4–2. The Royals continued the onslaught against Stanley, ultimately batting around and scoring six runs. The Sox were drubbed in their home opener, 8–2.

Nipper had another strong outing in the next game against the Royals but was outdueled by 1985 Cy Young Award–winner Brett Saberhagen in a 1–0 loss. Clemens would pick up the first Fenway win of the season the next day on a five-hitter with Baylor snapping a 2–2 tie in a big way with a grand slam in the bottom of the eighth to give the Sox a 6–2 victory. Clemens was 2–0, the Red Sox were 4–5.

They were 8–8 on April 26 when Nipper went to the mound in Kansas City and continued his early roll by besting Saberhagen with a complete game four-hitter in a 6–1 win. This time the Sox knocked Saberhagen out in the fifth inning after piling up eight hits, including Bill Buckner's first homer of the year. No doubt Nipper was the early surprise of the Boston starting rotation. Not an overpowering pitcher, he relied on throwing a wide assortment of breaking stuff and changing speeds. Think Eddie Harris, the fictional, crafty Cleveland Indians pitcher in the movie *Major League* who tells his manager in the ninth inning of the playoff tiebreaker with the Yankees, "I've thrown every piece of junk I've got at them, skipper, I have enough for one more hitter." Manager Lou Brown congratulates Harris for a job well done but still pulls him for Ricky "Wild Thing" Vaughn, who blows three fastballs past big Clu Haywood.

Al Nipper was Boston's real-life junk baller. Just turned 27 and in his third full season, he'd pitched to a slightly better than league average ERA through his first 55 career starts while winning just over half his decisions. Like most back-of-the-rotation starters who lacked great stuff, it mostly came down to control with Nipper. When he was able to put the ball where he wanted to, he was effective. When he wasn't, it could make for a long night for the Boston outfielders.

The Sox would get a two-day break—a rainout followed by a scheduled off-day—before returning home to open a series against the Seattle Mariners on April 29. As it happened, the Celtics would have a home playoff game that same night, probably a big reason why a lot of people who might have shown up to Fenway didn't make it. Before that night was over, they'd wished they had.

***

The Celtics' run through the 1986 NBA playoffs included three memorable events: Michael Jordan's national coming-out party in Game Two of the first round, Boston's 36–6 third quarter in the closeout Game Five over Atlanta in round two, and Jerry Sichting scrapping with Houston's Ralph Sampson in Game Five of the Finals, which ended in a disappointing loss but one that allowed the team to celebrate the title in front of their home fans in the next game.

It was nice of Jordan and Sampson to provide some drama, because there wasn't much otherwise. The Celtics pretty much treated the playoffs as a mini version of the dominant season they'd just completed, putting up separate winning streaks of six and seven games on their way to winning 15 of 18 overall.

Jordan didn't wait a moment to begin firing away in the opening round, no doubt knowing that a player of his caliber was just what could give an underdog team a fighting chance in a short series. It was reminiscent of two years earlier when superstar scorer Bernard King had carried the Knicks on his back to push the Celtics to seven games in their 1984 second-round series before falling short. Jordan put the ball up 36 times and poured in 49 points in the first game to help the Bulls stay close for a while. But the Celtics' big guns (Bird finished with 30, Johnson with 26) wore Chicago down in the second half and helped them pull away for a 123–104 win.

It isn't often that a 49-point performance in an NBA playoff game at Boston Garden is destined to go down as an afterthought in basketball annals. But that's just what Jordan's night became before Game Two was over. Unlike Game One, a locally televised Thursday night affair in which there was little doubt about the outcome despite Jordan's individual brilliance, the second game had all the bells and whistles—Sunday afternoon, national television, double overtime, and Jordan taking it to even another level.

From the get-go, Jordan was focused and in control. He shaked and he baked, he stutter stepped, he got to the rim, he created space for his jumper. With some help from Orlando Woolridge, the big forward from Notre Dame who scored 24, Jordan led Chicago to a seven-point halftime lead. By the end of the third quarter, he had 36 points and the Bulls still led by three. It wasn't as if the Celtics weren't doing a lot of what they normally did. The offense was clicking about as well as ever. Bird was on his way to a near triple-double including 36 points, McHale to 27 points and 15 rebounds, and Walton to 15 rebounds of his own along with 10 points in his 25 minutes. But they couldn't pull away from the Bulls because Jordan wouldn't let them. Even the best defensive guard in the league, Dennis Johnson, made no real difference this time. Ainge took a turn guarding Jordan and actually did a bit better, but no one was really going to contain him.

It was a fast, frenzied game with the referees whistling a ton of fouls—Walton and DJ would both foul out with Bird, Ainge, and Parish all getting hit with five. With Boston up two in the final seconds of regulation, McHale was called for a very cheap foul as he ran out and challenged Jordan's jumper at the horn. Jordan responded to the gift by coolly sinking both free throws, his 53rd and 54th points of the game, to force overtime.

With Chicago up two near the end of OT, Ainge drove the lane for the tying layup and then Jordan missed on an open look in the closing seconds. It was on to a second overtime. It was turning into a big game for Ainge—all 24 of his points came after halftime as he helped the team find another gear to keep up with Jordan. After Sichting and Ainge hit consecutive jumpers to put Boston up four in double overtime, Jordan came back with a jumper and a drive to tie the game 131–131 with just over a minute left. For Jordan it was now a playoff record 63 points, close to half his team's total, as he tried to will the Bulls to a big road win in this opening series.

They almost got there, but on the next Celtics' possession Sichting drilled another clutch jumper to put Boston up two after McHale drew a double team in the post and found him open near the top of the key. Then a Jordan 15-footer rolled out, Parish rebounded with 30 seconds left, and the Celtics worked most of the shot clock before Bird found Parish on a pick and roll for a short baseline jumper and a four-point lead with nine seconds remaining. Chicago's last shot missed and the Celtics had survived, 135–131.

Afterward, all the talk was naturally about Jordan. It wasn't just the points but how he got them—the speed, the smoothness, all of it coming within the flow, hardly anything forced. "He was so quick, so fast, it was like seeing Dominique when he first came in," says Wedman. "Larry said that if he ever reached 70 he's retiring." Up until this point in his young career, Jordan was seen as an exciting young player and a deserving Rookie-of-the Year from the previous season, but he wasn't His Airness just yet. It was this mesmerizing postseason performance on national TV that put him on a different level, really the first big step in the building of the Jordan brand into the biggest thing in sports, one that still endures two decades after his retirement.

Credit the Celtics for sticking together and turning it up a notch after the relatively easy win the fans might have expected didn't materialize. And the near upset didn't shake their confidence. The Celtics went into Chicago and had their way with the Bulls in Game Three, containing Jordan this time and building a 28-point lead through three quarters in a 122–104 win behind McHale's 31 points and Ainge's 20 points and seven assists. So the series did wind up as the three-game sweep most people expected. But it has to go down as the most memorable first-round sweep in NBA history. People still talk about Game Two, that Sunday afternoon when the country truly met Michael Jordan.

The Celtics returned to the Garden and kept rolling in the first two games of the next series against the Atlanta Hawks, the 50-win club that had played them pretty tough during the season despite no wins to show for it—Boston had beaten Atlanta in all six games during the season but never by more than seven points. The Hawks' Dominique Wilkins led a roster long on size and athleticism (Kevin Wills, Cliff Levingston, Tree Rollins) but short on outside shooting beyond guard Randy Wittman. They were solid at point guard with starter Doc Rivers, the same guy Danny Ainge would hire to coach the Celtics 18 years later, and backup Spud Webb, the 5′6″ wunderkind blessed with lightning quickness and a vertical leap that had won him the 1986 NBA Slam Dunk Contest in February.

But, of course, this was 1986. As solid as the Atlanta Hawks were, the Celtics were just at another level. They cruised to wins in the first two games at the Garden, clogging the middle and cutting off lanes to force the Hawks to shoot a lot more jumpers than they liked to. Wilkins shot just 4-for-15 in Game One, a 103–91 Celtics' win that wasn't really that close, while the backcourt rotation of Rivers, Wittman, and Webb combined to hit just 9-of-35. Dennis Johnson, in addition to harassing Webb and Rivers all day, went for 16 points and 14 assists while Ainge connected on 8-of-10 shots for 17. The Hawks shot the ball much better in Game Two, but the Celtics got 36 from Bird and seven steals from Johnson to go with his 15 points and nine assists in a 119–108 win. They headed to Atlanta with a 2–0 series lead and a five-game winning streak to start the playoffs.

***

A few hours before the Celtics wrapped their Game Two win, Roger Clemens had found himself mired in gridlock on Storrow Drive as he tried to make his way to Fenway Park for his start against the Seattle Mariners. Not just heavy traffic, true gridlock. As in 40 minutes without moving.[3] A Celtics playoff game and a Sox game on the same night had turned the usual slow rush hour into a late-April nightmare. Panicked, Clemens considered bailing from the car and running to Fenway on foot. Luckily a police officer recognized him and zipped him off in an escort. When he arrived at the clubhouse about 30 minutes before game time, pitching coach Bill Fischer called him over and told him he was scratching him from the start. Clemens managed to talk him out of it, then got dressed in record time and headed to the bullpen for a rushed warmup. With Clemens's pitches all over the place, Fischer told John McNamara to have a long man ready, that Clemens would be lucky to make it out of the first inning.

No more than 13,000-odd fans were on hand at Fenway on this Tuesday night in April to see Clemens oppose Seattle right-hander Matt Moore. It was a tough night for a big draw: The weather was cool, the nondescript Seattle Mariners were in town, and the Celtics were in the playoffs. Still Clemens was on edge and feeling rushed after missing out on his usual pregame routine. When the game started, he was a little bit better, but his pitches were still kind of all over the place, enough to go to 3–2 counts on Seattle's first three hitters, including his former University of Texas teammate (and soon to be Red Sox teammate) Spike Owen. But Clemens didn't lose any of them. He blew full count fastballs by each of the first three Seattle hitters, Owen, Phil Bradley, and Ken Phelps. A lot of first-inning pitches, but still three straight Ks.

Clemens had started his season strong, winning his first three starts and getting his first double-digit strikeout game in his previous outing against Detroit. But this was the night that brought the big shift in Boston's perception of Roger Clemens from good, promising young pitcher who had some trouble staying healthy to a guy who could be the best in the game, really something special. It didn't hurt that he was facing a lineup of free swingers that led the A.L. in striking out by a wide margin.

Throwing free and easy, mostly fastballs and mixing in sliders and curves, he began to hit his spots inside and out, occasionally getting some borderline calls in his favor from home plate umpire Vic Voltaggio who was inclined to ring up right-handed hitters on pitches that may or may not have caught the outside black. Steve Krasner, who was in the press box covering the game for the *Providence Journal*, remembers: "Voltaggio's right arm just kept going up, the hitters had no chance."

Clemens whiffed Jim Presley and Ivan Calderon in the second and another future teammate, Dave Henderson, in the third. With each early inning that passed, he was more and more calm. "By the third inning the game was slowing down," Clemens says. In the fourth, after Owen led off with a single for Seattle's first hit, Clemens whiffed Bradley and Phelps. Cleanup hitter Gorman Thomas then hit a foul pop-up near first base. With regular first baseman Bill Buckner dealing with a sore shoulder, McNamara had flip-flopped him with DH Don Baylor, who hadn't played much first base during his career. Baylor drifted over toward the dugout, reached out, and dropped the ball. Instead of inning over, Thomas continued with a full count. Clemens's next pitch was a fastball at the knees. Thomas took a step toward first, but Voltaggio rang him up (the pitch looked good). Four innings, nine Ks for Clemens, and an assist for Baylor.

And he was still just getting warmed up. "It was easy to stay strong in that weather," he says of the cool April night. "As a pitcher your legs should never get tired." Clemens whiffed his next five hitters before Owen flied to center to end the sixth. Meantime the Red Sox weren't doing much against Moore as the game remained scoreless. "Moore was their best pitcher, he was nasty, and the wind was blowing in," remembers Dwight Evans. They had their first big chance in the bottom of the sixth when Buckner doubled off the Green Monster to put runners on second and third with one out. But Moore wiggled out of trouble by getting Rice to ground out with the infield in and then striking out Baylor.

In the top of the seventh, Clemens blew away Bradley and Phelps to open the inning, giving him a career-high 16 strikeouts, very much within striking distance of the major league record of 19 in a nine-inning game, a record shared by three (still active) legends, Tom Seaver, Nolan Ryan, and Steve Carlton. When he threw two fastballs past Thomas, the crowd stood and roared, looking for number 17 and for the end of the inning. But all it takes is one. Thomas was ready for Clemens's next fastball and sent it to the deepest part of the park where it just cleared the centerfield fence for a home run. It was just the second hit for the Mariners, but they led 1–0. Suddenly Clemens was looking at the possibility of setting a strikeout record and losing a game on the same night.

But after Bradley grounded out to end the inning, Clemens's teammates went about making sure that wouldn't happen. The bottom of the seventh began with two quick outs. But then Steve Lyons singled, Glenn Hoffman walked, and Dwight Evans, despite his respect for Moore, hit a 1–0 pitch over the left-center field fence. Boston led 3–1. Meantime, Clemens's teammates mostly started avoiding him in the dugout. "It was like a no-hitter, where everyone stays away from you," he says.

With Clemens still looking as strong as he had in the first inning, the big drama was over his chase of the record over the final two innings. Sitting on 16 strikeouts, Clemens fanned Ivan Calderone on three pitches. After Danny Tartabull punched a single to right field, Clemens got a roar from the crowd by blowing a fastball past Henderson for his 18th strikeout. Pinch-hitter Al Cowens flied out to deny Clemens the record-tying strikeout in the eighth inning.

In the ninth, Clemens faced the top of the Seattle order, sitting on 124 pitches without so much as a suggestion that he might come out. He got two strikes on Owen, bringing the crowd to its feet. They exploded when Owen waved at a high outside fastball for Clemens's 19th strikeout. One to go for the record, Bradley at the plate. The count reached 2–2 as the crowd stood, clapped, and screamed. Clemens threw a fastball about knee-high on the inside corner that Bradley took for strike three. "A new record!" yelled Boston TV man Ned Martin. Bradley had taken the golden sombrero (four straight strikeouts), and Clemens had become the new single-game strikeout king. The first pitcher in big league history to strike out 20 hitters in a nine-inning game. And from the guy who couldn't throw a strike in the bullpen before the game, no walks.

Even with all the empty seats, Fenway sounded like the seventh game of the World Series. It didn't much matter when Phelps grounded out to end the game, denying Clemens a chance to finish with a flourish. Tom Seaver, Steve Carlton, and Nolan Ryan no longer had the single-game strikeout record. Roger Clemens, a veteran of exactly 39 big league starts, had it. And in a start he almost didn't make. Bruce Hurst dubbed him "Rocket" right after the game, a moniker that stuck for the rest of his career. "Hursty said that pitching had always been a second-class citizen at Fenway and now that's changed," Clemens remembers.

It was shaping up to be quite the early spring in Boston. Exactly nine days and three miles separated Roger Clemens's strikeout record and Michael Jordan's playoff scoring record. Both 23 years old, both soon-to-be giants of the sports world who were just entering their peaks. One of those combination of events that you appreciate well enough at the time just for the sheer athletic performance but where the historic significance doesn't truly sink in until years later.

There was little question now: For the first time in several years the Red Sox had a bona fide stopper. "It planted the seed that Roger Clemens was 'whoa.' It told the team that every time Clemens went out, they expected to win," Krasner says. Does that make for too much pressure for a 23-year-old who hadn't even completed his first full season in the big leagues? Clemens says, nah, not really. "I was pretty much on a mission," he says. "I expected to win."

It was an event that etched its way into fans' memories. From Rich Chaiton of Medway: "I remember watching the 20-strikeout game thinking, this guy is different. A Texas strong boy like Nolan Ryan who pitched like Tom Seaver. He could be a Hall of Famer. By June I was thinking they could win the World Series, mainly because of Clemens."

John Cascione of North Providence, Rhode Island, was a local law student living in Charlestown in 1986. He was listening on the radio and wanted to head over midgame, but it never happened. "We didn't have cable, didn't have NESN. I'm listening to the game on the radio. By the middle of the game he's got about 10 strikeouts and I said to my roommate, let's go down to Fenway. Tickets are cheap, the place was mostly empty that night. But he didn't want to do it and I didn't want to go by myself."

Cascione wasn't alone in his thinking. Clemens remembers that he "heard later that the night brought the most tickets the Red Sox ever sold *during* a game, people were coming over from the Garden."

After four starts Clemens was 4–0 with a 1.62 ERA and 39 strikeouts in 33 innings. Years later Clemens would tell journalist Gordon Edes that after the postgame interviews ended and the media had cleared out, Bill Fischer walked over to him and said, "Show up whenever you want."

Chapter 6

May–June 1986

On May 2 the Atlanta Hawks came out with strong energy in their first home game of the Celtics series. In what everyone knew was essentially an elimination game—there would be no coming back from a 0–3 deficit—they played hard in front of their energetic home crowd at The Omni. Also in Atlanta's favor: Bill Walton was sitting this one out with a sore knee after banging into Tree Rollins in the previous game.

So for Boston it was the classic Game-Three-on-the-road setup, a tough one to win when you're shorthanded and your opponent needs the game more. K.C. Jones responded by shortening his rotation, playing four starters for more than 40 minutes and just eight players altogether. The game was tight all the way, with Boston leading by four at the halftime break and by one at the end of the third quarter. Dominique Wilkins glided and twisted his way to 38 points, using his power to score inside and his quickness to beat defenders along the baseline. With Doc Rivers dishing out 14 assists to go with 18 points and big Kevin Willis scoring and rebounding inside, Atlanta hung right with Boston all the way to the end. But it still wasn't enough. Bird flirted with another triple-double, just missing with 28 points, 12 assists, and nine rebounds, and McHale poured in 25 despite foul trouble. Ainge, the only starter who didn't play 40 minutes, had his jumper going enough to finish with 23 points in 35 minutes.

The Celtics maintained their slim lead through the final quarter to win 111–107. Just one game, but one of those games that signaled the Celtics playing on a higher level than ever in 1986. One of those games where a fan might easily think, okay, I could see losing this one on the road, they'll still be up in the series and probably regroup in the next game with Walton back. And yet the team didn't approach it that way. They dug down and got the win to pretty much put the series away.

As it turned out, Walton did not make it back for Game Four. And, unfortunately, neither did anyone's jump shot. With Bird (5-for-19) setting the pace, the Celtics clanged their way to 34% shooting, a rare brick-laying display that cost them a series sweep. With Spud Webb supercharging Atlanta's offense with 21 points and 12 assists in 24 minutes off the bench, the Hawks rode a strong second half to a 106–94 win. For the first time in 10 games dating back to November, the Hawks had beaten the Celtics. They were officially still alive in this second-round series, but the next game was back at Boston Garden. Everyone knew what that meant.

On Tuesday night, May 6, the Atlanta players emerged from the visiting Boston Garden locker room at halftime facing a 66–55 deficit. Not promising, but not out of the game. On the first possession after the break, Randy Wittman hit a jumper to make the score 66–57. Then this happened:

- Dennis Johnson hits a cutting McHale in the lane for a basket.
- Bird hits McHale inside for two.
- DJ inside to McHale again for two.
- Ainge hustles the ball up court and feeds DJ on the wing for a jumper . . . 74–58.

Meantime the Boston defense consistently clogged the middle so that Atlanta's lineup of big men and athletic slashers had nowhere to go. They just didn't have the outside shooters to adjust with. The Hawks could barely get off a shot with a good look, and when they did it just didn't fall. As the onslaught continued:

- McHale feeds Bird for a lefty layup.
- An Ainge steal leads to a Parish putback of a McHale miss . . . 78–59.
- A Wilkins layup with a little over five minutes remaining in the quarter makes it 78–61 and would be the last Atlanta points of the period.
- Parish scores inside and then blocks Jon Koncak at the other end.
- A McHale dunk off a beautiful inside feed from Parish pushes the lead to 30.
- Bird's lefty hoop in the lane off the backboard is immediately followed by an Ainge steal and three-pointer.

It was officially overkill, as if nearby Division II Merrimack College had sent its varsity over to the Garden for a scrimmage. The final insult came when Atlanta's Johnny Davis missed the final shot of the quarter and a frustrated Kevin Willis was whistled for shoving Kevin McHale to the ground right at the horn. That sent McHale to the line at the other end after the clock had expired, where he added the last two points of the quarter. The final third-quarter tally was 36–6. The scoreboard read 102–61. The final was 132–99, and the series was emphatically over. Walton, incidentally, tested his knee for seven minutes and seemed to feel okay (he grabbed eight rebounds). He'd be good to go for his usual minutes the rest of the way.

As much as the Celtics' earlier sweep of Michael Jordan and the Bulls might have been the NBA's most memorable first-round series ever, their series with the Milwaukee Bucks may well have been the league's most forgettable conference final ever.

Coached by old friend Don Nelson, who owned five championship rings from his playing days in Boston, the Bucks were a very good team that just didn't match up well with the Celtics. The team's strength lied in its perimeter players. The big men, guys named Alton Lister, Randy Breuer, and Paul Mokeski, didn't have the skills to hang with the Celtics' famed front line. It didn't help that their best player, Sidney Moncrief, was day-to-day with a bum foot. The Bucks had been pushed to the limit in the previous round against Philadelphia, pulling out the seventh game at home by one point.

With Moncrief sitting out the first game, the Celtics won a blowout in which K.C. Jones ultimately emptied the entire bench—Vincent, Carlisle, Thirdkill, and Kite all got at least nine minutes. The Bucks had a better effort in Game Two—Breuer and Lister had good games—but the Celtics crafted a methodical 11-point win in which all five starters scored at least 20 points.

When the series shifted to Milwaukee, the Bucks essentially duplicated the Atlanta Hawks by putting up a spirited effort in front of the home crowd, leading by as many as 13 points in the third quarter before the Celtics heated up and went ahead midway through the fourth and held on for a 111–107 victory. Parish (28 points, 12 rebounds) and McHale (29/11) overpowered the Bucks' front line while Bird put up his first playoff triple-double. The downside: Scott Wedman suffered broken ribs courtesy of a collision with Terry Cummings's knee, he'd be out for pretty much the rest of the postseason. Just as the NBA Finals beckoned, the team would have to do without one of its valuable bench veterans.

Wedman was naturally disappointed but rolled with it okay, mostly content to know he'd had plenty to do with the team getting there: "It is what it is. When McHale was out, I started and played really well. It would have been great to be healthy but I had a good run."

Even without Wedman the Celtics wrapped up the sweep the next day when Bird and Ainge combined to bury 8 of 11 three-point shots, Bird getting 17 of his 30 points in the Celtics' big fourth quarter in a 111–98 win. Regular season and playoffs combined, Boston had beaten Milwaukee, the No. 2 team in the East, nine times in nine tries in 1985/86.

A nice bonus: With Parish in foul trouble for a good part of the game, Walton played a season-high 30 minutes, collecting nine points and nine rebounds. His health looked fine as the team looked ahead to the Finals.

***

Beginning with Al Nipper's impressive win in Kansas City and Roger Clemens's historic game two nights later, the Red Sox launched into the month of May ready to become the hottest team in the league. For the fans it was a nightly party: As the Celtics chewed through their NBA playoff opponents, the Red Sox chewed through American League opponents, mostly from the Western Division. Every night, it seemed, someone was winning.

The Sox finished the rest of their homestand by winning five of seven against Seattle, Oakland, and California. Clemens showed no ill effects from his high pitch count in the 20K game as he beat the A's on a three-hitter. The club then headed west and won another five straight to bring their record to 20–10. In the trip's first game at Seattle, Jim Rice, Wade Boggs, and Marty Barrett picked up three hits apiece, including Rice's fifth homer, in an 11–5 win. Barrett added two more hits the next night including a big two-run triple in the seventh inning, when the Sox scored all of their runs to beat the Mariners 4–2.

A month into the season, Barrett had the batting average at .344. He'd cool off from that pace, but the California native and Arizona State product was on his way to the best season of his 10-year career, one that he would cap off with a scorching postseason. Barrett was a contact hitter who liked to hit to the opposite field. He had little power and he rarely struck out, whiffing just 31 times in more than 700 plate appearances in 1986. His ability to handle the bat would soon spur McNamara to move him up in the lineup from his customary seventh or eighth into the lead-off spot, allowing McNamara to move Evans, who had been leading off, into the middle of the order where his power could do more damage. By early August, McNamara would tinker one last time by flip-flopping Barrett and Boggs, leaving Barrett in the two-hole and Boggs, the league's premier on-base machine, leading off the rest of the way. Barrett would wind up the year hitting .286 with a .353 OBP, playing in 158 games.

The strong West Coast trip included a 6–5 win in Oakland on Sunday afternoon, May 11 in which Boyd allowed homers to Bruce Bochte, Carney Lansford, and super rookie Jose Canseco, already his 10th of the year. But Boyd allowed just one additional hit over his seven innings as the Sox pecked away with 10 hits and six walks, taking a 6–4 lead into the bottom of the ninth. Bob Stanley served up Lansford's second homer of the day and then allowed two more base runners before Joe Sambito nailed down the final out with the tying and winning runs on base for his third save of the year.

Rich Gedman finished the day 4-for-4, all singles, and then drew an intentional walk in the top of the ninth to set up Marty Barrett's RBI single for Boston's final run. In the final game of the trip three days later in Anaheim with the Sox trailing the Angels 4–2 in the top of the eighth, Gedman blasted a three-run homer off reliever Ken Forsch to put them in front. After California tied it in the bottom of the eighth, the Sox promptly rallied for three more in the ninth to win 8–5. Gedman's blast had preserved Roger Clemens's win streak—he was now 6–0 despite not having his best outing in this one.

More than anyone else on the Boston roster, Rich Gedman was the guy living the dream. He was the kid from nearby Worcester who had watched the Red Sox 1967 "Impossible Dream" team capture their improbable American League pennant less than a week after his eighth birthday.

"I knew all the players and their stances," Gedman says of the '67 team and beyond. "Dad loved watching the Red Sox. Life for me as a little boy was baseball with no time for anything else."

He became a star at St. Peter–Marian High School, catching, pitching, and playing first base. As a junior in 1977 he led the Guardians to a state championship at the same time his girlfriend, Sherry Aselton, now his wife, pitched the softball team to its own state title.[1] But high school baseball in the northeast didn't normally get the kind of respect it did in the warm-weather hotbeds. Gedman was not drafted by any major league clubs, and Division I college interest was minimal.

"I got some letters of interest but no one was knocking the door down. I probably would have wound up at a community college," he says. "My family was not much into schooling—baseball was first, the best road for me to go." So when his local club, the Red Sox, offered to sign him as an undrafted free agent and start him at the bottom of the chain, Gedman jumped at the chance. "I told Dad I'd give it so many years and if it didn't work out, I'd go back and get my education. I was a kid doing what he loved to do."

As Sherry finished out her last year of high school and then went on to pitch for the University of Connecticut, Rich headed to the Instructional League and then to Class-A ball in Florida to begin his journey to the big leagues. It would be a short one. Scouts told him that concentrating on catching would be his ticket. He wasn't a professional-quality pitcher, and solid lefty-hitting first basemen weren't that hard to find.

"My first year in the Instructional League there were seven catchers. In A-ball there were two catchers older than me. It wasn't like today—there were no specialty coaches. You had to learn how to block the ball. You didn't really block the ball as a kid, you reached for it."

Walt Hriniak, the future big league hitting coach whom Gedman would later gravitate to for his offensive game, was a former professional catcher who was a young coach in the Instructional League at the time. "Walt Hriniak worked with the catchers. I remember getting black and blue. He taught the little things like keeping your hand forward, don't let your bones get exposed," Gedman says. "Walt was a great teacher. He took a kid under his wing and looked out for him. A lot of players come in and then leave after a short time. If not for Walt I would have been one of those guys."

Gedman turned out to be the polar opposite of those guys. "He was a grinder, he just worked and worked," says Steve Krasner. Gedman moved up quickly, a level each season from Class-A Winter Haven, Florida, to Double-A Bristol, Connecticut, and then to Triple-A Pawtucket, Rhode Island. "Growing up in Worcester, every minor league stop took me closer to home," he says. Not to mention closer to Boston. At Pawtucket Gedman got more invaluable catching instruction from pitching coach Mike Rourke, a Rhode Island native and former big-league catcher who would have a long career as a pitching coach in the majors and minors. "Mike Rourke was very good with catchers. He taught me how to move, block pitches, and emphasized moving the hips."

When the Red Sox expanded their roster in September 1980, Gedman got the call. Not quite 21 years old, some two years and three months after graduating from St. Peter–Marian, he was playing at Fenway. Carl Yastrzemski, the man who had carried the Red Sox to their 1967 "Impossible Dream," was now a teammate. So were Fred Lynn, Jim Rice, and Dwight Evans. "It was a culmination of your dreams. Fenway was the greenest of the green. To walk up the steps in a Red Sox uniform was unbelievable," he says. "To be in the same room with these guys, it was like, 'What am I doing here?'" Gedman spent most of his time out in the bullpen, listening and soaking up as much information as possible. His brief 1980 stint with the big club bought him a three-week overlap with Carlton Fisk, the incumbent star catcher who would bolt to the Chicago White Sox after the season. Gedman remembers: "Fisk always had this stoic walk, he commanded respect. If he didn't say much, he was still a big presence."

His first at-bat came on September 7 against the Mariners when manager Don Zimmer sent him up in the bottom of the third to pinch-hit in the DH spot for—of all people—Carl Yastrzemski. The Sox were already trailing 8–1 after a big Seattle second inning, and Yaz, according to Gedman, had a bit of a sore back. "He probably went to the manager and said, 'Let the kid play today,'" says Gedman. "Yastrzemski was always good to me. He could be tough but with me there was a gentle kindness. Getting that call to hit was like floating on air." He flew out that first time up but wound up banging out a pair of singles before the day was over.

He would see Triple-A just briefly in 1981 but otherwise he was up for good. Over the following three years Gedman shared major league catching duties with Gary Allenson, a solid pro behind the plate who didn't have the offensive potential Gedman had. As he continued to work on the defense, Gedman's key tutor in the majors would eventually be veteran catcher Jeff Newman, who came over from Oakland in the Tony Armas–Carney

Lansford trade after the 1982 season. "Jeff Newman really helped me with the exchange," he says, referring to the process of getting the ball from the glove to throwing hand more quickly.

After hitting .294 in 81 games in 1983 Gedman took over as the regular catcher in 1984 at age 24. A lefty hitter with an open stance who could hit to all fields, he popped 24 homers with a 118 OPS-plus and showed good defense. He was even better in 1985 when he made the A.L. All-Star team by hitting .295 with a 126 OPS-plus and 18 homers. And the defense just kept getting better. In the early part-time years, Gedman averaged about 24% success at throwing out base stealers, a bit below average. That ballooned to over 40% in his first two full-time seasons in 1984 and 1985. Then in 1986 Gedman would gun down just about half of the runners who tried to steal on him (54 of 109) and finish a close second to Bob Boone in defensive WAR among American League catchers. At 26 he was one of the best in the business. Bill Ballou, from the *Worcester Telegram & Gazette* remembers Gedman "once throwing out Rickey Henderson by five feet. How many guys could do that? As well as he could hit, he could catch."

But just when it seemed like he was headed toward being one of baseball's top catchers for several years to come, it would all derail pretty quickly after the 1986 season. Gedman couldn't come to terms with Red Sox brass on a 1987 contract. He was one of 10 free agents who, under the rules that year, had until January 8 to sign with their current teams if another team didn't offer a contract (this became known as the collusion era); otherwise, they had to wait until May 1 to sign. Gedman didn't sign by the deadline and hence missed the early part of 1987. When he did come back, he wasn't nearly the same, hitting .205 with one homer in 165 plate appearances that year. His career continued downhill from there: another mediocre year and a half in Boston and then two-plus years of part-time duty in Houston and St. Louis before retiring in 1992 at age 31. Right after 1986, with more than 500 major league games behind the plate under his belt, the wear and tear was already catching up to him. Guys like Carlton Fisk and Ivan Rodriguez who go on catching forever are exceptions in baseball. Shelf lives are generally short for those who play the most physically demanding position on the field.

As a coach these days back near home with the Red Sox's Triple-A club in Worcester, Gedman says he was a bitter person for a while as the injuries started to eat up his career. "After the '86 season I went to Japan [as part of a barnstorming tour] and broke my cheekbone. Then in 1987 I was in the best shape ever but I didn't have the six weeks needed to get into baseball shape. In '88 I broke my toe on a foul ball and then came back too soon."

Still, quite the run for an undrafted high school player who was never supposed to be a big leaguer in the first place. And the chance to handle the 1986 pitching staff was a career opportunity. "The pitchers were a close-knit group.

Clemens, Hurst, Nipper, and Oil Can were the type to talk and ask questions. Then when Tom Seaver came over, his influence was incredible. Amazing the things he could still do at his age. When you're around a guy like Tom Seaver you want to be great because that's what he was used to."

Following their big West Coast trip, the Sox lost the opener of the next home stand against Texas 4–1 despite a great effort by Hurst, who struck out 14 but was touched for three solo homers. But right after that the Sox won six in a row, lost a tough 3–2 game in Texas when Stanley allowed two in the bottom of the ninth, and then won another four in a row. The stretch included a 17–7 romp over Minnesota at Fenway on May 20 when Clemens endured a shaky outing by giving up five runs. But Boggs picked him up by going 5-for-6 to raise his average to .383 and Tony Armas, sliding over to right field to give Evans a day off, rapped out four hits.

By May 28, after Oil Can Boyd beat Cleveland on the road for his sixth win thanks to nine combined RBI from Rice and Baylor, the Sox were 31–14 and leading the division by two games over the Yankees.

Don Baylor did a little bit of everything in the Cleveland game: three-run homer in the sixth, hit by a pitch and scoring a run in the seventh, sacrifice fly in the eighth. The home run was already his 10th of the season, with the on-base percentage at .352. Beyond the stats lay the intangibles. Baylor had always been a respected clubhouse leader, known for bringing teams together and enforcing fundamentals. Placing a value on leadership isn't easy. This wasn't high school baseball. How much difference does a "good in the clubhouse" guy really make to a professional ball club, particularly one with a lot of veteran players like the 1986 Red Sox?

The answer, if you ask them, is a lot. Baylor was more than just a right-handed bat. He was the new heart and soul of the Red Sox. The spring training deal for Mike Easler became a bigger deal than most had expected. When seeking out reasons for the Red Sox taking off in '86, Clemens's emergence as a genuine stopper has to top the list. Beyond that, says Dwight Evans, "The biggest thing was trading Mike Easler to New York for Don Baylor. He was the kind of guy you hated as an opponent but, on your team, you loved him. He really brought us together." Baylor implemented the "kangaroo court" in the Boston clubhouse, a mock trial in which he acted as judge and jury to convict and fine players for fundamental mistakes. "It penalized *mental* errors. Giving up a home run on a 0–2 pitch, an outfielder not hitting the cutoff man," Evans says. Evans hit it off with Baylor pretty quickly and the friendship endured. Eight years later, during Baylor's second season managing the expansion Colorado Rockies in 1994, he'd hire Evans as a coach. "A very intelligent guy, we were close on and off the field," he says.

Gedman remembers how much the focus tightened when Baylor came aboard. "He brought a lot of veteran guys together and set goals. The kangaroo court teaches the game, helps you focus on the game. It helped everyone to be better. If you could do *something* [i.e., something small like advancing a runner or throwing to the correct base], you could make the team better. We played for each other. We played not to let the other person down." The approach made it easier to focus on each game as it came and not get too concerned about the big picture, which can get overwhelming during a long season. "Don't get too far ahead, just win a series. Donnie brought a lot of that," says Gedman.

Nothing personified Baylor's unselfish approach more than his knack for crowding the plate and then taking first base after being plunked by an inside pitch. The hit by pitch became as much a Baylor trademark as home runs and kangaroo courts. Eight times he led the American League, including a career high 35 in 1986. "I hit behind him a lot that year. He was always trying to get on base for you. He would take pitches, get hit a lot," says Evans. Baylor would hit only .238 in 1986, but his 62 walks and 35 HBP pushed his on-base percentage to .344 to go along with his 31 homers and 94 RBI. Says Evans: "I loved to hit with guys on base."

As May gave way to June, the Red Sox continued to roll. A 6–4 win over Cleveland on June 4—Baylor homered and was hit by a pitch—was Boston's 5th victory in a row, their 9th in 10 games and, going back to Nipper's win in Kansas City in late April, the team's 28th win in its last 35 games. They were 36–15 and 4½ games in front. Around town, you could feel that fans didn't know whether to be giddy or shocked. Who did these guys think they were, the Celtics? Of course the Red Sox were no strangers to hot starts and lame finishes. It had happened just last year. The big collapse of 1978 was only eight years old, still fresh in many memories. Somehow, though, it didn't feel the same this time. They weren't slugging like some past Sox teams but they were more balanced—getting on base, not striking out a lot, getting good pitching. The best pitcher in the game this year was on hand to extinguish losing streaks. Generally speaking, not the type of team prone to the big collapse.

But there was still a long way to go, and the big roll was not without its costs. The starting pitching was suddenly thinning out with injuries. Nipper had gone out on May 18 against Texas after suffering a nasty gash on his knee as he tagged out Larry Parrish covering home plate after a wild pitch and caught an inadvertent spike as Parrish slid into the plate. Luckily Parrish had just missed the ligament, but the cut was deep enough to keep Nipper out for several weeks.

Then on May 31 in Minnesota, it was Hurst, off to an excellent start at 5–3 with a 2.99 ERA and second in the A.L. in strikeouts, who felt a sharp pain pushing off his left leg in the fifth inning. He had aggravated his groin. He was taken out and would miss more than seven weeks. And so McNamara would have little choice. It would be Jeff Sellers, Rob Woodward, and Mike Brown, three young right-handers who were all quite mediocre and who would all split their seasons between Boston and Pawtucket, making a lot of starts in June.

***

The other thing happening as late May gave way to early June: The Celtics were in the NBA Finals, but not the one everyone was expecting; the one that NBA fans were all pumped up for. Over in the Western Conference the Lakers were out, bounced by the Houston Rockets in the conference finals in a shocking five games. After 62 wins during the season and another five straight to start the playoffs, L.A. first hit some turbulence against Dallas, who beat them in the third and fourth games of their second-round series to forge a 2–2 tie and then just missed getting a big win at The Forum (116–113) that would have given the Mavs the series lead. After holding off Dallas in six games, the Lakers won their first game against Houston but then dropped four straight, something they hadn't done all year. The series ended in the fifth game at The Forum when Ralph Sampson took an inbounds pass in the frontcourt with a second on the clock, tossed the ball toward the rim in an awkward motion and then watched it rattle in for a two-point win.

So Celtics-Lakers III was not happening. Everyone, players and fans alike, had to readjust their collective mindset away from Magic, Worthy, and Kareem and toward Houston's imposing Twin Towers of Sampson and Hakeem Olajuwon. The pair had pretty much manhandled the Lakers inside during the conference finals. Olajuwon, the 23-year-old rising star on his way to becoming an all-time NBA big man, had made Kareem look awfully old and slow during their series as he dominated the paint to average 31 points and four blocks a game. The Rockets didn't have anyone else who would turn your head, although perimeter guys Lewis Lloyd, Rodney McCray, and Robert Reid could occasionally come up with a hot hand. Guard Mitchell Wiggins and forward Jim Peterson provided the key depth. As an added twist, the Rockets were coached by Bill Fitch, the guy the Celtics were happy to be rid of for the past three years but whose chops as an NBA coach couldn't be denied as he led his second team to a final.

Ask anyone with the Celtics whether there was any kind of emotional letdown after the anticipated matchup with the Lakers went up in smoke, and they'll say, no, not really. Playing for an NBA title is all the motivation needed, and there's no controlling your opponent from round to round. The one slight exception was Wedman's observation that "the only person who was disappointed was Bill Walton; he really wanted to play against Kareem."

With Wedman out, Jones would bump Bird's minutes well into the 40s with David Thirdkill occasionally spelling him for a few minutes per game.

Of course Walton and the rest of the front line would have their hands full with Hakeem, who went for 33 points and 12 rebounds in Game One to keep Houston close for a half. But the Celtics opened things up with a big third quarter for a 112–100 victory in which every starter scored at least 18 points and Walton kicked in 10 points and eight rebounds in 18 minutes. The confounding part for the Rockets was Sampson's game—he missed 12 of 13 shots and finished with 2 points. It kept with the pattern for Sampson (though this was an extreme example), a guy who was prone to dominating at times and disappearing at other times. For all his enormous potential, Sampson's 15 points and nine rebounds a game for his nine-year career can only be called a disappointment. In fact the stats would say that Joe Barry Carroll, who rose to the top spot of the 1980 draft after Sampson had turned Red Auerbach down to stay in school and whose time in the NBA was best known for not living up to expectations, had the better career.

Boston cruised at home again in Game Two to take a commanding series lead, riding Bird's 31 points including 3-of-5 trifectas to a 117–98 win. And so the Rockets predictably found themselves in the same spot as the Bulls, Hawks, and Bucks in these NBA playoffs—unable to win at Boston Garden and needing to take that third game at home to maintain a fighting chance. And as it turned out, the Celtics didn't have an easy time at the Summit, Houston's loud arena since 1975. Unlike the earlier playoff rounds, the NBA Finals worked on a 2-3-2 home court schedule, so the Rockets would get the next three on home turf. The first two both went down to the wire, making for a fine line between a Boston sweep and a 2–2 series tie.

The Celtics looked primed to take the big 3–0 lead as they ran double teams at Olajuwon all night in Game Three and got a big game from McHale (28 points, 11 boards) to lead by 11 in the third quarter and by 8 with about three minutes left.[2] But they went cold down the stretch as Houston crawled back. Sampson, benefiting from all the attention the Celtics were paying to Olajuwon, was the antithesis of his Game One self with 24 points and 22 rebounds. As great an all-around game as Bird had (a 25-point, 15-rebound, 11-assist triple-double), he shot just 10-for-26 and missed a key runner near the end that would have put his team up by 3. He then fouled Olajuwon on the rebound and watched Hakeem sink two free throws to put Houston ahead. They would squeak out the win, 106–104.

Two nights later it was more of the same. The Summit was just as loud and the game just as good. After one quarter the game was tied. At halftime it was Houston by one. After three quarters it was Boston by one. With just over two minutes left and the score tied, Walton passed from the post out to an open Bird, who drilled big a three-pointer. After the Rockets scored it was Walton hitting the offensive glass and putting back a Johnson miss to put Boston back up by three. Then two big defensive plays by the Celtics forced Houston turnovers in the final minute to preserve a 106–103 win. You had to applaud the Rockets' effort, but a split of the two nail-biters just wasn't going to do it for them. The Celtics were up 3–1 and sitting on two more potential home games. Everyone knew that the Houston formula for an upset was based on winning all their home games while hoping to get one at Boston Garden. But two at the Garden? It wasn't going to happen. Still the Rockets were determined to go down fighting, literally—inspired to end their home season on a positive note even if they knew deep down that they wouldn't win the series. And as it turned out the most memorable moment of the series was still ahead.

The pace was fast and the energy high to begin Game Five as the teams traded baskets early on. Bird had a hot hand, making his first four shots. The Celtics were still running double teams at Olajuwon, which freed things up for Sampson. Once again Houston had the "good Sampson," as the big man drove the lane, hit the boards, and hit from outside to make five of his first seven shots.

But they wouldn't have the good Sampson, or any Sampson, for long. Early in the second quarter with Houston up three, Jerry Sichting found himself guarding Sampson in the low post just as the ball got down to the Rockets' end of the floor. Giving away 15 inches, Sichting bodied up on Sampson, trying to hold his ground. There may have been a bit of pushing on Sichting's part for which there could have been a whistle, but nothing flagrant, nothing beyond what you normally see between two guys battling for position in the post. But Sampson apparently didn't see it that way. He turned out of the post and took a big swing at Sichting. Suddenly players were everywhere. Sampson took another swing at Sichting after the initial separation. Then he tagged Dennis Johnson with a left hand and just missed with a right. Johnson and Olajuwon also exchanged a couple of swings although neither seemed to connect. Ultimately Walton swooped in and tackled Sampson low, bringing him to the ground. Walton's maneuver actually seemed to deescalate things by taking Sampson off his feet and putting an end to the flying fists.

Sichting, the former high school quarterback, remembers: "I had played football. I didn't mind contact. I was boxing him out, but he was frustrated, that's why he swung at me."

The question was, what was so frustrating about such a routine sequence? It was a bizarre move on Sampson's part. Here he was playing well, his team was playing well and holding a small lead, and then he was gone, ejected in the second quarter. Just from a little bit of pushing. Jan Volk floats a possible explanation: "Sometimes big guys don't like playing against little guys. It becomes a different game." Like that pesky mosquito that keeps bothering you, you just want to slap it away.

But when the dust cleared, it was the Rockets who emerged from the melee with more energy. It became one of those situations when a team responds to being shorthanded by digging deeper and rallying. And that energy from the home crowd doesn't hurt. "The bad part was we had momentum; we would have won that game. We should have wrapped it up in five," Sichting says. Olajuwon played like a madman in the paint the rest of the way, finishing with 32 points and 14 rebounds. Frontcourt sub Jim Peterson stepped into Sampson's spot and grabbed 12 boards while sharpshooter Mitchell Wiggins came off the bench for 16. Houston built an 11-point lead by halftime and a 21-point lead by the end of the third quarter. The final was 111–96. Bird would later say that his team lost its composure a bit, a true rarity for the 1980s Celtics.

Still, as nice as it was for Houston to finish the home season with a win and extend the series, few people thought they had done anything more than delay the inevitable. The NBA's dominant team could smell a championship, and they were headed home to the building in which they virtually never lost.

The crowd arrived early on Sunday afternoon June 8, 1986. Boston Garden was rocking well before the Celtics and Rockets would tip off. They were there for two things: to see their club wrap up its 16th world championship and to harass Ralph Sampson, the new public enemy No. 1 in Boston. And really the two went hand in hand—throwing one of the Rockets' biggest potential weapons off his game figured to go a long way toward a win. The players were serious and focused; the Game Five meltdown was not sitting well. To them the series had already dragged on longer than it should have and it was time to wrap this thing up for good. Bob Ryan says that Larry Bird would tell him afterward that "I was never more prepared to play a game in my life."

And so it went. In what Ryan calls a top-three Larry Bird game of all time, this is what the Celtics' leader and NBA's top player would do to the Houston Rockets in Game Six:

- On the first Houston possession guarding Rodney McCray he drops back into the passing lane and steals McCray's pass, leading to transition layup by McHale.
- A minute later, step back jumper for two.
- Picks up Sampson on a switch along the baseline and smothers him like a blanket to force a travel.
- Next offensive possession, a tough offensive rebound in traffic and put back for 10–4 lead.
- By the middle of the first quarter all five Celtic starters have scored. Bird then steals a pass in the lane and dribbles all the way up the court to feed Ainge for a fast break layup and a 20–9 lead.

- Late in the quarter he grabs a defensive rebound and fires a quick pass ahead to Parish running the floor, although Robert Reid hustles back to knock ball away from Parish just before he could go up for layup.
- After a Rockets' run tightens the game late in the first quarter, Bird dives on the ground in the defensive paint to cause a jump ball, then wins the jump against Olajuwon by faking his initial jump (like a pump fake on a jump shot) to throw Olajuwon's timing off . . . then at the other end fakes McCray out of his shorts in the post and drives to the hoop to draw a foul on Olajuwon.
- Early in the second quarter he emerges from a defensive scrum with the ball, rushes ahead to create a three-on-one break and passes ahead to DJ who flips back to Bird for a layup. The Celtics are up nine; Bird has 12 with six assists.
- Two possessions later he fires a bullet pass from the perimeter into McHale for a dunk ("Vintage Larry Bird!" bellows Dick Stockton).
- Late in the half he hustles for an offensive rebound, just keeps his feet inbounds at the baseline, and shoots a backward pass to McHale for another dunk (McHale already has 20 at this point with many openings created by Bird).

All the while Ralph Sampson was a nonfactor, not scoring until the last two minutes of the half. Says Jerry Sichting looking back: "It went on that way for two or three years. After that incident, he couldn't play in Boston." Talk about a case of serendipity: The player who had spurned Red Auerbach six years earlier now pretty much couldn't play in Auerbach's building,

At halftime Bird had 16 points, eight rebounds, and eight assists. The Celtics were up by 17 points despite uncharacteristically missing 10 of 19 free throws. They were completely controlling the inside. Even the Twin Towers were no match for the white and green front line in this game. As the game continued in the third quarter:

- Bird grabs a rebound and fires a quick outlet pass to DJ who pushes it up court and feeds Ainge for a layup . . . 64–45.
- With five minutes left in the third Bird drills his first three for a 20-point lead. Right after that he makes a move to the hoop, fakes a jumper, and hits McHale on a pick and roll which ends up with two free throws.

Bird had his triple-double before the third quarter ended: 19 points, 11 boards, 10 assists. By the end of the quarter the lead was 82–61, the crowd was ready to celebrate, and Bird still hadn't come out of the game. Wedman was in uniform but his ribs really weren't ready for NBA contact. The only question was whether Jones would give him a token appearance near the end.

- Early in the fourth quarter Bird catches a pass inside with Olajuwon right on him and only a few seconds left on the shot clock. He dribbles quickly out to the corner behind the three-point line, turns around, and drills his second trifecta. The Celtics are up 25. It's all over.
- The last detail worth noticing: Up 28 a little way into the fourth quarter, Bird is still playing intense defense on Rodney McCray as if he's in a seesaw game.

The final was 114–97, only that close because the Rockets scored at will over the final five minutes after the Celtics had stopped playing defense.

Anticipating a big crowd rush at the final horn, the starters filed into the locker room before the game ended, some raising their fists in triumph to the crowd as they went, while Jones emptied the bench. Wedman, armed with heavy padding under his jersey, did get on the floor for the final two minutes though he didn't score, missing his only shot.

Most of the player stat lines seemed appropriate for the 1985/86 Celtics' final game. Bird with the triple-double (29/11/12), McHale with 29 and 10 rebounds, Ainge hitting seven of nine from the floor and scoring 19, Parish with a solid double-double (11/11) and Walton putting up his typical game off the bench with 10 points and eight rebounds in 17 minutes. Dennis Johnson scored a bit below his average but still had a nice all-around game with 10 points, five rebounds and five assists while putting in 46 minutes.

And so the Boston Celtics' 16th championship was in the books. The NBA's greatest franchise to that point had just completed its greatest season yet. Bob Ryan is adamant that no Celtics club, not even the best of the Russell dynasty, equals the 1985/86 squad for one season, and it's easy to agree. Long-term dynasties and single-season greatness are two different things. No single Russell team matched the '86 team for winning percentage or went 50–1 at home. As far as expanding beyond Boston, Ryan believes the only team that merits debate with the Celtics are the recent Golden State Warriors, the historical divide being the adoption of the three-point shot as a big weapon, which changed the way the game is played and the way rosters are built. "I believe the '86 Celtics were the greatest team of the pre-three-point era," he says, meaning the era before the three became as significant a part of the game as it is now. "I'd love to be able to see them play the Warriors."

Cases could be made for a few other championship teams. The best of the Michael Jordan Bulls champions went 72–10 in 1996 and 69–13 in 1997. The 1972 Lakers of Jerry West and Wilt Chamberlain also went 69–13 and won a record 33 straight along the way. Wilt's 1967 Philadelphia 76ers team with Hal Greer and Chet Walker finished 68–13. Both the 1983 76ers and 1987 Lakers made it to 65 wins. But the precise ranking of history's top handful of teams can be debated another time. Wherever the '86 Celtics rank, it's high. And for a basketball purist, there was probably never a more enjoyable team to watch.

The Celtic and Laker teams of the 1980s—and you could probably throw in the Pistons of 1988–1990—were really the last great teams built before the effect of the NBA salary cap fully kicked in, a dynamic that mostly forced front offices to build around a couple of stars and surround them with a bunch of roll players. The Michael Jordan–Scottie Pippen Chicago teams were built this way. Great teams, but you didn't see five Hall of Famers on the roster. The same goes for the Shaq–Kobe Lakers of the early 2000s. Both of those teams were three-peat champions—in fact the '90s Bulls three-peated twice and might have won eight titles in a row if Jordan hadn't run off to play base-ball for a while. Yet to see those teams pull off such a rare feat with so many average players putting in significant minutes speaks to the era as much as anything else. Rings are rings, but it's hard to escape the feeling that all those rings in Chicago and Los Angeles were more about strengthening the career portfolios of Michael Jordan and Kobe Bryant than about the teams.

The funny part for Boston is that the full effect of historical greatness doesn't really sink in right as it's happening. When a club strings together several strong years like the 1980s Celtics did, it's hard to fully differentiate one year from another, at least right in the moment. Through their seventh year of the Larry Bird era, the Celtics had just played in their fourth NBA Finals and won their third championship.

For one season after another (aside from one) winning 60 games and mak-ing it to the conference finals is the usual routine. If they make it to the finals, all the better, and if they win it all, great, fantastic. Following the final horn in Game Six against the Rockets, the natural reaction in Boston was celebra-tion, not much different from 1981 and 1984—we took it all the way this year, and that's awesome. Horns beeped on the streets of Watertown and no doubt in plenty of other towns. People had plenty to rehash at work the next day; many made plans to go to the downtown parade the day after. What you didn't really think about was how that Game Six horn signaled the official end of the 1986 Boston Celtics, and how there would never be another team quite like it.

***

The Red Sox's big roll did hit a snag when both Jeff Sellers and Mike Brown absorbed losses in Milwaukee in early June as the Sox lost three of four to the Brewers. Predictably it was Clemens who helped them avoid the sweep on June 6 when he tossed a four-hit shutout with eight strikeouts to win 3–0. Wade Boggs drove in all three runs with an RBI single in the third and a two-run double in the eighth. A week into June Clemens was 10–0, 2.38 and Boggs was hitting .404.

No, Wade Boggs wouldn't hit .400 for the season. By the end of the year, he'd have to settle for .357 and his third American League batting title, on the way to five. Now in his fifth season, Boggs was reaching that point of almost being taken for granted. He'd been a hit machine from the beginning, the batting average never dropping below .325 or the on-base percentage below .406 since breaking in with the Red Sox in 1982. But he wasn't so much a natural as he was a self-made product of constant, obsessive work.

Boggs, born in Omaha, Nebraska, hailed from a military family and attended high school in Tampa, Florida. His habits reflected the orderly, disciplined military life.[3] He adopted the Ted Williams approach to hitting, developing discipline at the plate, learning the strike zone, and laying off almost anything out of it. A so-so fielder in the minors, he took countless ground balls and turned himself into one of the majors' best glove men at third base. Steve Krasner remembers Boggs's Pawtucket days: "His range was a step to his left, a step and a half to his right, and then look up at the press box to see if it was scored an error," he says.

There were the quirky superstitions. During the season Boggs ate chicken every day. Literally. Before night games he ran his pregame sprints at 7:17 p.m. sharp. Always. A lot of ballplayers are superstitious, maybe sticking with the same undershirt during a hot streak or taking care not to touch the white chalked foul line when running on or off the field between innings. Boggs took it to a new level. He was the ultimate creature of habit—if it worked it worked, and you didn't mess with the formula.

He wasn't supposed to be this good. Not to traditional scouts who saw that he lacked the big-time strength, speed, and athleticism they were used to seeing from top prospects. To the establishment, Boggs didn't have the natural "tools," didn't look the part of a future big leaguer. "The Sox had once left him exposed in the Rule V draft when he was in the minors," says Krasner. "Any team could have had him for $25,000 but he went unclaimed." So long did it take Boggs to win over the doubters that he spent six years in the minors. But by hitting well over .300 each year, including .335 at Triple-A in 1981, they couldn't keep ignoring him. He made it up to the Red Sox the following year and just kept hitting. Initially filling in at first and third, a Carney Lansford injury brought Boggs regular playing time at third for a stretch of the '82 season. He wound up hitting .349 in 338 at-bats, and Lansford was traded to Oakland the next winter.

Still not everyone was a big fan right away. Some in the media, like Mike Barnicle, didn't like the way Boggs seemed to care more about his batting average than the win column, as they saw it. Boggs was certainly obsessed with his stats. Krasner remembers the time he narrowly missed a batting title in the minors and how much it upset him. "He made an out on the last day of the 1980 season and lost the batting title by .0007," says Krasner. "Losing out late just ate at him. His manager Joe Morgan said, 'If this kid didn't win his batting title his head would explode.'"

Of course obsessing over your own numbers doesn't necessarily mean you don't care about winning too. The two go hand in hand after all. Few things helped the Red Sox win more than their best hitter consistently producing and getting on base. As much as it's a team game, you probably don't want the best hitter on the planet trying to ground one to the right side to move a runner over, you want him taking his rips.

In 1986 Wade Boggs not only led the American League in hitting at .357, he led it in on-base percentage at .453 while finishing second to Don Mattingly with a 157 OPS-plus (on-base and slugging combined, adjusted for league average and ballpark). Defensively, the advanced stats say he turned enough left-side ground balls into outs to rank eight runs above the average third baseman, just two fewer than Gold Glove winner Gary Gaetti of Minnesota. His 8.1 WAR led all everyday players in the American League. Boggs reached base 312 times in 1986, by far the most of any player in either league.

Wade Boggs was much like Larry Bird in 1986. Similar in age, talent, and work ethic. Both of them all-time players at their career peaks in Boston. A difference is that in baseball the star can't control the game as much he can in basketball because the star can only come to the plate when it's his turn like everyone else. Boggs never got Bird's multiple rings, but it wasn't for lack of trying.

After muddling along for a bit in their next seven games (three wins, four losses), the Red Sox arrived in New York for their first series of the year against the Yankees. At 40–21, they led the second-place Yanks by 3½ in the A.L. East. Adding to the challenge was that Wade Boggs wouldn't be available for the series after a truly bizarre injury in his Toronto hotel room in which he reportedly fell onto the arm of a couch as he tried to take off a cowboy boot.[4] The fall bruised his ribs; he would miss six games. Ed Romero would fill in at third.

The atmosphere was ripe. It was mid-June, almost summer. The weather was warming up, school was almost out. Both the NBA Finals and Stanley Cup Finals were in the books, and it was now all about the daily rhythms of the baseball season. With the two traditional rivals leading the division, the season held the potential for another '77 or '78, those classic Yankees–Red Sox battles to the wire. Even without a weekend—the series was played Monday through Wednesday nights—all three games at Yankee Stadium would draw at least forty thousand fans.

In the opening game Clemens faced off against veteran Ron Guidry, who was eight years removed from his historic Cy Young Award season that Clemens was in the middle of emulating but still just one year removed from his big 22–6 season in 1985. But for Yankee fans packing the house, the game turned out to be a dud. The Sox jumped on Guidry for three in the top of the first keyed by a two-run single by Jim Rice, the man who had shared the limelight with Guidry in 1978 with his dominant MVP season (five play-ers—Rice, Evans, Stanley, Guidry, and Willie Randolph—remained from the famous Red Sox–Yankees 1978 showdown season that would culminate in Bucky Dent's homer). Rice added RBI singles in both the third and fourth innings as the Sox bolstered their lead to 7–1. The final score was 10–1 as Clemens cruised with a complete game four-hitter.

The Sox picked up where they left off the next night with five first-inning runs against 41-year-old knuckleballer Joe Niekro as Buckner and Evans both homered. After the Yankees scored a couple of their own early runs Evans homered again in the third to put Boston up 7–2. This one would pack some excitement, though. Rookie right-hander Rob Woodward was hanging in there despite a couple of runs and a lot of base runners until McNamara removed him with two men on in the fifth. The Yankees got one that inning and then got one in the sixth and two in the seventh against Steve Crawford, helped along by a Barrett error.

Holding onto a 7–6 lead, Stanley allowed singles to Don Mattingly and Mike Easler and a walk to Gary Roenicke to load the bases with two out in the bottom of the eighth. McNamara summoned left-hander and New York native Joe Sambito, once a relief star with the Houston Astros who was near-ing the end of his career, to face the Yankees' lefty-swinging third baseman Mike Pagliarulo. The move worked just as it's drawn up with Sambito whiff-ing Pagliarulo for the third out.

But the tension was far from over. With Sambito still in there in the bot-tom of the ninth, Butch Wynegar and Willie Randolph opened with singles to give the Yankees two men on with none out. When Dale Berra followed with a third straight single, the Yankee comeback looked inevitable. But Rice charged the ball and came up throwing, firing a strike to Gedman to get Wynegar at the plate (why Wynegar, a catcher and slow runner, was going with no outs is anybody's guess). The runners moved up on the throw, giving the Yankees second and third with one out and their big hitters coming up. Sambito walked Rickey Henderson, loading the bases. But Sambito didn't flinch. Don Mattingly flied to Evans in right field, too shallow for Randolph to tag at third, and then Dave Winfield grounded to Ed Romero at third to end the game. The Yankees had left the bases loaded in both the eighth and ninth innings, left 15 men on for the game, and the Red Sox escaped with a 7–6 win.

The next night was tight, too, a good pitching duel between Oil Can Boyd and Bob Tewksbury that was 2–2 into the ninth. Against reliever Bob Shirley, Barrett singled and Romero doubled to put runners at second and third. It would be a pretty nice series for Romero, who reached base five times and scored four runs in the three games filling in for Boggs.

After Buckner popped up, young right-hander Brian Fisher replaced Shirley and intentionally walked Rice with the open base. Baylor came up and made him pay with a big double over Henderson's head in center field that cleared the bases. In the bottom of the ninth Boyd allowed a lead-off single to Easler (both he and Baylor were excellent with seven hits apiece in their first series against each other since the trade) but then retired the next three batters for a 5–2 win and a huge series sweep. Boyd's ninth win and fourth complete game pushed Boston's lead over New York to 6½ games in the American League East.

***

A few hours after the tired but happy Red Sox had returned home on their late-night flight from New York, Celtics' general manager Jan Volk was awakened at home by a ringing telephone. It was not quite 7 a.m., and a local television producer was on the line. The news: Len Bias, the University of Maryland basketball star just chosen by the Celtics with the second overall pick in the NBA draft two nights earlier, was dead. The news was too crazy to believe, especially in the fog of the early morning.

"He told me he [Bias] had had a heart attack. At first I thought it was some wild story and went back to sleep," Volk says. "Later I called Red, and he knew about it from [Maryland coach] Lefty Driesell."

Soon the story became clearer. Len Bias had died of heart failure induced by cocaine. Following his whirlwind trip north, first to New York for the draft and then to Boston to meet with Celtics officials and the local media, he was celebrating with friends back in Maryland. The partying went on through the wee hours of the night; beer and drugs were both involved. While snorting coke in his dorm room, Bias suddenly went into cardiac arrest. His friend called 911, he was taken to a nearby hospital, but he couldn't be saved.

Jeff Twiss, the Celtics PR man, heard about it the same way Volk did. "My phone rang at 7 a.m. A TV news producer says, did you hear the news? I'm like, no, I just woke up, what is it? He told me Len Bias died. I scrambled to get ready."

The death of Len Bias was one of those shocking moments in which sports fans remember where they were when they heard the news.

John Molori: "I was at home, my cousin Shane who was a Sixers fan and hated the Celtics called and told me that Len Bias died. I remember people like Billy Packer and other college basketball commentators said he was better than Michael Jordan. We all thought he was the perfect segue to the next phase. One of the saddest things in Boston sports history. That was the guy they wanted. We all do the 'what-ifs.' They gave the Lakers a run in the 1987 finals, but put Len Bias on that team. . . ."

And from Rich Chaiton of Medway: "We were so excited because the Big Three was aging and we didn't know if Walton would go more than another year." But he'd also been watching the sports news in recent years like anyone else. And a lot of it had been filled with drug stories, enough that he wasn't entirely shocked by the Bias news. Baseball's highly publicized Pittsburgh drug trial that had nabbed a lot of big-name players who had bought cocaine from an accused dealer was still less than a year old. And a few of Bias's fellow 1986 NBA draft picks would eventually see their careers derailed by drugs, notably Roy Tarpley and Chris Washburn. "My first thought," says Chaiton, "was that they all do it."

He was far from alone. The image of a pretty big drug culture in sports certainly existed at the time. Of course it was hard to sort out all the particulars from one case to another. Bias was 22 years old, a finely tuned athlete and not known as a drug user. That didn't necessarily mean he hadn't taken drugs before, but who knew? Three NBA teams, including the Celtics, had administered physicals to him before the draft, at least one of which included a drug test. He'd passed them all.[5] Certainly Red Auerbach hadn't seen this coming, hadn't seen any red flags. He knew Lefty Driesell well, and there were certainly no warnings from him. "I can still hear Lefty's voice," says Bob Ryan. "He said, 'Lenny's only weakness is ice cream.'" Ryan had just sat with Bias during his interview in Boston, and for a while he could hardly process the news that followed. "It was almost surreal, he had the nice suit on, his family members with him. No one knew there was a problem."

Auerbach generally said all the right things, focusing on Bias and his family more than on his ball club. Twiss says that for all his scrambling, the media-savvy Auerbach didn't need a lot of his help in the end. "He'd call me in to say, 'Does this sound good?' That type of thing."

Len Bias was going to be the next great Boston Celtic. An explosive 6'8" and 210 pounds, he had succeeded Michael Jordan as player of the year in the ACC in 1985 and won it again in 1986. He could run the floor, get to the rim, and shoot the midrange jumper. And a lot of people did compare him to Jordan as a talent.

"A *mean* player," says Jan Volk. "He played hard and mean. He was a fourth-year senior, so he had a lot of maturity to his game. The scouting report said he was Michael Jordan with a better outside shot and not quite as good a handle going to the hoop."

Would Len Bias have been as great as Michael Jordan? That wouldn't seem likely, considering that Michael Jordan may have been the greatest player of all time and certainly ranks among the top handful. Holding Bias to that standard is probably a stretch. But Jordan or not, there wasn't anyone who didn't expect Bias to be an NBA star. This had been a classic tale of the rich getting richer: the NBA's dominant team, which had just completed its championship less than two weeks earlier, adding a stud with the second pick in the draft, a pick Auerbach had secured two years earlier from Seattle in the trade for Gerald Henderson. It was another Auerbach deal that had turned up roses. The Sonics had been a .500 team at the time of the trade, but two years later they had sunk enough (31–51) to land in the lottery, where the pick the Celtics had snagged turned to gold.

And now shockingly, it wasn't gold anymore. Who knows exactly how much the loss of Len Bias set the Celtics back. Probably a lot. The chance to inject his youth into the talented but aging front line would have been the perfect prescription to cut back on the minutes that Bird, McHale, and Parish were logging as they aged. Maybe the back problems that Bird began to endure in the late 1980s would have been put off a bit further. Maybe the Celtics don't cede Eastern Conference supremacy to the Detroit Pistons by 1988, and maybe they win another couple of titles.

"Boston went from color to black and white that day," is how Lesley Visser puts it. "I had just interviewed him at the draft, he was so young, so gifted."

***

John Molori recalls the days at Fenway Park that stuck out as his favorites in 1986. "We went a lot on Saturday afternoons. It seemed like Clemens would always pitch a three-hitter and Dwight Evans would homer and they would win." That would have included the Saturday afternoon June 21 game against the Baltimore Orioles. In a sign that the team was now grabbing more national attention, particularly if Clemens was pitching, NBC flip-flopped its schedule to air Red Sox–Orioles as its primary *Game of the Week* telecast, beamed to most of the country, while moving Yankees–Blue Jays to the secondary slot.[6]

Clemens didn't quite pitch a three-hitter, but he did toss a six-hitter over eight innings in the 7–2 win, his 13th of the season without a loss. And it was Evans who sent the Sox on their way right ought of the gate with a three-run blast off young Baltimore right-hander Ken Dixon to cap a four-run first inning. Evans would add a pair of singles to finish his day 3-for-4 with four RBI. He was heating up with the weather. The homer was just his eighth of the season but his third in the past four games. At age 34 he was on his way to another strong offensive season, once again eclipsing anything he'd done with the bat in his 20s. By the end of the year Evans would wind up hitting a pretty pedestrian .259, but his .376 on-base percentage and 131 OPS-plus both just missed the league's top ten. He'd hit 15 of his 26 homers after the All-Star break.

Nicknamed "Dewey" since his minor league days, Dwight Evans's career arc didn't fit the usual pattern. Most hitters approach their peak at a young age, have their good run for a number of years, and then tail off as they age. Evans pretty much did the opposite. In the younger years he played great right field, had the great arm, but he was pretty much average offensively. A complementary guy in a strong Boston lineup that included Jim Rice, Fred Lynn, and Carlton Fisk. It was later, right around age 30, that he became a force at the plate.

"I came up at 20. I was probably too young," Evans says. "We really didn't have hitting coaches. They'd say, 'Get a fastball and try to pull it.' There was no one to really bounce things off of." The standard advice, he says, was just to relax at the plate. "But I really didn't know how to relax. I'd talk to Rod Carew, and he would talk about how to relax. The key is moving a little bit in the box, wave the bat a little. It's when you're standing still at the plate you get tired."

Along with Rich Gedman, Evans became a Walt Hriniak devotee. Hriniak didn't become the Red Sox hitting coach until 1985, but some players had begun picking his brain well before that during his time as a bullpen coach who threw a lot of batting practice. His hitting theory centered on keeping your head down, dropping the hands and hitting the ball up the middle. If you got an inside pitch and pulled it, fine, but the middle of the field was your starting point, your center of gravity.

"My natural thing was hitting up the middle, stay in the middle of the field. That was my mantra," Evans says. He worked with Hriniak tirelessly, even adopting the suggestion that he lift the heel of his front foot in the box with the toe pointing straight down, which helped keep his weight back. Everything in place for the swing.

"I really did work my rear end off," Evans says. "People would always talk about me as a right fielder and I'd say, 'I can hit too.'"

The results during the second half of his career were pretty startling. Breaking-in full time with the Red Sox in 1973, Evans played for almost a decade without reaching 30 home runs in a season. Only three times did he even reach 20. Then from 1982 to 1987 he just about averaged 30 homers. His batting eye improved to the point where after never walking more than 69 times in a season from 1973 to 1980, he led the A.L. three times beginning in 1981 and drew at least 96 walks four more times beyond that. The on-base percentage topped .400 three times in the 1980s and wound up at .370 for his career—higher than Ichiro Suzuki and just a few points behind Pete Rose. Add 385 home runs and the strong defense during his younger years (the numbers say the defensive range did drop after age 30 though they still rate quite high for his career) and his 67.2 WAR ought to have gotten him many more Hall of Fame votes than the 51 he got. As much as he was generally respected as a good player, Evans was never quite seen as elite.

MLB Network anchor Brian Kenny, in his excellent book *Ahead of the Curve*, which among other things looks back at the careers of some past players in an analytical way, noted that initial perceptions of a player can be hard to break, even if his game changes as he goes. That Evans spent so many years as a good field-decent hit guy during the first half of his career that his reputation became cemented that way even after his offensive game took off later. During the years he spent patrolling the Fenway Park outfield with Jim Rice and Fred Lynn, Evans was always seen as the little brother to the two higher-profile stars. That perception never seemed to change very much even after Lynn left and Evans went on to clearly have the best career of the three.

John Molori saw it differently: "Dwight Evans was one of my favorite players of all time. He was the top right fielder of his time. Right field at Fenway was very difficult with the distance and with that corner." As right fielders of the time go, adding up both offense and defense, the numbers—OPS-plus, WAR, defensive metrics—show Evans ranking a little way behind Reggie Jackson, clearly ahead of Dave Parker, whose shelf life as a star was short, and about even with Dave Winfield, who is in the Hall of Fame largely because he hung around for several average seasons late in his career to compile 3,000 hits.

Tony Gwynn, who came up nearly a decade after Evans but did overlap with him for nine years, would rate higher—barely. It's one of the enduring biases of Hall of Fame voting—standing out in one facet of the game usually gets you more attention than building your value with the all-around game. Tony Gwynn was a hit machine, winning battle titles and churning out 200-hit seasons. He was easily defined: "One of the great pure hitters of all time." With Dwight Evans it was more a mixture of this and that—on-base, power, and defense.

Jackson, Winfield, and Gwynn are all in the Hall of Fame. Parker isn't, but he got a lot more votes and stayed on the ballot a lot longer than Evans did. Evans never came close to election from the writers, and he came up a few votes shorts from a Modern Era Committee in 2019. Here's hoping he gets his due soon.

The Yankees got some measure of revenge against the Red Sox when they took two of three at Fenway in late June. The 1986 version of the Yankees may not have had the balance of the championship teams of the late '70s—the pitching certainly wasn't the same—but their stacked lineup could smash you to pieces on a given night. They hammered both Boyd and Woodward in the first two games of the series to roll up a pair of lopsided wins. The Sox salvaged the final game of the series after welcoming Al Nipper back to the mound for his first outing in almost six weeks. He had a shaky start, allowing two first-inning runs and then watching the Yankees load the bases before he induced Willie Randolph to ground out to escape further damage. The Sox responded by sending nine men to the plate in the bottom of the first to quickly knock out young right-hander Doug Drabek, the future Pittsburgh Pirates ace who was just cutting his big-league teeth at the time. In a move that their fans would lament for years afterward, the always impatient Yankees would deal Drabek to Pittsburgh after the season for veteran pitcher Rick Rhoden and then watch Drabek's career take off. But on this night making just his third major league start he was knocked around for four hits, two walks, and five runs while retiring one batter. Tony Armas supplied the key hit with a two-run single. After one inning the Red Sox led 5–2.

The Sox didn't score again the rest of the night and Nipper battled through another couple of runs but he made it through seven innings and departed with a 5–4 lead. Sambito held the lead with a stellar relief job, striking out the side in the eighth and then picking off Rickey Henderson in the ninth before recording the final out. The Sox led the second place Yankees by five games in the A.L. East.

They followed the victory with a three-game sweep in Baltimore (Clemens improving to 14–0 and Sellers getting his first win of the year with a complete game) and then took the first two games of the next series against the Blue Jays at Fenway to run the latest winning streak to six games. The wildest one came on Monday night, June 30, when the Jays knocked Nipper around for eight runs and 11 hits by the sixth inning (George Bell and Lloyd Moseby both took him deep) only to see Boston keep counterpunching with three in the first, two in the fifth, and four in the sixth. Barrett rapped out four hits, Boggs three, and Rice three, including a homer. After six innings the score was 9–9. Bob Stanley turned in his best relief outing of the season with three scoreless innings to keep the score tied into the bottom of the 10th. With two on and two out, reliever Jim Acker hit Don Baylor with a pitch—Baylor's second HBP of the night—to load the bases. Evans then took ball four from Acker to force in the winning run, 10–9. It was Evans's third walk of the night to go with his two-run single. The lead over the Yankees was now eight games.

It was becoming a pattern—one of 18 games the Red Sox would win in their final turn at bat in 1986. The team was good, but there was some magic going on too. "We could beat teams in different ways, win the 9–8 games and 1–0 games," says Gedman. And the 10–9 games. Says Steve Krasner: "Just one of those things, they caught lightning in a bottle. It's just magic, sometimes things just fall for you."

The game wasn't quite the only thing that fell for the Red Sox on the final day of June. Earlier that morning, splashed across the front page of the *Boston Globe*, was news of a big trade.

PART III

July to October, 1986

Chapter 7

July–August 1986

On his way to Boston and set to start on Tuesday night, July 1, was Tom Seaver, obtained from the Chicago White Sox for fourth outfielder Steve Lyons.[1] The news wasn't exactly unexpected. Bolstering the pitching was a common move for a contending team, and Seaver rumors had been circulating for a while. With the White Sox fading out of the American League West race and Seaver publicly expressing his desire to head back closer to the Greenwich, Connecticut, home he'd kept since his heyday with the Mets, he was an obvious candidate for a trade. The Yankees were a possibility, but ultimately White Sox GM Ken Harrelson, who as it happened had once led the American League in RBI for the 1968 Red Sox, took Lou Gorman up on his offer of Lyons.

Seaver would be reunited with John McNamara and Bill Fischer, his manager and pitching coach in Cincinnati.

The trade generated a lot of buzz because of Tom Seaver's stature in the game; it was just cool to see an all-time great putting on a Red Sox uniform in what would turn out to be his final major league season. On the field, everyone knew the trade wasn't *that* big because Tom Seaver was 41 years old and he wasn't an ace anymore. But that was okay. The Red Sox had their ace in Roger Clemens. They had some talent lined up behind him. Seaver didn't need to be an ace, and said himself that no team that considers itself to be a legitimate contender should have a 41-year-old at the top of the rotation. He was there to take his turn every fifth day and add some depth. As for any wisdom and leadership qualities he could bring to a fairly young staff—sure, he'd be happy to help anyone who asked. But he also joked that the best thing he could do for Roger Clemens was to make sure he got to the park on time. He wasn't there to be a second pitching coach; he was there to pitch. Still, as true as it was that Clemens was doing just fine before Seaver hit town, he does credit the veteran for some of the subtleties he picked up just from observation. "I got to witness the best power pitcher ever to do it. You would see him struggle to throw the fastball at 88 and then suddenly with runners

121

on second and third he would pop 94; he knew when to dial it up," Clemens says. "You have to pay attention to detail. You won't always have great stuff. Probably 100 wins of my career came without all three pitches working."

The move made plenty of sense because even though Seaver was not the pitcher he'd been in his prime, he could still be effective. With brains and guile and stuff that could still be pretty good he had tossed 238 innings and won 16 games the previous year, including career-win No. 299 at Fenway Park and No. 300 five days later in front of many of his old Mets fans at Yankee Stadium. The Sox rotation was looking thin at the moment beyond Clemens and Boyd, with Hurst still out, Nipper beginning to struggle following his comeback from the knee injury, and the fill-ins—Sellers, Woodward, and Brown—only showing so much. So the veteran Seaver was brought in to shore things up.

More than thirty-two thousand people were on hand—nearly a sellout—for Seaver's first home game at Fenway. His debut against the Blue Jays was not the best game he would have in a Red Sox uniform. Facing a tough lineup he struggled with a lot of base runners—his only one-two-three inning would be the sixth—but he made it through seven innings before departing with a 9–4 lead. The lineup supported him with a four-run first inning highlighted by Evans's three-run double and a three-run third inning with RBI singles by Gedman, Barrett, and young outfielder Kevin Romine, who had just been called up the previous day to replace Lyons. Crawford and Sambito struggled in the final two innings but the Sox hung on to win 9–7. Seaver hadn't been great but he did what the team had brought him in to do: pitch seven innings and keep them in the game.

It was the night following Tom Seaver's Red Sox debut that something pretty extraordinary happened. The incarnate Seaver, Roger Clemens, lost a game. Entering his start against Toronto 14–0 with a 2.18 earned run average, Clemens was about as masterful as ever most of the way. George Bell's fourth-inning solo homer was the only hit he allowed through seven innings while striking out eight. But with lefty Jimmy Key mostly keeping the Red Sox lineup in check, Clemens nursed a narrow 2–1 lead in the eighth when he was pulled after allowing a walk and two hits for a run that tied the score. Stanley came in and allowed a single to Bell and a sac fly to Jesse Barfield for two more runs and a 4–2 Toronto lead. That would be the final score, leaving Clemens 14–1. McNamara's decision to lift Clemens in a tie game became a sure indicator that he didn't always see eye to eye with Fischer, his pitching coach. After the game, Clemens remembers, "Fish yelled at McNamara, 'You leave that kid in to lose his own game.'"

It was an amazing run. Think about a pitcher taking every turn, beginning in early April and not losing a game until July. Making 16 starts and getting to at least the eighth inning in 14 of them. Averaging a strikeout per inning in a league where the pitcher doesn't hit, in a contact era when the typical pitcher averaged 5.8 Ks per nine innings.

And, of course, the run was far from over. It was all coming together. Long before he was winning multiple Cy Young Awards in Toronto, New York, and Houston, long before he threw a bat near Mike Piazza in a World Series game, and long before anyone was connecting him to performance-enhancing drugs, Roger Clemens was the Red Sox's young phenom. After beginning his career with some shoulder problems, he was enjoying the breakthrough year. He was taking to living in Framingham. Off days were sometimes spent golfing with Larry Bird and other Celtics. It was clear by now that the Red Sox not only had the guy they were hoping for, but much more.

"He was like Yaz in '67. It's unusual in baseball for one player to carry a team to first place," says Bill Ballou. "But Clemens was that guy, such a remarkable year. With Clemens they knew they wouldn't lose many games in a row. It just boosts everyone's confidence, you play much more relaxed."

Teammates noticed his dedication and work ethic, the effort to keep fit and healthy. It was clear that Clemens wasn't a guy inclined to coast on talent; he put the work in to maximize it. "A very hard worker," says Dwight Evans. "He would go out and run around the Charles, and big runs, five, six miles or more at a good pace." Clemens remembers: "Boston is an easy city to run in. Everyone loved to run and you've got all those paths by the river. Pop the head set on and go."

The Red Sox celebrated July Fourth at Fenway with a win over Seattle but also with a stark reminder of their biggest weakness, a shaky bullpen. They got a strong start from Jeff Sellers, who tossed seven shutout innings and led 6–0 behind homers from Evans and Gedman. But when McNamara pushed him into the eighth, Sellers allowed two walks and a three-run homer to Danny Tartabull. Sambito came in to finish the eighth unscathed but then allowed a walk and a two-run homer to Jim Presley in the ninth. Boston held on for a 6–5 win, but the bullpen had to be concerning them.

The Sox finished out the long home stand by going 5–4 against the three West Coast teams leading up to the All-Star break. Included was Seaver's second straight win when he allowed just an unearned run over seven innings in a 7–3 win over the Mariners. But the highlight of the home stand came on Thursday night, July 10, in a wild game against the California Angels (shades of October). Both teams used six pitchers—highly unusual back then—in the back-and-forth marathon that went 12 innings and lasted four and a half hours.

Trailing 3–1 in the sixth, the Sox rallied against California starter Ron Romanick for three runs to take the lead on Buckner's two-run homer and Evans's RBI single. Al Nipper was having a good Al Nipper game, not over-powering but mixing pitches and hitting enough spots to limit the damage. He lasted into the eighth inning when Wally Joyner doubled and Brian Downing singled him in for the tying run. With the bullpens taking over, the game remained 4–4 into the 12th inning.

Steve Crawford got the first two outs in the top of the 12th but was removed after feeling a burst of pain in his right shoulder as he struck out Gary Pettis.[2] That brought on Mike Brown, and it didn't go well: triple, wild pitch for a run, walk, walk, single for a run, double for a run. Trailing 7–4, Boston's long night seemed lost.

But the Angels were down to young reliever Mike Cook, a recent callup pitching in his fourth big league game, to close things out in the bottom of the 12th. He came close, getting two outs after yielding a lead-off single to Barrett. Even after Rice deposited one way beyond the Green Monster for a two-run homer, Cook and the Angels still led by a run with the bases clear and two out. The game appeared to be over when Baylor lofted a pop-up into short left field. But old Fenway friend Rick Burleson, who had just entered the game at third base an inning earlier, dropped the ball. Cook then walked Evans and gave up a line single to right to Gedman that drove in the tying run. Worse for the Angels, first baseman Wally Joyner bobbled the relay throw for an error, allowing the runners to move up to second and third. On came right-hander Todd Fischer to relieve Cook with the winning run on third.

Rey Quinones stepped up to the plate with a chance to win the game. But Quinones never saw a pitch. As he came set, Fischer moved his glove ever so slightly before stepping off the rubber. Plate umpire Joe Brinkman stepped out and called a balk, and Evans trotted home with the winning run. Another night at Fenway, another win in the final at-bat, this time a four-run rally in the bottom of the 12th. For Todd Fischer, it was his ninth and final appearance in a big league game.

Unfortunately, one player who wasn't around to celebrate the dramatic win was Dennis (Oil Can) Boyd. A little bit earlier he had been given the news that he hadn't been chosen for the upcoming All-Star Game in Houston, news that he didn't take well. According to various news reports, Boyd threw a major tantrum in the clubhouse, including tossing clothes out of his locker. He screamed at anyone, including teammates, who tried to calm him down, and then stormed off. As the Red Sox played their game against the Angels, he was in his car on the way back to his Chelsea neighborhood. He had taken his ball and gone home.

Such was the conundrum of Oil Can Boyd. Talented, volatile, unpredictable. Funny and charming one day, angry the next. "Mercurial, moody," says Bill Ballou. "But sometimes he could be the most pleasant conversationalist." His nickname came from the drinking that had been a regular staple for him since his teen years growing up in Meridian, Mississippi, swilling from those big metal cans that resembled oil cans. There were drugs too. He'd later admit to regular crack use, including during the 1986 season. Steve Krasner never saw any drugs while covering Oil Can but says, "It wouldn't surprise me."

Boyd had been something of an underdog prospect from the beginning, not drafted until the 16th round in 1980 out of Jackson State University. He was always too skinny, carrying some 155 pounds on his 6–1 frame. But he could pitch. Boyd had a big repertoire: fastball, curve, slider, change. Not overpowering, exactly, but he had that ability to mix things up and change speeds. Similar to Al Nipper but with better stuff. When he had it going, he was fun to watch, flamboyant and animated on the mound, pumping his right arm after a strikeout. Traditionalists thought Boyd's occasional antics were bush league but really he was just a bit ahead of his time—his act was pretty tame by today's standards.

He made it up to Boston in 1982, became a regular in the starting rotation by late 1983, and progressed steadily over the next couple of years. By 1985, with Clemens hurt and Hurst having his ups and downs, Boyd was Boston's most reliable pitcher. Even if his personality was a little bit volatile, it wasn't enough to outweigh what he was giving the team on the mound.

This explosion after the 1986 All-Star snub was bad though. A big scene in the clubhouse, walking out on the team . . . what to do with that? The Red Sox initially suspended Boyd for three games, but soon, after he'd exacerbated his troubles with a little altercation with the local police, pushed it much further, sidelining him for almost a month while he underwent a series of physical and psychological tests. "They were a condition for coming back," says Krasner, whose clearest memory of Boyd during his absence was chatting with him on his front lawn as Boyd held the leashes of a couple of big, threatening dogs.

Remembers Rich Chaiton: "He was a good pitcher but he was nuts. The guy he reminded me of was Roger Moret," he says, referring to another skinny Red Sox pitcher from about a decade earlier with good stuff and a fragile psyche who was later sent for psychiatric testing by the Texas Rangers.

Boyd didn't get a lot of sympathy from the press. Will McDonough in the *Boston Globe* called him "a 26-year-old teenager."[3] In a different season Boyd might have pitched his last game in a Red Sox uniform. But the team was in first place, there was a pennant to win, and Boyd, despite where his head may have been, still had that good right arm. Says Ballou: "Had they not been in contention they probably would have cut ties with him, but they had a chance to win so they had to suck it up. He could throw all sorts of different pitches from all sorts of angles, but he didn't have the emotional maturity."

Lack of emotional maturity seems like a good way to put it. Boyd came off like a guy who wanted what was his, as he saw it. If he cared about the team, he really didn't show it. He wasn't going to the All-Star Game, so nothing else seemed to matter.

Even on the merits, Boyd's anger at not being picked for the American League squad didn't really fly. He was a guy whose opinion of his own talents always seemed a bit inflated. A good pitcher who fancied himself a great pitcher. He was certainly a pretty solid candidate for the 1986 All-Star Game, but his reaction suggested that he thought himself to be a slam dunk choice, which he wasn't. By the second week of July he was 10–6 with a 3.71 ERA that was a bit better than average. In 18 starts and 128 innings he'd allowed 127 hits and 20 home runs. That's a lot of dingers, but all in all he had pretty solid numbers, especially for a guy pitching half his games at Fenway. But All-Star selections are rarely perfect. Borderline candidates get left out all the time. The biggest constraint for American League manager Dick Howser of Kansas City, who had the task of picking the pitching staff, came from dealing with the television-driven rule that every team was required to have at least one player in the All-Star Game. As it turned out two of the starting pitchers he chose, Milwaukee's Teddy Higuera and Texas's Charlie Hough, went as the lone representatives of their teams (by all accounts Higuera was having a better year than Boyd anyway; it was a closer call with Hough).

So the Sox would have to ride out some drama from Oil Can as best they could. The good news was that they hit the All-Star break at 56–31 and seven games ahead of the Yankees in the American League East. Boyd wasn't going to Houston but four other Red Sox were, five if you count John McNamara as a coach. Wade Boggs, hitting .363 with a .468 on-base percentage, was voted the starter at third base. Jim Rice, hitting .334 with a .385 OBP, was taken by Howser as a reserve despite only nine homers. Howser also took Rich Gedman, who was having a so-so offensive year but playing great defense, to back up starting catcher Lance Parrish.

And Roger Clemens, 15–2 with a 2.48 ERA, would start on the mound for the A.L. in a triumphant homecoming in front of family and friends at the Astrodome. Despite working on just two days' rest following his Saturday win over the Angels, Clemens didn't disappoint. He took game MVP honors by tossing three perfect innings in the American League's 3–2 win over the National League, striking out Ryne Sandberg and Darryl Strawberry. The Mets' Dwight Gooden, whose team was leading everyone out of sight in the N.L., started and took the loss after he was tagged for an early two-run homer by Detroit's Lou Whitaker. Fans in New England liked the look of the graphic on the T.V. screen at the end of the game, which below the final line score read: W-Clemens, L-Gooden. A foreshadow of October, they hoped. It was starting to feel that way.

But, of course, it's a long season, and baseball can be a streaky game. Coming out of the gate to begin the second half, the Red Sox went to the West Coast and stumbled through their worst stretch of the season by losing 8 of 10 in Seattle, Oakland, and California. Clemens was still playing stopper—only his wins over the Mariners and Angels saved the Sox from a winless trip. Nipper was roughed up twice on the trip and Sellers was lit up for eight runs in his only start. Seaver started three times and pitched okay but wound up with two losses and a no-decision. The toughest loss was on July 17 in Seattle when Seaver allowed one run in six innings in a game the Sox eventually lost in extra innings when Stanley, after two scoreless innings, served up a two-out grand slam to Jim Presley in the bottom of the 11th.

The final game out West matched Seaver against his old National League rival Don Sutton in a Sunday matinee in Anaheim. Both 41 years old, both already past the 300-win plateau and, really, both could still pitch. Sutton outdueled Seaver that day to win 3–0. Boston's lead was already down to three games over the Yankees.

The trip was disappointing but not without its encouraging developments. Late July brought a couple of nice boosts to the pitching staff. On July 20 hard-throwing Calvin Schiraldi was called up from Pawtucket. The organization's plan to convert him to a reliever seemed to be working. Schiraldi had been pretty much killing it in Triple-A, blowing away hitters to the tune of 59 strikeouts in 44 innings with a 2.86 ERA. He debuted with two-plus innings in a loss to Seattle, allowing one run. He'd soon become McNamara's go-to late-inning guy the rest of the way. The next day in Oakland it was Bruce Hurst finally making it back to the mound for the first time in almost eight weeks. He was a bit rusty as expected, walking three and serving up homers to Tony Phillips and Dave Kingman before departing in the sixth in a 5–2 loss. But more importantly the groin didn't give him any trouble. He was healthy and feeling good. Winning more games on the trip would have been nice, but the Sox were leaving the West Coast with a better rotation and better bullpen than when they'd arrived.

Schiraldi's promotion and gradual assumption of the late-inning role (the term "closer" wasn't really used yet) allowed the Red Sox to bump Bob Stanley into more of a setup role for which he was probably better suited. A right-hander whose signature pitch was a palm ball, Stanley's stuff was designed to get hitters to beat the ball into the ground, not so much to swing and miss. That left a lot to chance—sometimes those grounders were gobbled up by the infielders, sometimes they would sneak through for base hits. In close, late-game situations, a power arm like Schiraldi's that was likely to whiff a couple of hitters was closer to a sure thing to finish out the game.

Schiraldi's high octane relief was a welcome sight for Red Sox fans, who generally got heartburn when Stanley was called in late. "Tie 'em up, Stanley," John Cascione called him for the number of wins Stanley seemed to pile up as a result of blowing saves first. "Like a softball player" is how Rich Chaiton described Stanley's portly build.

It was true that Stanley was not having his best year in 1986. By the end of the season he'd allow 109 hits in 82 innings with a 4.37 ERA, not the kind of numbers you're looking for in one of your top relievers. For much of his career, though, Bob Stanley has to go down as one of the more underappreciated players the Red Sox ever had. Since coming up in 1977 he'd been durable and flexible, adapting to whatever role the club asked of him—long relief, short relief, starting. He's one of only 15 pitchers in major league history to record at least 100 wins and 100 saves. Twice an All-Star, Stanley appeared in 637 games in a Red Sox uniform—85 of them starts—still the club record for a pitcher. His best seasons came in 1978 when he went 15–2 with a 2.60 ERA over 141 innings (with a 160 ERA-plus, meaning 60% better than league average after factoring in ballpark), and 1982, when he threw 168 innings out of the pen, led the league with a 140 ERA-plus, and got some Cy Young votes. He would ultimately put up a 118 ERA-plus with a 115–97 record and 23.9 WAR over a 13-year career. And how's this for a comparison: In career innings, ERA-plus, and WAR, Stanley stands virtually identical to his contemporary Rollie Fingers, who is in the Hall of Fame because he was utilized almost exclusively as a late-inning specialist who chalked up a ton of saves, a stat which Hall of Fame voters seem to love.

Stanley's struggles in 1986 might at least partly be chalked up to the supporting cast. The key middle infielders, Barrett at second base and the combination of Hoffman, Quinones, and eventually Spike Owen at short, didn't have the range that a ground-ball pitcher like Stanley enjoyed when the quicker Jerry Remy and Rick Burleson played behind him. Whatever the combination of reasons, it just wasn't happening for Stanley in '86. To his credit he never made excuses, never brought up the defense. "Always affable, he had that deep voice," says Steve Krasner. "When he gave it up, he was right there answering questions."

The sudden presence of Schiraldi to take some pressure off Stanley would be a huge plus as the season approached the home stretch. Schiraldi picked up his first save on August 3 at Fenway when he relieved Nipper against the Royals with none out, a runner on first in the ninth, and the Sox holding a 5–3 lead. With the tying run at the plate, he whiffed Frank White and Steve Balboni and then induced Jorge Orta to ground out.

But the Sox had their struggles during some of the late July and early August dog days, mainly because their bats were tired. This wasn't a team with a deep bench. Most of the regulars were playing almost every day and were bound to hit a tired stretch by midsummer. Right after the Royals' series, they dropped the next game to the White Sox 1–0, a tough loss for Clemens who tossed a complete game four-hitter.

The following night, August 5, marked the return of Oil Can Boyd to the mound. More than thirty-five thousand people turned out at Fenway on a

Tuesday night, ready to forgive and forget. He got a nice reception for his first game in almost a month but the night was mostly low key. The past was the past, everyone seemed to say in one way or another. Now it was time to just let Boyd pitch. Team doctor Arthur Pappas told the press that Boyd didn't go through any particular treatments during his time in the hospital but mainly used the time to rest and decompress.[4]

He was cool and composed on the mound and did very well, only to suffer nearly as tough a loss as Clemens had the night before. A couple of mistakes wound up in the seats, a two-run homer by Carlton Fisk in the fifth and a solo shot by Harold Baines in the eighth for all of Chicago's runs. Boston's recent offensive woes continued as Richard Dotson and Gene Nelson held them to three hits in a 3–0 loss. Their lead in the American League East was down to 2½ games over the Baltimore Orioles, a hot team of late that had jumped past the Yankees into second place.

The bats finally woke up in a big way the following night in support of Hurst, who pitched his first real gem since coming back from the groin injury. This was the night that John McNamara decided to go ahead and flip-flop Boggs and Barrett in the order, inserting Boggs into the lead-off spot with Barrett hitting right behind him.

So what happened? Boggs led off the bottom of the first with a walk and Barrett followed with a two-run homer. As the inning continued, the next four Red Sox all reached against Chicago starter Floyd Bannister, who was pulled after four runs without retiring a batter. In the second inning the Sox loaded the bases against long reliever Bill Dawley before Buckner cleared the bases with a double to right field. The Red Sox led 7–0 after two innings on the way to a 9–0 win. Maybe the lineup shift was a coincidence, but Barrett wound up the night with three hits while Boggs reached base all five times up with three walks and a pair of singles. Hurst, meantime, went all the way on a three-hitter, striking out four and walking none.

It was good to see Bruce Hurst rounding back into form after a couple of shaky starts had followed his return from the injured list. He had already built on his late-1985 success with a strong first half, and no doubt he was anxious to show that any midseason slump was little more than an injury-induced hiccup. In his 11th year of pro ball and his 5th full year in the majors, Hurst's journey to becoming a premier pitcher in the American League was almost complete. But it almost didn't happen. "Two or three times in the minors he was ready to walk away," says Steve Krasner, who covered Hurst in both the minors and majors and calls him one of the nicest guys you'll ever meet.

On the field Hurst had always made good progress in the minors, putting up mostly solid numbers at every stop after the Red Sox drafted him in the first round out of high school in St. George, Utah, in 1976. But Hurst struggled with the lifestyle. A Mormon who lived his life with high moral values, he didn't mesh with a pro baseball culture that revolved so much around the road, drinking and chasing women. Part of him wanted to keep pitching, part of him wanted to go home. Finally Joe Morgan, his manager at Pawtucket, got him to face the fact that baseball life would probably never be perfect. "Morgan told him, this is your career, you can't have it both ways," says Bill Ballou. "They gave him a couple of weeks off to figure it out." Hurst stayed; he wouldn't walk away again until his retirement in 1994. And he never changed his lifestyle either. From his battery mate, Rich Gedman: "He was a different person, he made you a better man."

Two nights after Hurst's masterpiece Seaver went the distance at Detroit with nine strikeouts in a 5–1 win, kicking off a three-game sweep and a five-game lead over the Yankees and Orioles. The bats were back in a big way. After sleepwalking through 59 runs over a 21-game stretch, the Boston offense piled up 134 runs in the next 21 games. Okay, that figure was skewed a bit by a crazy night in Cleveland when the Red Sox scored 12 first-inning runs and won 24–5. But even taking away that game, they scored enough over the 21 games to nearly double the previous 21. So go the ebbs and flows of the baseball season. Hitting is contagious, they say.

On August 10 in Detroit, Gedman, resting in favor of Marc Sullivan behind the plate, came off the bench in the top of the eighth and pinch-hit a grand slam off Willie Hernandez to cap a five-run inning and a 9–6 comeback win. Two nights later the division lead dropped back to 3½ games when the Sox lost both games of a doubleheader in Kansas City. McNamara used Stanley to start the nightcap and he did well for five innings before allowing three runs in the sixth in what would be a 6–5 loss.

But that was as close as the competition would get. The Sox won the next two in Kansas City—Gedman, Armas, and Evans homering in an 11–5 win on August 14 to give Nipper a win despite a shaky outing—and then returned to Fenway for a quick home stand to take two of three against Detroit.

On Sunday, August 17, with their lead at five games, the Sox won a game and made a post deadline deal to strengthen the roster for the stretch run. Against the Tigers at Fenway, Calvin Schiraldi relieved Bruce Hurst in the sixth inning of a 4–4 game and got his first win by allowing one run the rest of the way. Boston's winning rally came in the bottom of the sixth on an RBI double by Barrett, followed by a two-run double by Baylor.

After the game GM Lou Gorman announced that he had agreed to deal his struggling young shortstop Rey Quinones along with (currently) Triple-A pitchers Mike Brown and Mike Trujillo to the Seattle Mariners for shortstop Spike Owen and outfielder Dave Henderson. Quinones had pretty much lost his grip on the shortstop job; utility man Ed Romero had been starting there a lot over the past couple of weeks. The team had always loved Quinones's tools. He'd shown plenty of pop at the plate during his quick rise through the

Red Sox's minor league system, and he was still just 22 years old. But the team was in first place and needed to solidify things. Owen, though still just 25 himself, had a few years of big league experience under his belt and figured to bring a steady presence, if not much of a bat (he was at .246 without a homer). Quinones could continue his learning curve with the Mariners, who were on their way to finishing in the A.L. West basement.

Henderson, just turned 28 and in his sixth season, would fit in well as a fourth outfielder. He was having a pretty nice year in Seattle, hitting .276 with 14 home runs. Outfield depth was an issue as the club looked to hold its lead over the final seven weeks. Tony Armas was having a mediocre season both offensively and defensively, and Steve Lyons had been sent to Chicago in the Seaver trade.

Gorman had pulled off a nice deal by showing patience. The Mariners had reportedly been looking to land Boston's two top outfield prospects, Ellis Burks and Mike Greenwell, for Henderson and Owen.[5] Gorman wouldn't go for it, and he eventually got Seattle general manager Dick Balderson to go for Quinones's potential. Greenwell had already seen a bit of big league action in both 1985 and '86; he'd even wind up on the postseason roster as an extra lefty bat at McNamara's disposal. Burks would have to wait for the following spring, but both he and Greenwell would become forces in the Boston lineup by 1987.

As it turned out, neither Henderson nor Owen would do much for the Red Sox during the rest of the regular season. Both hit under .200 with Owen showing shaky defense to boot. Really, he was no better than Quinones. Of course seven weeks is a pretty small sample as baseball goes. Henderson, as everyone would later find out, would prove to be the sleeping giant.

The Red Sox moved on to Minnesota and took two of three against the Twins. Seaver turned in another strong outing with a three-hitter in a 3–1 win, followed two nights later by a Clemens two-hitter in a 9–1 rout. The Red Sox were 71–49 and 5½ games in front. After slumping for a little while after the All-Star break, the team was back to doing what it needed to do. They hadn't relinquished the division lead. When they stumbled, they bounced back. They were winning series one at a time; in their past six series, dating back to August 1, the Sox had won four, lost one, and split one. Steady as she goes. Overall they had now won 6 of 8 and 10 of 15.

The Yankees had recently enjoyed a brief hot streak with five wins in six games to move back into second place and stay within striking distance. But their chase of the Red Sox the rest of the way was mostly futile. This season brought a historical turnabout in the rivalry. Fans in years past remembered Red Sox teams with powerful lineups that were good enough to challenge but were often held off by better-balanced Yankee clubs with deeper pitching. All of that flipped in 1986. The Yankee lineup could mash with Rickey

Henderson, Don Mattingly, Dave Winfield, and some other solid hitters including their DH Mike Easler, who was having a good season. But they just didn't have the pitching to match. Their best pitcher, lefty Dennis Rasmussen, wound up the season statistically about even with Boston's third best pitcher, Oil Can Boyd. As for that super stopper at the top of the rotation: the 1978 Yankees had Ron Guidry; the 1986 Red Sox had Roger Clemens (the Yankees still had Guidry in 1986, but not nearly the same one). That was about the size of it.

The Boston lineup backed Clemens with 14 hits in the August 20 blowout of the Twins. Boggs ripped a single, double, and triple, Baylor and Evans both went deep, and Jim Rice unloaded for two doubles and a homer in what was probably his best game of the season.

Rice had been gliding along seemingly unnoticed for most of the season, unusual for a player of his stature who had been such a key figure in Boston for more than a decade. But there was a lot going on this year to take up a Sox fan's attention: Clemens's rapid climb, Baylor coming over and asserting himself as team leader, Boggs gunning his way toward another batting title, the legend Tom Seaver showing up at midseason, all capped off by the Oil Can Boyd drama in mid-July.

Jim Rice seemed to be floating under the radar a bit in 1986, yet he was steadily putting together one of the five best seasons of his 15-year Hall of Fame career. He was doing it less dramatically than usual, without the long ball. The homer against the Twins was his first in 11 games and just his 12th of the season. He'd wind up the year with 20 home runs, the fewest of his career at that point aside from the 17 he popped during the strike-shortened 1981 season.

But make no mistake, he was producing in a big way. Playing virtually every day and hitting third or fourth in the lineup, Rice had the batting average at .330 and the on-base percentage at .379. With Baylor hitting behind him he was using the whole field, going the other way more often. When he did pull the ball, he was hitting more shots off the Green Monster than over it this year—his 39 doubles were just about twice his 1985 total. By the end of the year he would hit .324, 5th in the league, with a .384 OBP, while collecting exactly 200 hits and driving in 110 runs. He finished 10th in the A.L. in both on-base percentage and slugging percentage, making him the only player in the league other than Don Mattingly to finish in the top 10 in both categories. His 5.7 WAR also ranked 10th.

A bit less noticed: By not looking to pull the ball all the time, Rice was cutting down on the ground-ball double plays, those dispiriting rally killers that had always been a weakness of his offensive game. Not that it was all his fault. As a big, strong guy with average speed who hit the ball hard, those one hoppers he'd shoot to third or short would get to an infielder quickly, leaving plenty of time to turn two. Rice had grounded into 35 DPs in 1985, the fourth year in a row he'd led the league. But in 1986 he nearly cut that in half to 19. This year Rice was all about sustaining rallies, doing it better than most players in the American League even if he wasn't challenging for the home-run crown. At 33, this would be his last big year in the majors before vision problems curtailed his career.

Producing quietly seemed to be the way Rice liked it. One thing he didn't have was much of a relationship with the local press. Not that he couldn't be affable when he wanted to be. You'd occasionally see him do a pregame network interview on a national telecast where he would come off just fine, perfectly friendly. But it was usually a different story with the locals. "He was always suspicious of the Boston media," says Steve Krasner. "He would sit in front of his locker with his arms folded as if to say, 'I dare you to ask a question.' He was extremely intimidating."

"Moody, he could be difficult," says Ballou. "But he could also be very insightful if he thought the question was good."

Remembers Bob Lobel: "I talked to the back of his head many times." Krasner does credit Rice for one thing in his postgame routine. "When he hit a home run or drove in a big run, he was hard to find. But if he hit into a double play or struck out, he was at his locker right away to answer questions."

The Sox got themselves stuck in neutral for a little while as August wound down, losing five of eight against Texas and Cleveland. The lead was 3½ games over Toronto, the latest A.L. East team to move into second place in a division that had become very topsy-turvy everywhere but at the top. The most encouraging development came from Boyd, who after slumping through a couple of starts shut down the Rangers on August 26 on a complete game four-hitter with 10 strikeouts in an 8–1 win.

Then just before Labor Day, the Red Sox hit the accelerator. Against the Indians at Fenway on August 30 they jumped on veteran knuckleballer Phil Niekro for four second-inning runs and a 4–0 lead. Clemens cruised along, his one key mistake resulting in a two-run homer by Cleveland DH Carmelo Castillo in the top of the fifth. But in the bottom half it was Tony Armas blasting a three-run shot against Niekro to make the score 7–2. Clemens allowed four hits and struck out 11 in his seven innings for his 20th win of the season. Schiraldi finished out the 7–3 win with two perfect innings, six up and six down with four strikeouts.

It was the victory that not only got Roger Clemens No. 20 but proved to be the catalyst for Boston's final big push and launched 11 wins in a row. They continued the home stand by beating Cleveland again the next day 4–3 on Baylor's walk-off single in the bottom of the ninth, and then stomped on Texas and Minnesota with back-to-back three-game sweeps. The town could feel it: The Red Sox weren't going to blow anything this year.

Chapter 8

September 1986

The hot streak included a Hurst 9–0 shutout of Minnesota on September 7 in which Rice capped off a five-run third inning with a grand slam off of Twins' lefty Neal Heaton. For Hurst, who struck out seven without walking a batter, the shutout launched the start of what would be a nice September roll. After battling through some ups and downs in August following his groin injury, he was rounding into the form that would take him through a memorable run in October.

The next night in Baltimore four hits by Boggs and four RBI from Evans powered a 9–3 win in which the Sox got six in the top of the 11th inning to break open a 3–3 game. Schiraldi threw three scoreless innings for the win in relief of Seaver, who had another solid outing. By the end of the winning streak on September 10, the Sox were 85–54 and 8½ games ahead in the A.L. East. It was all over but the shouting.

When they dropped two of three in New York shortly afterward—Seaver and Nipper both getting lit up pretty good—it didn't much matter because Boston's big lead had sucked any potential drama out of a September matchup with the Yankees.

At least any pennant race drama. A visit to Yankee Stadium is usually bound to bring something memorable, and in this case it was a tussle with some fans over a stolen cap, which was aired on national television. In the bottom of the eighth inning on September 13 with the Sox trailing the Yankees 11–6, Rice and Owen collided hard near the left-field line on a shallow foul pop-up by the Yankees' Dan Pasqua. Rice made the catch, but the smaller Owen was shaken up pretty badly. As the trainers attended to him while teammates looked on, a fan reached to the ground over the short wall and grabbed Rice's cap, which had fallen off during the play. Owen got up after a few minutes and walked off under his own power, done for the day. At about the same time Rice noticed that his hat was missing and saw who had it. He jumped the wall and raced about 10 rows up into the stands to confront the offending fan. Security rushed in to keep other fans back, and Red

Sox players rushed out from the dugout, several of them joining Rice in the stands. Ultimately there was no fight, Rice got his cap back, and the guilty fan was escorted out by security without his souvenir. Just another Saturday afternoon in the Bronx. Owen would sit out the next day, but he was back in there when the Red Sox returned home to face Milwaukee.

The home cooking was welcome and worked wonders after the strange weekend in New York. After the Sox pummeled the Brewers four straight at Fenway—Clemens winning his 23rd, Boyd his 15th, and Hurst his 12th, all on complete games—the Sox were 90–57 and 10½ games in front on September 18.

They lost four of five to delay the inevitable clinching a bit. That would come on Sunday, September 28, a beautiful afternoon at Fenway with Oil Can Boyd on the mound against the Blue Jays. The Red Sox wasted little time, pecking away with base hits and walks while taking advantage of three Toronto errors to roll to 10–2 lead by the end of the fourth. The packed house was abuzz all afternoon; by the seventh inning they were doing the wave. Boyd was touched for a two-run homer in the fourth and a run scoring single in the fifth, both by Lloyd Moseby. But his energy seemed to grow in tandem with the fans as everyone anticipated the final out that would bring Boston its first A.L. East title since 1975.

With the crowd behind him Boyd retired his final 11 hitters to close out the game. By the ninth, with the score 12–3, the players in the Sox dugout were on the top step. The relievers in the bullpen had their arms on the outfield wall as they eagerly peered in toward the field. With the crowd on its feet, Boyd dropped a curve on Rick Leach for a called third strike, Boyd's ninth whiff of the day. On the next pitch Manny Lee hit a routine fly ball to Jim Rice in left—two out. Then it was Kelly Gruber popping up a 1–0 pitch to the right side of the infield. Fittingly it was Bill Buckner, 36 years old and completing his 134th game at first base on weak knees and bad ankles, who squeezed it for the last out. Buckner and Barrett leaped in the air, the dugout and bullpen emptied, and the players ran to the mound to mob Oil Can Boyd, the man who had nearly abandoned them in July. The 1986 Boston Red Sox, picked by most prognosticators to wind up the season in fourth or fifth place, were the American League East champions.

The big question: Was the team really that good, or was it a dream year in which everything went right? It's hard not to believe that a little of both were at play in 1986. It was a good team for sure, although today's analytic gurus would have no problem pointing out the luck factor compared to 1985. History shows that adding up the number of runs a team scores during a season and comparing it to the number it gives up is a pretty strong predictor of how many games the team will win. Interestingly for the Red Sox, their numbers were little changed from 1985 to 1986. By overall run disparity, the formula says they should have won 89 games in 1985 (they won 81) and 90 games in 1986 (they won 95). A club that should have improved by one game improved by 14. The telling signs of luck are there. Not only did the 1986 team win 18 games in its final turn at bat, but check the records in one-run games:

- 1985: 22-27
- 1986: 24-10

None of this is to suggest that Boston's big season ought to just be written off as "lucky." Perhaps those Don Baylor kangaroo court sessions truly made the difference in some of the close games. But in acknowledging that luck and randomness play at least some role in any sports season, the Sox just had more of it on their side in 1986 than they did in 1985. Hey, nothing wrong with that. For a fan, enjoying that occasional magical season where things break your way is pretty much the point. Sox fans had been through more than their share of near misses. It was time the baseball gods took their side, right?

And there were a few interesting team stats that shed some light on their success. Boston's 144 homers ranked just 11th in the American League but their .346 OBP ranked second and their 107 OPS-plus tied for third. They also struck out the fewest times of any team in the league, and by a wide margin. And so the Sox finished fifth in the league in runs despite the paucity of homers. As for the pitching staff: second in the league in complete games (36), second in strikeouts (1,033), tied for third in staff ERA (3.93). And all of that with three-fifth of their regular starting rotation—Hurst, Boyd, and Nipper—missing several weeks apiece.

Clemens finished his breakthrough season 24–4 with a 2.48 ERA and a league-best 169 ERA-plus in hitter-friendly Fenway. He had begun the season with shoulder questions and ended it as a major workhorse by pitching 254 innings, more than his 1984 and 1985 totals combined. His 238 strikeouts ranked second to Seattle's Mark Langston, his .969 WHIP (combined walks and hits allowed per inning) ranked first. At the end of the season Clemens would be voted the Cy Young Award and Most Valuable Player in the American League. One of the great pitching careers of all time had been launched.

Clemens's primary support staff was also looking sharp heading into the playoffs. Hurst won five straight in September before losing his final five-inning tune-up against the Yankees, finishing the season 13–8 in his 25 starts. His 2.99 ERA and 140 ERA-plus both ranked fourth in the American League. He was now doing what his former lefty rotation mates John Tudor and Bob Ojeda never did: win consistently at Fenway. While both of those guys went on to shed the Green Monster and win in their new spacious ball-parks in the National League, Hurst was the one who stayed. And now it was paying dividends.

Boyd managed to toss 216 innings despite his time away in the middle of the season, finishing a solid 16–10 with a 3.78 ERA. Nipper, whose ERA stood at 3.65 when he went out hurt on May 18, saw it balloon to 5.38 by the end of the season with a 10–12 record. Other than a couple of strong outings here and there, it had been a rough second half for Nipper. Tom Seaver fin-ished 5–7 during his three months in Boston, although the record could have been better with a bit more luck. Averaging more than six innings per start with a 3.80 ERA and 111 ERA-plus, Seaver had met the expectations of shor-ing up the back of the rotation. In the bullpen Calvin Schiraldi was everything the Red Sox wanted and then some. In 25 appearances since his call-up in July, he whiffed 55 hitters in 51 innings with a miniscule 1.41 ERA. Watching him stroll to the mound at crunch time had become a welcome sight. For the first time in a long time, the Red Sox had a genuine power arm to finish out games with.

Maybe the biggest surprise of all looking back: The Sox won 95 games despite negative WAR from their regular players at three positions: center field (Armas), first base (Buckner), and shortstop (every one of Hoffman, Quinones, and Owen). By pitching as well as they did and by getting enough offense from the other regulars, it all worked out. But shortstop just wasn't a strong suit, and Armas and Buckner were clearly fading veterans. Lou Gorman's smart move to get Dave Henderson would mitigate the center field situation for the playoffs. But no such luck at first base, where Buckner had been a fixture since the Sox got him from the Cubs for Dennis Eckersley dur-ing the 1984 season.

Some perspective on Bill Buckner: The popular narrative that has sur-rounded his name for years is that he was a borderline Hall of Fame player who cost the Red Sox a World Series title in 1986. In reality, neither is true. The error that would make Buckner famous didn't cost the Sox the World Series any more than about 100 other things did over the course of seven games. As for his long career before that—vastly overrated.

At 36 years old in 1986, Bill Buckner just wasn't a very good player. You had to admire his fortitude and his work ethic for the way he continued to go out there day after day on those bad wheels. The ankles, the knees, they all hurt. Tape and ice all the time. If nothing else, he was a gamer. "Ice packs every game," says Steve Krasner. "It pained *you* to watch him walk around the clubhouse."

He did hit a career-high 18 homers, a decent number for the low-wattage 1980s, and he did drive in 102 runs. Those numbers, particularly hitting that coveted 100 RBI mark, provided the illusion of a productive season at the plate. The problem with RBI as a measuring stick, as many modern analytic types now point out, is that it's derivative. Stick any average hitter into the middle part of the lineup every day with good on-base guys hitting in front of him and he'll probably drive in 100 runs. McNamara usually hit Buckner third in the order, that ideal RBI spot, while sometimes dropping him down against lefties. Either way he was following a group of hitters—Barrett, Evans, Rice, Baylor, and especially Boggs—who outdid the league average in on-base percentage by comfortable margins. But as for Buckner's own production at the plate—a .267 batting average, a meager .311 on-base percentage, and 98 OPS-plus (meaning below league average when combining on-base and slugging)—it was so-so at best. Age and health rendered him slow on the bases and a statue in the field. Add it all up and you had a player who came in below replacement level, meaning that an average, generic replacement called up from the high rungs of the minors would have likely done a bit better. There's little chance that Buckner sees the three-spot in any of today's analytic driven lineups.

As for his long career, this is a guy who won a batting title, hit .300 several times, and piled up more than 2,700 hits. You could make a Hall of Fame case for him, the thinking goes. He's at least close, right?

Well, no. Buckner's career didn't come within shouting distance of the Hall of Fame. Going back to his younger years in Los Angeles and Chicago and right on through his veteran days in Boston, Bill Buckner did one thing very well—he made contact. A solid line drive hitter who rarely struck out, Buckner did hit over .300 a few times and finished his career at .289. But there just wasn't a whole lot to the rest of his game. Little power, little speed after the early years in L.A., and defensive metrics that were okay in his young outfield days and turned south as he transitioned to veteran first baseman. Mostly he was a singles hitter who didn't walk a lot. Buckner's on-base percentage wound up at a ho-hum .321 for his career and peaked in the .340–.350 range in his handful of best seasons.

His 1980 season with the Cubs is the perfect microcosm. Buckner hit a career-best .324 that year to take the N.L. batting crown. Historically, winning a batting title in the major leagues carries a lot of prestige—once a batting champ, always a batting champ. The thing was, Buckner decorated the nice batting average with just 10 homers and 30 walks. The average may have been No. 1 in the league but the .353 OBP didn't break the top 10. Throw in mediocre defense and a 119 OPS-plus that was solid but not All-Star level, and you see why Buckner was basically an average player with a 1.5 WAR in 1980. A batting champ and an average player at the same time. Yes, it can happen.

Buckner wound up with a career 100 OPS-plus, right at league average, surpassing 120 once. His pedestrian 15 WAR over a two-decade career was about the same as fellow first basemen Nick Johnson, Kevin Millar, and Matt Stairs. Even his peak seasons never got him to a 4.0 WAR, generally considered the standard for an All-Star.

Casting Bill Buckner as a near Hall of Fame player who cost the Red Sox a championship just doesn't hold up to scrutiny. Really, he was an average major league player who lasted a long time (hence all the hits) and who happened to miss a grounder in a World Series game that wound up being hyped way beyond its significance.

With the division wrapped up, McNamara mixed in his bench guys to share time with the regulars over the final week at Fenway against Baltimore and New York. The Sox closed the season with four straight losses to the Yankees to finish 95–66 and 5½ games ahead of them in the division.

After going 7-for-12 in the Baltimore series to raise his average to .357 and open up a seven-point lead over Don Mattingly in the batting race, Wade Boggs decided to protect his lead by sitting out the entire Yankee series. With Mattingly at .352 going into the final game, his long-shot hope rested on going 6-for-6 on the last day of the season. Yankee manager Lou Piniella hit Mattingly in the lead-off spot to maximize his chance of getting to the plate six times, and Mattingly did proceed to lead off the game with a homer off Jeff Sellers. But the long shot didn't come in. Mattingly would settle for a 2-for-5 day and second place in the batting race. Boggs had his third American League batting crown in five big league seasons. The Sox would have just one day off before opening the playoffs at home.

As they set out to go for a championship, one topic the Red Sox players weren't thinking about, at least not very much, was 1918, the year of the last Red Sox World Series championship. It was now 68 years and counting. The Sox had only made it *to* the World Series three times since—in 1946, 1967, and 1975—and lost in seven games all three times. The word "curse" hadn't become a regular staple just yet. That term would take off a few years later after publication of the book *The Curse of the Bambino* by *Boston Globe* writer Dan Shaughnessy, which traced the team's championship draught back to the 1920 trade of Babe Ruth to the Yankees. But whether you called it a "curse," a "draught," or a "hex," Boston's championship futility was ingrained in the local mindset. It was practically part of New England culture. But not so much with the players.

"Not at all. We didn't really care" says Dwight Evans. "But it was great to see them finally win in 2004. We were almost the team that did it." Says Clemens: "I knew the history but I really didn't pay any attention to it. I just thought it was great to get guys like Dewey and Rice back to the dance." Steve Krasner remembers the reaction he'd get when the topic came up. "It was 'Stop bringing that crap up, we're just here playing,'" he says. After all, most of the players weren't from New England. Although one who was says that while he didn't think much about 1918, he couldn't help but feel it tug at him a little bit. "To a degree it was motivation, you want to be the team that does it," says Worcester native Rich Gedman. "The opportunities were there. We were trying to chase history."

Chapter 9

October 1986

The American League Championship Series against the California Angels was not going to be easy. In winning the A.L. West by five games, the Angels featured a core of playoff-tested veterans like Reggie Jackson, Doug DeCinces, Brian Downing, and Bob Boone mixed with younger athletic guys like Wally Joyner and Gary Pettis. The pitching staff too had an impressive array of old and new, led by a pair of talented 25-year-old right-handers, Mike Witt and Kirk McCaskill, helped along by veterans Don Sutton and John Candelaria.

The Angels were managed by Gene Mauch, a respected veteran manager whose only career blemish was not getting to a World Series.

The 1986 season would mark one of the rare occasions during baseball's four-division pre–wild card era (1969–1993) in which the four division winners advancing to the playoffs, the Mets, Astros, Red Sox, and Angels, were truly the game's four best teams. The American League in particular tilted toward a top-heavy East during much of the era, producing some Western Division champs that might have done well to finish third or fourth in the East. But no such mismatches in 1986. The result was three postseason series—Red Sox–Angels, Mets–Astros, and then Red Sox–Mets—that would go down among the most memorable ever. "Up and down, up and down. That whole postseason really messed with your emotions," says Clemens. And yet at the same time, "There was nothing like playing baseball in New England in October, when the air is cool and the leaves are turning color," he says.

One potential problem for Boston: Tom Seaver had hurt his knee late in the season and wouldn't pitch in the playoffs. Seaver wasn't a top-tier player at this point in his career, but the starting pitching now had a bit less depth.

Unfortunately, Clemens didn't have much in the playoff opener, surrendering five early runs to the Angles in an 8–1 loss to Mike Witt, who went the distance on a five-hitter. Clemens had taken a line drive to his pitching elbow in his final regular season start—not enough to seriously hurt him but enough to make him tentative, he says. "I started the game off gingerly and they made me pay for that." The Sox returned the favor the next afternoon when they jumped on McCaskill and two relievers for 13 hits for a 9–2 blowout behind Hurst. The late afternoon sun turned this one into a funky game: five errors, plus second baseman Bobby Grich losing a ball in the sun that fell for a double for Evans, and McCaskill losing a high chopper back to the mound in the sun that gave Boggs an infield single.

In Game Three in Anaheim, Boyd started against Candelaria and pitched very well for six innings before tiring in the seventh and giving up home runs to Dickie Schofield and Gary Pettis. The Angels won 5–3 to go up a game in the series.

It was the next game that was just bitter, one that had even the hardiest Red Sox fans thinking that the magic was about to dry up. Down a game, McNamara shortened the rotation by passing on Al Nipper in Game Four and starting Clemens on three days' rest against veteran fourth starter Don Sutton. Clemens answered the call by looking like his usual self, tossing eight shutout innings and carrying a 3–0 lead into the ninth thanks to Buckner's RBI double in the sixth (off his onetime L.A. Dodger teammate Sutton) and Barrett's RBI single in the eighth followed by an unearned run on an error.

But Clemens couldn't quite close it out. Doug DeCinces homered to lead off the bottom of the ninth, putting California on the board. Then one-out singles by Schofield and Boone chased Clemens and brought Schiraldi. His first hitter, Pettis, hit a deep fly ball to left that Jim Rice misjudged, then watched helplessly as it sailed over his head and bounced against the wall for a double. Another run was in, with runners at second and third. After an intentional walk to load the bases, Schiraldi whiffed Bobby Grich on a hard fastball, a huge out that got Boston within one out of a victory. Then, almost incredibly, Schiraldi threw a 1–2 breaking pitch to Brian Downing that didn't break quite enough and plunked him on the left leg. Tie game. Reggie Jackson came up with a chance to win it for the Angels—his kind of spot—but he grounded out to send the game to extra innings.

McNamara stuck with Schiraldi through the 10th and into the 11th, when Grich drilled a base hit to left with a runner on second to win it for the Angels. The Sox had let a pivotal game get away and trailed in the series three games to one. Several Boston players lingered in the dugout as the Angels celebrated, Schiraldi burying his head in a towel.

But sports can be funny. Today's big disappointment can turn into tomorrow's game for the ages, complete with that moment that winds up seared into fans' memories for life. The Red Sox were faced with a quick turnaround after Game Four—a day game after a night game—making it all the more difficult to shake off such a tough loss.

Hurst started against Witt and stayed in control for five innings. He carried a 2–1 lead into the bottom of the sixth thanks to Gedman's two-run homer in the second. But the previous night's hero, Grich, came up with a man aboard and lofted a deep fly ball to center field. Dave Henderson, who had entered the game just an inning earlier after Tony Armas had been shaken up attempting a catch at the wall, drifted back close to the outfield wall, lined up the ball, jumped, got his glove most of the way around the ball, and then hit the wall before he could close the glove completely. The ball came loose and carried over the fence for a home run. Hurst got down on a knee behind the mound and lowered his head. California led 3–2.

They bumped the lead to 5–2 against Stanley in the seventh on a couple of hits, a walk, and a sacrifice fly. Meantime Witt was cruising along nicely, allowing just four hits and no runs since Gedman's second-inning homer. But much like Clemens the night before, there was the matter of that pesky ninth inning. (The concept of the "closer," whose entry in the ninth in a save situation was nearly automatic, hadn't arrived in baseball just yet. Front-line starters, particularly true aces like Witt and Clemens, pitched into the ninth inning routinely if they still looked reasonably strong.)

Buckner led off the ninth with a base hit. Witt struck out Rice for the first out, and then went 3–2 on Baylor. On a pitch low and away that might have been ball four, Baylor reached for it and muscled the ball out to left-center, where it cleared the wall over a leaping Pettis. It was a 5–4 game. Mauch left Witt in to pitch to the right-handed Dwight Evans, who popped up to third for the second out. One out left in the season. Mauch then played the percentages by bringing in lefty reliever Gary Lucas to face Gedman, who had a 4-for-4 day going against Witt. But the move immediately backfired when Lucas's first pitch sailed up and in and plunked Gedman on the left hand as he tried to bail out. With the tying run now at first, out went Lucas and in came right-hander Donnie Moore to face the righty-swinging Henderson, batting for just the second time in the game and third time in the series.

Moore got ahead of Henderson 1–2. The crowd was up and screaming; the players in the Angel dugout were on the top step, ready to charge onto the field. Henderson fouled off a couple of pitches to stay alive, the noise dying down and rebuilding each time.

"There were about sixty thousand people there and they were getting loud. Some fans were already spilling onto the field," says Evans. "Cops were in our dugout, we had to sit back behind them."

Moore then threw a forkball that didn't dip quite enough. Henderson swung and drilled it over the left field fence. A no doubter. The Red Sox dugout exploded as a giddy Henderson backpedaled his first few steps toward first base before doing a 180 and completing his trip around the bases. The rest of the building went quiet. Boston had scored four in the ninth to lead 6–5.

"When Henderson hit the ball we had to look through the legs of these cops," Evans says. "After that the cops got out of there in about 15 seconds."

It was one of those moments when fans remember where they were right down to the details. Paul MacDonald of North Andover: "A big group of us are in a restaurant celebrating my dad's 50th birthday. We go into the bar to look at the game. The Sox are behind, we're saying this is it, they're going to choke again. And then bang, huge cheer goes up in the room."

Rich Chaiton of Medway: "I was at the Patriots game with a group of people. We were listening on the radio tail-gaiting. We all went crazy."

John Cascione, the law student in Charlestown by way of North Providence, was in the midst of getting philosophical after the eighth inning as he got set to watch what he figured would be his team's last few at-bats of the season. A nostalgic baseball promo featuring Humphrey Bogart came on, one aimed at reminding us all of the romance of the game and how ingrained it was in our culture: *You take your worries to the park and you leave them there . . . a hot dog at the game beats roast beef at The Ritz.* "I'm thinking, yeah, he's right, baseball is still great," Cascione says. "Then Baylor hits the home run, then Gedman gets hit, then when Henderson hits the home run, I screamed."

John Molori was still a senior at BC, working his internship at Channel 7, where, as usual, he was tracking his highlights for the crew to use on the news later that night. "I'm watching the game; things are going kind of slow. Then Henderson hit the home run, and we all jumped in the air. Another guy was there I didn't know that well, I think I kissed him on the cheek."

As much as everyone was soaking in the moment, the game wasn't actually over yet, and the Angels weren't giving up. In the bottom of the ninth they strung together three singles against Stanley, Sambito, and Crawford for a run that tied the game and put the winning run on third with one out. After the tremendous comeback in the top half of the inning, the Sox had given up the lead and were right back on the cusp of going home as Rob Wilfong danced off third base as the winning run. Just a medium fly ball would end the series. But after intentionally walking Brian Downing, Crawford got DeCinces on a fly to shallow right and Grich on a soft liner back to the mound. Another bullet dodged. It was on to extra innings.

The Sox got a chance in the top of the 10th when they put runners on first and third with one out. But Moore got Rice to ground into a double play. In the bottom half, Pettis launched a long drive to left field with two out and a runner on first that Rice ran down and caught right against the wall. By now everyone watching needed their heart rates checked.

In the top of the 11th, Moore, into his third inning, hit Baylor with a pitch to lead off (that was Baylor, again getting on base any way he could). Evans followed with a base hit and then Gedman, trying to sacrifice, beat out the bunt for an infield hit to boot. That sent Henderson up against Moore for the second time. Henderson hit one to center, not over the wall this time but deep enough for the sac fly to score Baylor with the lead run. Schiraldi came on and got the Angels one, two, three, in the bottom of the 11th, and the Red Sox were headed home with a 7–6 win.

"The ALCS was just so insane," says Lesley Visser, part of the *Boston Globe* crew on hand who had just written up a piece after the game that focused on Gene Mauch's continued frustration trying to get to a World Series. "After the Game Five win, the paper flew all the writers in first class on the red eye back to Boston. We mostly drank on the red eye."

California still led the series three games to two, but the vibe in the air seemed to assure everyone that the Red Sox would complete the comeback at Fenway. How could they lose now? Says Clemens: "I remember telling Oil Can Boyd, you get us to Game Seven and then I've got it."

But Oil Can nearly imploded right out the gate in Game Six. A hyped-up Boyd labored through a very difficult first inning in which he threw more than 40 pitches, allowing run-scoring doubles to Reggie Jackson and Doug DeCinces and then hitting Bobby Grich with a pitch to load the bases. Gedman was out at the mound to settle him down and Nipper was already warming in the bullpen. As much as the momentum had seemed to turn in their favor, it was still the Red Sox who needed this game, not the Angels. Boyd was one hit away from a big first-inning hole and probably an early exit. He threw 10 pitches to Angel second baseman Rob Wilfong, who at one point fouled off seven in a row. Finally Wilfong swung at a fastball and popped it up to Buckner at first base. The ballpark breathed a collective sigh of relief, the score still only 2–0.

And that would be the low point for Boston for the rest of the series. They got the two runs right back against McCaskill in the bottom of the first to tie the game, and then erupted for five in the bottom of the third. No long ball— the Sox just pecked away, killing McCaskill slowly with line drives. Single, single, double, single with an error by the cutoff man, another single. . . . The crowd was getting delirious as Red Sox players kept rounding the bases.

Boyd settled down after his rocky first inning, not allowing another run until Brian Downing's solo homer in the seventh that made the score 8–3. Stanley finished the final two innings, allowing an unearned run in the eighth as the Sox won 10–4.

Game Seven brought no early anxiety, or any anxiety. Clemens, despite battling a touch of the flu that day, cruised for seven innings. Boggs delivered a two-run single in the second, Rice knocked John Candelaria from the game with a three-run bomb in the fourth to send the crowd into bedlam, and Evans poked a homer over the monster off Sutton in the seventh. Schiraldi pitched the final two innings and closed out the 8–1 blowout by striking out the side in the ninth.

It was on to champagne and TV interviews in the clubhouse. The MVP trophy was presented to Marty Barrett, who seemed to be in the middle of almost every rally as he went 11-for-30 in the series.

Super Bowl, NBA Finals, and now a World Series. All in nine months. Party on, Boston. The signs in the stands and the headlines in the next day's papers carried the October rallying cry: Bring on the Mets.

Dwight Evans is perfectly happy to look back at the World Series now. But that wasn't always the case. "I didn't talk about or watch the 1986 World Series for about 25 years," he says. "People would always say what a great World Series it was and I'd say, what are you talking about? But then I realized the fans' view. What a series it was to watch, even though you're disappointed to be on the other side."

The 1986 World Series wasn't necessarily set up to be an instant classic—you never know how a series will go—but it felt that way. It was, after all, Boston and New York, a pair of intense, side-by-side fan bases that intersected somewhere around Hartford. Even though the Red Sox rivalry was with the Yankees, it was hard to resist the story line of a club focused on smashing its 68-year "curse" against an opponent that had recently displaced the Yankees as the Gotham villain that everyone loved to hate. Most of the country would be rooting for the Red Sox, including about half of New York.

"Walking around the city, coming out of a restaurant, people would say, 'Beat those Mets,'" says Evans. "Yankee fans, they hated the Mets. It made me think about what New York must have been like when they had the Dodgers, Giants, and Yankees."

The Mets were a deep, talented team led by veterans Keith Hernandez and Gary Carter that had swaggered its way to 108 wins during the regular season, 22 more than any other team in their division and 12 more than any other team in the majors. They led the National League in runs, on-base percentage, slugging percentage, ERA, rowdy fans, curtain calls, and (it seemed) brawls. And not all of the brawls were necessarily on the field. Back in July four of their players had been arrested in Houston for scuffling with police at 2 a.m. in a local bar. The bad-boy image was a strange one for a franchise whose traditional identity had mostly been that of lovable underdog. But the rebuilding job that had followed the club's dark years of the late 1970s and early '80s had brought not only talent but intensity and attitude. It started with manager Davey Johnson, who had told his team in spring training that he expected nothing less than domination—a directive that was carried out on the field mostly by Wally Backman, Len Dykstra, and Ray Knight.

As an added subplot, the series was a dream matchup for Red Sox GM Lou Gorman, who had actually helped build more of the Mets' roster than the Red Sox's roster during his time as Frank Cashen's right hand during the rebuilding. His deal to get his old prospect Calvin Schiraldi from the Mets for lefty starter Bobby Ojeda had been a win-win in 1986, with Ojeda winning 18 games flourishing in spacious Shea Stadium while Schiraldi injected that much-needed boost to the Boston bullpen since coming up in July. Now they would both be in the World Series.

Las Vegas had the Mets as heavy favorites, but a closer look made you wonder why. The Mets' one clear advantage over the Red Sox was depth. They had a deep starting rotation that was filled at the back end by talented young veterans Sid Fernandez and Rick Aguilera and a deep bench manned by Kevin Mitchell, Lee Mazzilli, Tim Teuefel, Howard Johnson, and Danny Heep. Depth goes a long way during the 162-game grind, which would explain the Mets winning 13 more games than the Red Sox during the season. But in a seven-game series, it's less of a factor. When you're down to a handful of games for the world championship, it's the main horses seeing almost all of the action. And it was hard to see much difference there. Boston's front three starters (Clemens, Hurst, Boyd) certainly stacked up well against their Met counterparts (Dwight Gooden, Ron Darling, and Ojeda). As far as the starters at the other eight positions, it was very close. The Sox would have to do without their designated hitter, Baylor, in the four games at Shea, and the Mets had a bit more flexibility to platoon at a couple of spots with Teuefel and Mitchell spotting Backman and Dykstra against lefties. But overall there was little to choose between the two lineups. Tony Armas was on Boston's active roster but he wasn't at 100%; it would be Henderson in center field.

Like the Red Sox, the Mets were coming off a tough and exhausting league playoff series. Houston's Mike Scott had dominated them twice to help his club split the first four games. The Mets needed to win the next two to avoid seeing Scott in a Game Seven. They used every ounce of physical and mental energy to do it, winning Game Five in 12 innings and Game Six in 16 innings. By the skin of their teeth, they were National League champs.

The two teams looked exhausted as the series opened. The energy inside Shea Stadium seemed low, as if everyone needed a bit more time to recover from the previous round. Hurst and Darling dueled to a scoreless tie into the seventh when Gedman hit a grounder to second that went right between Teuefel's legs to score Rice from second base. That was it; the Red Sox won 1–0.

The game featured one interesting call by McNamara that's worth noting, the kind that shows how managers only get second guessed for a questionable move when the move doesn't work. With the Sox clinging to their 1–0 lead in the top of the ninth, they put runners on second and third with two out. The Mets walked Spike Owen intentionally to get to Hurst in the pitcher's spot. McNamara now had a tough call: A hit in this spot would pad the lead with just three outs to go, but taking out Hurst, who had dominated the Mets all night, seemed risky. McNamara went for it by pinch-hitting young Mike

Greenwell for Hurst. Greenwell flied out, leaving the score 1–0 with Hurst now on the bench. The game was in the hands of Schiraldi, who began the bottom of the ninth by walking Darryl Strawberry. You could almost hear the "oh no, here we go" groans throughout New England. But Schiraldi recovered quickly to get three straight outs, striking out pinch-hitter Danny Heep to end it. Had Schiraldi blown the lead and the game, McNamara's decision to remove Hurst probably would have been panned to this day. But it worked out, so it's pretty much forgotten.

The series went through its momentum shifts over the next few games. The Red Sox pounded Gooden the next night in a 9–3 route, hammering out 18 hits with Henderson and Evans going deep, although a shaky Clemens was pulled in the fifth inning when the score was still closer. Crawford and Stanley shut the Mets down over the final four-plus innings as the Sox pulled away. They were up two games and headed home. Things couldn't be looking better.

But the Mets returned the favor in the next two games. Dykstra led off Game Three with a homer off Boyd, kicking off a four-run first inning. Looking comfortable at Fenway, the Mets went on to a 7–1 win behind Ojeda, who came through in a must-win outing against his old club. Still up a game, McNamara went with Nipper in Game Four to keep his front-line starters on full rest for the remainder of the series. Nipper did fine despite a 17-day layoff, allowing three runs in six innings. But the Mets got another strong start from Darling and late homers off Crawford by Dykstra and Carter to build a 6–0 lead. The Red Sox got two off reliever Roger McDowell in the eighth, but that was it—the final was 6–2. The series was tied, with the road teams winning all four games. (It's interesting that the team thought to have the deeper starting rotation was the one to shorten its rotation in the series. New York manager Davey Johnson decided it was better to avoid Sid Fernandez, a lefty who gave up a lot of fly balls, at Fenway Park against the right-handed power of Rice, Evans, Baylor, and Henderson. So as Nipper went for the Red Sox to keep everyone rested, Johnson had his starters going on short rest going forward.)

The extra day seemed to work for Hurst, who shut down the Mets again in Game Five. The Sox hammered Gooden for a second time with nine hits and four runs by the fifth inning. The 4–0 lead felt like 8–0 with the way Hurst was dealing. After Hurst shut them out through the seventh to run his series' scoreless streak to 15 innings, the Mets finally nicked him for a couple of late runs. But McNamara stuck with Hurst even as the Mets got the tying run to the plate in the ninth, probably because of the lefty-on-lefty matchup against Dykstra, who struck out swinging for the final out of a 4–2 Sox victory. The Red Sox were one win away from shattering 1918 and had Roger Clemens set to go on five days' rest in the next game.

What's to say about Game Six that you haven't heard a thousand times? Believe it or not, there are probably at least a few interesting details that managed to fade into oblivion over the years as the legend of the "Buckner Game" grew and grew to become the defining narrative of October 25, 1986.

It was Clemens against Ojeda in front of a jacked-up Shea crowd. Clemens dominated the early innings, allowing one base runner through the fourth with six strikeouts. Meantime the Sox had Ojeda on the ropes throughout, scoring a run in the first on Evans' RBI double and another in the second on Barrett's RBI single. The Mets put together their first rally to tie the game with two in the fifth on a pair of base hits, a stolen base, and a walk, helped along by an Evans bobble that allowed Ray Knight to go first to third on a single and set up the second run.

Ojeda would yield 10 base runners in his six innings (eight hits, two walks), but he limited the damage by constantly worming his way out of trouble. The biggest Boston culprit: Bill Buckner. He came up in the first inning with one on and one out and flied out. He came up in the second with two on and two out and flied out. In the fifth he came up with a man on and none out and flied out again.

In the top of the seventh with the score still 2–2 Buckner came up against Roger McDowell with Barrett on first and grounded out. At least that out moved Barrett to second base to set up the Mets' costliest error of the night. When Rice grounded one to third, Ray Knight fielded the ball but threw wide to first base, the ball glancing off Hernandez's glove and trickling away. Barrett raced to third with Rice on safely at first. Instead of two out and a runner on second, Knight's error had given the Sox runners at the corners with one out. Evans then battled McDowell to a full count, which spurred McNamara to send Rice from first base on the next pitch. Evans hit a grounder to second, normally a tailor-made double-play ball. But with Rice running on the pitch, the Mets couldn't turn two. They settled for the out at first as Barrett scored the go-ahead run. The Sox nearly had more when Gedman grounded a single to left, but Mookie Wilson—never known for having a great arm—dialed up a strong and accurate throw to Carter to get Rice at the plate.

In the next inning, Buckner came up against Jesse Orosco with the bases loaded and two out and flied to center. His stranded runner count was at seven.

Clemens was done after seven innings, the reason being a point of contention to this day. McNamara, who passed away in 2020 at age 88, always maintained that Clemens asked out due to a cut that had begun to develop on his pitching hand. Clemens, as he has for years, vehemently denies that he ever asked out of the game. "I got a blood blister on my middle finger in the fifth inning; it only affected my slider. I was ready to go fastball-curve the rest of the way," he says. "Watch the tape, I'm on deck getting my helmet on. Bill Fischer made the comment that it was comical [that he would ask out of the game]." And, says Clemens, he never would have gone to the manager to ask out of the game because he rarely talked with the manager anyway. "I didn't answer to John McNamara, I answered to Fish," he says.

With Clemens cooling his heels in the dugout, the Mets tied the game against Schiraldi in the eighth and almost won it in the ninth but stranded two base runners.

In the top of the 10th, Henderson, who was killing it all series—he'd wind up hitting .400 with a pair of homers—greeted Rick Aguilera with a long home run to left field. The Red Sox were up 4–3, and they would add another big run thanks to some shoddy Mets defense. After Aguilera stuck out Owen and Schiraldi (who probably would have been lifted for a pinch-hitter after his two innings but would stay in now that the Sox had the lead), Boggs hit a deep fly ball to left that Wilson misjudged. He ran straight over toward center instead of back and over at a 45-degree angle. By the time he realized how deep the ball was and started back, it was too late—the ball was over his head and bouncing off the wall. Officially it was a double all the way—there was no error on Wilson on a ball he never got to—but it could well have been caught. When Barrett followed with his third hit of the night, Boggs scored to give Boston a 5–3 lead.

And then the fateful bottom of the 10th. Schiraldi got the first two outs and NBC was prepping for the champagne celebration in their clubhouse. The Shea Stadium scoreboard inadvertently flashed a "Congratulations Red Sox" message for a few seconds. Hurst had already been named series MVP. The curse was all but vanquished. Then, Carter single, Mitchell single, Knight single. It was 5–4 with runners at first and third. On came Stanley to relieve Schiraldi with Mookie Wilson at the plate. Stanley threw one inside for a wild pitch (some still believe a passed ball by Gedman—close call) that tied the game and sent Knight to second. Then Wilson hit the bouncer that skipped past Buckner, and the Mets were 6–5 winners.

Of course the whole world remembers Buckner's error because it happened on the last play. But didn't Evans's error earlier in the game, which cost the same number of runs (one), count just as much? Who remembers that the Red Sox took the lead in the seventh inning, thanks to an error by Knight, without which there probably would not have been a 10th inning? And the second run in the Boston 10th courtesy of Mookie Wilson playing Boggs's fly ball into a double? It was at least as poor a defensive play as Buckner's, but mostly buried from memory. Heck, how about the Sox winning the first game of the series on a ball through Tim Teuefel's legs? The glove giveth and the glove taketh, but no one play decides a seven-game series. If Buckner was a Game Six goat, blame his bat more than his glove. One well-timed hit among all those at-bats with runners on base could have brought the Red Sox a relatively stress-free victory without all the late-game drama. And he wasn't the only one: the Sox left 14 men on for the game.

Evans recalls pondering the championship just minutes before the collapse. "After Schiraldi got two outs I looked up and over and saw the 'Congratulations Red Sox' message. Later [Angels catcher] Bob Boone told me he was yelling at his TV, 'How does it feel?!'" The whole thing was indeed a bit eerie—a team that had just crawled back from the dead a week and a half earlier now seeing its fortunes reversed so quickly. Gedman doesn't say if he thinks he ought to have gotten Stanley's wild pitch, but he regrets what came a moment later when he chased the ball back toward the backstop and didn't quite grab it cleanly on the first try. "If I had picked up the ball cleanly and thrown it to Bob Stanley the game would have been over," he says. The replay doesn't quite back Gedman up on that one, given how far back from the plate he was relative to where Kevin Mitchell was as he raced in from third. But that's what sticks in his memory.

Lesley Visser was just on her way from the press box to the visitors' clubhouse to capture the celebration when the Mets' rally started. "At the elevator someone yells out, hold on, Carter singled. Then it was, oh, Mitchell singled," she says. Visser was having reflections of a phrase that Tip O'Neil once told her some years before: "Red Sox fans live with a Calvinist sense of guilt, we spend our entire lives waiting for the other shoe to drop. And here it was happening right in front of me."

By the time it was over, Visser wound up in the home clubhouse talking to Knight and others about the wild finish. "Keith Hernandez said that Stanley went with the wet one but overthrew it," she says. During his career Bob Stanley's name would occasionally get tossed around in articles about spitballs, common for almost any guy whose pitches tended to sink. He never said he applied anything to a ball beyond the sweat he'd wipe from his brow, which is perfectly legal. In this case, the ball didn't sink, it sailed inside, and so who knows? If anything, Stanley would have been better off with a pitch in the dirt, which would have compelled Gedman to get down and block it. But there's no blocking a waist-high pitch that runs way inside. Gedman's only play was to reach for it, and he was just a tick late.

John Molori, working his usual intern rounds at Channel 7 that night, has his own special memory of the game.

"There was a girl at BC who was a fellow communications student and fellow intern. I had a car and I would usually give her a ride to the office. I was pretty into her, but I was pretty shy at that age. Finally I get the nerve to ask her out and she says yes. So we're set to go out sometime the following week. She was from the New York area and she's a Mets fan. We're in the office the night of Game Six. The inning unfolds, the play happens. She's jumping

up and down and really got into our faces with 'You always choke,' that type
of thing. I left her there, didn't drive her back. I never talked to her again."

Fans lamented McNamara not bringing Dave Stapleton in for defense
at first base, as he sometimes did that year (though not always). Sure,
McNamara could have had Stapleton in the game, but that was never really
the point. Remember, the Mets had already tied it up before Buckner's error
and may well have won anyway. And the issue on the last play wasn't the
poor range that the hobbling Buckner dealt with. He got to the ball just fine,
and once he did that he was just as unlikely to miss it as Stapleton would
have been. In this case, he just did. That's baseball. If Evans doesn't bobble a
grounder in the outfield, if the Sox don't leave 14 men on, if the Mets don't
get three straight hits off Schiraldi before the last two plays . . . it all counts
the same. Says Gedman: "We had plenty of chances to make it not close."
Adds Steve Krasner: "I don't really remember the players defending him or
blaming him. It was more like, 'That's just the way the sport goes.'"

There has long been a general assumption that a Game Seven loss was
inevitable for the Red Sox after the disheartening sixth game. But that wasn't
necessarily so. The game had more than its fill of twists, turns, and shifts
in momentum with the Red Sox hardly looking like an emotionally hun-
gover team.

The Boston players seemed ready to move on to Game Seven pretty
quickly. Steve Krasner says, "Players can't ride that emotional roller coaster
like fans. Players are generally good at 'Today's a new day.'"

First, the game was delayed a night by rain, allowing the players more
time to digest the tough loss and for McNamara to skip Oil Can Boyd and
start Bruce Hurst, the man who had confounded the Mets all series. The Mets
scored a break from the delay too—Ron Darling would now start on his usual
four days of rest instead of three. (Krasner, incidentally, has a theory that the
rainout helped build the Buckner saga: The media needed something to talk
about for two days between games, and the final play of Game Six was a
natural starting point.)

Hurst would be going on three days' rest, which wasn't ideal but wasn't all
that unusual at the time. He had recently gone on three days' rest during the
ALCS when McNamara decided to shorten his rotation in that series, with
decent results.

Unfortunately, in what has to go down as one of the most self-absorbed
acts in sports history, Boyd was reportedly so upset at being passed over that
he spent the afternoon drinking, leaving him in no shape to pitch in relief if
needed, a possibility that figured even more prominently with Hurst going
on short rest.[1] This was the seventh game of the World Series—all hands
on deck with no time for individual egos. But Oil Can's ego didn't allow
him to see that McNamara's decision was certainly rational, even obvious.

Boyd was a solid pitcher, but Hurst presented the tougher matchup against the Mets' lineup. The Mets were generally not quite as potent against lefties, who kept their sparkplugs, Dykstra and Backman, on the bench and could better neutralize Keith Hernandez and Darryl Strawberry in the middle of the order. And Hurst in particular just seemed to have their number; two runs in 17 innings speaks for itself.

But perhaps the biggest lesson of Game Seven was the reminder that it's hard for a pitcher to dominate the same team three times in just over a week. Darling found that out early. He had pitched as well or even better than Hurst during the series, allowing just a single unearned run over two starts and 14 innings. But the Red Sox jumped on him for three runs in the second when Evans and Gedman opened with back-to-back homers and Boggs added an RBI single later in the inning.

Johnson lifted Darling for Fernandez in the fourth, a move which proved to be the first momentum-turner in the Mets' favor. It was a moment to acknowledge that while depth may not matter as much in the postseason as it does during the regular season, it can still matter. Fernandez had the fastball and big curve working as he blew through the next two-plus innings with four strikeouts without allowing a hit. When plate umpire John Kibler rang up Spike Owen to end the top of the sixth, the fans erupted. Fernandez's brief dominance had brought the crowd back to life and bought the Mets a chance to come back still within striking distance.

In the bottom of the sixth, it was Hurst's turn to finally run out of gas. He surrendered a one-out single to pinch-hitter Lee Mazzilli and another to Wilson, followed by a walk to Teufel. With the bases full and the crowd on its feet, Hurst threw a high fastball on a 0–1 count to Hernandez, who belted it into left-center field for a single that scored two runs and left runners on first and third. Carter then hit a short fly ball to right field that Evans dove for and seemed to initially catch until the ball squirted out of his glove at the last second. Evans had time to throw to second to get Hernandez, who was hanging back close to first thinking the ball might be caught before belatedly heading to second. But the run scored from third to tie the game, effectively making the play a sacrifice fly. The Mets had finally put together a rally against Hurst.

McNamara went to Schiraldi in a 3–3 game in the bottom of the seventh, and he just didn't have it this time. His first batter, Knight, greeted him with a home run over the left-field wall to give the Mets their first lead. After a couple of singles sandwiched around a wild pitch scored another run, Schiraldi was pulled for Sambito, who allowed one more run on a Hernandez sac fly. The Mets had six straight runs and a 6–3 lead and finally seemed to have things under control.

But the 1986 World Series wouldn't have been complete without at least one more momentum shift. In the top of the eighth against McDowell,

Buckner singled, Rice singled, and Evans drove both of them in with a double up the right-centerfield gap. Just like that it was 6–5, and the Sox had the tying run on second with none out. But Johnson brought in Jesse Orosco, who bailed out McDowell by getting three straight outs to strand Evans and keep the Mets in front.

With Boyd on the shelf, McNamara brought in Nipper for the bottom of the eighth, a big spot in which the Red Sox were trying to keep it a one-run game. But Darryl Strawberry, who had been quiet for most of the series, greeted Nipper with a home run to right field and then hotdogged it with a painfully slow trot around the bases. The Mets added one more in the inning to restore the three-run lead at 8–5.

Still, your gut told you that the series couldn't end without some final drama, without one last momentum change before the season was done for good. And then you felt almost shocked when it didn't happen. Orosco got the Red Sox one, two, three in the top of the ninth. In fact the last out was the unlikeliest of all. Marty Barrett, the consummate contact hitter who hadn't struck out since Game One and who'd been spraying hits all over the field during the series (13-for-30 for a .433 average) whiffed on Orosco's final pitch for the last out.

And so the dream had ended just a hair short. "We were 23, 24 years old and we lived and breathed Red Sox," says Rich Chaiton. "Right then we thought, that's it, they'll never win." It is funny how people's perceptions can quickly change as a team has success, that the better a team does as it goes along, the higher the expectations rise. Back in spring training most any Red Sox fan would have signed up for a World Series appearance, win or lose. But after all the team had done since then, spring training felt more like eight years ago than eight months ago. The focus in the moment wasn't so much on a great season but on the frustrating loss at the end of it, especially Game Six. From Rich Gedman: "Looking back, it was special but it takes a long, long time."

The strange ending of Game Six aside, the guy who wound up incurring the most wrath from Sox fans was Calvin Schiraldi. Too timid, too scared on the mound, they said. Just not up for meeting the moment.

Schiraldi mostly had a good postseason, allowing one earned run in six innings in the ALCS and then closing out the 1–0 win in the first game of the World Series. It was later in the sixth and seventh games against the Mets that he faltered. It's amazing how things can turn on a dime in sports. From late July to late October, Schiraldi was the godsend who stabilized the Boston bullpen. Now after two shaky outings at the worst possible time, fans seemed to have little use for him.

Rich Chaiton: "There were two problems with him. He threw hard but straight. And he had that deer-in-the-headlights look."

And from Krasner: "He didn't have that presence, where you feel the game is over," he says. "He didn't have that cockiness, where it was 'Give me the ball.'"

Did Schiraldi lack confidence on the mound? Only he knows for sure. It's an easy claim for an armchair critic to make. This was a young guy with a bit of a baby-faced look, complete with those puppy-dog eyes that really got wide and sad right after Ray Knight took him deep in Game Seven. So, no, he didn't look the part of a pit bull, but whether that affected his pitching is anyone's guess. On the surface he hadn't shown any more cockiness during the summer when he was mowing down opposing lineups than he did in those last couple of outings in the World Series. So maybe it was just a case of missing on a few pitches or wearing down a bit by the end of the season, his first one going deep into October.

In any case, Schiraldi was never again as electric as he was during those two splendid months of 1986. He'd struggle some in 1987 and then find himself dealt to the Cubs along with Al Nipper in exchange for established closer Lee Smith. So maybe his critics had a point, or maybe the league adjusted to him and he failed to adjust back by changing his patterns or developing another pitch. In the end he was a shooting star in Boston, much like the whole local sports scene in 1986.

The other shooting star of course was Dave Henderson. This is a guy who played a grand total of 111 games for the Red Sox over parts of two seasons, hitting .226 with nine homers. And yet in Boston sports lore, "Hendu" pretty much walks on water. When you hit the biggest home run in team history (yes, bigger than those of Carlton Fisk and Bernie Carbo in the 1975 World Series, neither of which came in a spot where making an out ends the series) and follow it by killing the Mets over seven games, including another huge homer that would have stood up as the series winner if not for the bizarre bottom of the 10th, your place in team history is secure. "If Game Six or Game Seven had gone differently, Henderson would have been a David Ortiz–type figure," says Molori, even as he acknowledges that Big Papi had more postseason moments over a long period of time. But, yeah, Dave Henderson made himself a beloved figure in the same kind of way. Dwight Evans remembers his teammate as "a great guy, he always had that big smile on his face. And a great athlete, I remember how he could jump from the dugout floor right up to the field."

And so ended the wonderful and crazy year when everything got turned upside down, when nothing went according to plan. A team that was supposed to finish fifth in the American League East finished first. A team that was one strike away from losing the American League Championship Series wound up winning. And a team that was one strike away from winning the World Series wound up losing. That's why, of the three teams that vaulted Boston to the top of the sports world in 1986, "the Red Sox were probably the most special, they had the most drama," says Bob Lobel. Even the club that finally busted the curse 18 years later, the one with Schilling, Pedro, Manny, Big Papi, and Johnny Damon that made history by rallying from a 0–3 deficit against the Yankees and then sweeping the Cardinals for the first championship in most fans' lifetimes, may not quite measure up when it comes to capturing the imagination. According to Lobel: "People will still remember the 1986 Red Sox after they've forgotten about the 2004 Red Sox."

Epilogue

It was Bob Lobel who said that Boston's big year in sports needed to be appreciated in the context of what came before and what came after. And was he ever right.

The last time the New England Patriots or Boston Red Sox had won a post-season game before 1986? That would be Game Six of the 1975 World Series when Carlton Fisk homered off the left field foul pole in the bottom of the 12th to beat the Cincinnati Reds (the Sox would lose Game Seven). The next time the New England Patriots or Boston Red Sox won a postseason game after 1986? That was when coach Bill Parcells and QB Drew Bledsoe led the Pats to a win over the Pittsburgh Steelers in the AFC Divisional Round play-off on January 5, 1997—11 years to the day after Pat Sullivan's little scrape with Howie Long and Matt Millen in Los Angeles. That Pats team would go on to Super Bowl XXXI where they lost to Green Bay.

The next Red Sox playoff win came almost two years after that, when Pedro Martinez beat the Cleveland Indians in the first game of their 1998 American League Division Series, the first time the Sox walked off the field as winners of a postseason game since Bruce Hurst beat the Mets in Game Five in 1986.

The Celtics, as usual, proved to be the exception, contending for several more years after the 1986 championship, although they wouldn't get another title. They followed their sheer dominance in 1985/86 with a valiant effort in 1986/87 that got them to the brink of championship No. 17, but they didn't quite make it. Bill Walton's injuries returned—he'd sit for most of the year before giving it a whirl late in the season but he never really made it back. Kevin McHale, meanwhile, was gritting his teeth through the 1987 playoffs as he put in 40 minutes a game playing through the pain of a hairline fracture of his right foot. That's all on top of the death of Len Bias, which deprived the Celtics of their next-generation star. And yet they still almost did it—pulling out a tough Eastern Conference Final against Detroit before losing to the Lakers in six games in what would be their last NBA Finals appearance of the era.

And so it was the 1986 Celtics that gave the town its last sports title of the 20th century. By the time Adam Vinatieri booted his 48-yard field goal to beat the St. Louis Rams in the Super Bowl on February 3, 2002, Boston Garden had been torn down, *Cheers* had been off the air for almost a decade, the Big Dig that was transforming the city was well underway (though not nearly finished), Whitey Bulger was on the lamb in California, and Sullivan Stadium—now called Foxborough Stadium—had just hosted its last Patriots game.

Not that the '86 Pats and Red Sox teams didn't have some fight left in them.

Following their Super Bowl loss to the Bears, the Pats came back and duplicated their 11–5 record the following season but were immediately ousted from the playoffs in Denver. The interesting part was how they did it. The tough running game that was the Patriots' staple during their Super Bowl season disappeared almost entirely after John Hannah decided to retire and Craig James was hit by the injury bug that would soon derail his career. The Pats finished dead last in the NFL in rushing in 1986/87. And yet they won the division by thoroughly changing their game to ride Tony Eason's arm. This was Eason's one shining season, one where he broke out for over 3,300 yards and 19 touchdowns while completing more than 60% of his passes. It was just after that 1986/87 season that his physical breakdown began. Eason wouldn't start more than five games in any of his final four seasons before he retired in 1990. The wimp label that people hung on Eason mainly comes from those last few years when injuries kept nagging at him, but you can't forget his big 1986 season.

Meantime, the nucleus of Clemens, Boggs, and Evans led the Red Sox to a pair of follow-up division titles in 1988 and 1990, though they were swept out in four straight both times by the Oakland A's. Talented young outfielders Ellis Burks and Mike Greenwell proved to be the perfect weapons to offset the steady declines of Rice, Boyd, and Gedman, and the team finally got itself a good shortstop when Jody Reed came up from Pawtucket. Bruce Hurst had a strong 1988 season (18–6) to help the team win the A.L. East but then left as a free agent for the San Diego Padres and missed the 1990 division crown.

Jim Rice would play his last game in Boston in 1989, Steve Grogan and Dwight Evans in 1990, Larry Bird and Wade Boggs in 1992, Kevin McHale and Andre Tippett in 1993, and Roger Clemens in 1996.

The golden era was right around the corner—Brady and Belichick launching a dynasty, the Sox busting the 1918 curse four times over, the Celtics and Bruins each chipping in a championship of their own. For Boston, enduring those ups and downs over the years, like any sports city, is just what made 1986 so special. It was like a sudden, unexpected dynasty unto itself, all packaged within about 10 months. The sports bonus of a lifetime.

Not only a Super Bowl, NBA Finals, and World Series, but a year in which the Patriots, Celtics, and Red Sox all had their absolute best seasons in their franchise histories. The Pats have since surpassed that standard during the Belichick-Brady era. But the Celtics have never surpassed the 1986 squad, not that you can expect them to, considering that many call the '86 team the greatest in NBA history, and there is a good argument that the Red Sox haven't either.

A quick explanation on the 1986 Sox, who aren't generally considered to be quite that high up in the stratosphere. Sure, their 95–66 record, good as it was, wasn't exactly historic. And they didn't even quite win the World Series. But there's a bigger picture to consider. Given the caliber of the competition in a strong 1986 American League East—five of seven teams finished above .500 that year with no one doing worse than 73–89—any reasonable power ranking that includes strength of schedule would place the Red Sox far higher than the raw win total would indicate. Contrast that with the 2018 Red Sox team that went a seemingly dominant 108–54 and then blew through the postseason to a championship. They were better, right? You could make the case, but don't forget the perspective. This was the tanking era, one that brought historically wide chasms between the haves and have-nots across the league. Three American League teams won 100 or more games that year while three others lost 100 or more. Highly unusual. So the win total was certainly inflated. In short, the 1986 team separated itself from the pack by a wider margin than the 2018 team did.

As for winning the World Series: different years, different opponents. The 2018 Dodgers team that the Red Sox vanquished had a nice squad (92–71), but they weren't the 1986 Mets (108–54 in a balanced year), a team that by any measure stands among the top handful of all time. Logic says that losing the World Series by a whisker to an opponent like that doesn't necessarily push you below other clubs that won that final game. Of course it was a lot more fun for a Sox fan to see the World Series trophy handed to John Henry those four times between 2004 and 2018 than it was to see it whisked out of Shea Stadium visitors' clubhouse in 1986 during the 10th inning of Game Six just before it was to be handed to Jean Yawkey. But that doesn't mean Mrs. Yawkey's team wasn't better. The 1986 Red Sox have a solid case as the best team in franchise history.

***

Watching the 1986 World Series wasn't easy in the Watertown apartment filled with a mix of Met fans and Red Sox fans. During the series an extra friend or two would usually be there with the four of us, making for some pretty intense watch parties. The matchup we'd been anticipating since about the All-Star break, the one we figured would be so much fun, became a little bit uneasy as rooting interests firmly took hold. There had never been any conflict before—Red Sox fans and Mets fans were normally staunch allies that bonded over their mutual disdain for the New York Yankees. Here we had the Sox playing in their first World Series in 11 years and the Mets in their first in 13 years. It was good to see both teams make it after pretty lengthy droughts, but how much easier it all would have been had it happened, say, a year apart instead of right together. Rooting for the Red Sox to beat the Whitey Herzog Cardinals in 1985 or 1987 would have been a no-brainer. But in 1986 I had no choice; I'd have to root against them for the first time ever.

And, of course, nothing turned the stomach like Game Six, one that I didn't even make it through. When Ray Knight threw the ball away for his big error in the top of the eighth of a 2–2 game, I was done. I retreated to bed, not to be heard from for the rest of the night. Yes, I missed the end of what would be one of the most memorable World Series games ever.

My friends called me a sore loser, which was true, although they didn't realize that that was how I had always watched the Mets. When things got too dicey or tense, I'd launch into "I can't even watch" mode and walk away. Silly for sure, but that's how I rolled when the pressure really mounted and I was just a fan, helpless to do anything. To me this was nothing like the NFL when the Pats had begun their playoff run to the Super Bowl by beating the Jets, which I really didn't mind so much. Baseball was always my main thing; I was never a Jets fan like I was a Mets fan.

A lot of time has passed and we're all quite a bit older. It's much easier now to look back and see all of this more objectively and to appreciate the time in Boston for the firsthand view of the wild ride of 1986. Yes, the Sox should have had the World Series. From a Mets perspective the championship always felt a bit on the hollow side, knowing that the narrative would always ensure the 1986 World Series going down as one that the Red Sox blew more than one that the Mets won.

Waking up on Sunday morning, October 26, I still didn't know for sure how Game Six had turned out. Even though one of my friends had shaken me awake to tell me about the bottom of the 10th, I wasn't sure I believed him. I strolled quietly into the living room, and there was my answer. On the coffee table sat a half-empty bottle of champagne, along with a few filled glasses. The bubbly had been opened and poured, but never sipped.

Notes

INTRODUCTION

1. Chad Finn, "How Michael Jackson Helped Save the Patriots," Boston.com, June 26, 2009.

CHAPTER 1

1. Thepostgame.com, "Happy Birthday Craig James," January 2, 2015.

CHAPTER 2

1. NBA TV, via BTM Basketball Time Machine, via YouTube, no date given.
2. YouTube, "Uncle Sam's Reject Gaming," January 5, 2018.

CHAPTER 3

1. UPI, "New England Patriots Owner Testified Friday That . . . ," July 17, 1981.
2. Rick Gosselin, "The New England Patriots Have a Sudden Concern for . . . ," UPI, January 11, 1986.

CHAPTER 5

1. Dan Shaughnessy, "Designated Deal—Easler-Baylor," *Boston Globe*, March 29, 1986, p. 27.
2. Murray Chass, "Baylor Trade Talks Off," *New York Times,* December 14, 1985.
3. Southworth YouTube Channel, "A Conversation with Roger Clemens."

CHAPTER 6

1. Tyler Ash, "Rich Gedman," Society for American Baseball Research, https://sabre.org.

2. Bob Ryan, "Celtics Break Down in Fourth Quarter," *Boston Globe*, June 2, 1986, p. 31.

3. Steve West, Sabr.org.

4. Chris Jaffe, "Silver Anniversary of Bizarre Wade Boggs Injury," *The Hardball Times*, June 2011.

5. Jack McCallum, "The Cruelest Thing Ever," si.com vault, June 30, 1986.

6. Jack Craig, "NBC and NESN to Put Clemens under the Gun," *Boston Globe*, June 20, 1986, p. 47.

CHAPTER 7

1. Dan Shaughnessy, "A Fenway Fantasy Fulfilled," *Boston Globe*, June 30, 1986, p. 1.

2. Larry Whiteside, "A Wild Night for Red Sox, Boyd," *Boston Globe,* July 11, 1986, p. 39.

3. Will McDonough, "Message to Boyd: It's Time to Grow Up," *Boston Globe*, August 3, 1986, p. 46.

4. Leigh Montville, "Boyd Loses, 3–1, in Return," *Boston Globe*, August 6, 1986, p. 1.

5. Dan Shaughnessy, "Red Sox Notebook," *Boston Globe*, August 17, 1986, p. 52.

CHAPTER 9

1. Bruce Markusen, "Cooperstown Confidential: The Sad Saga of Oil Can Boyd," *Fangraphs*, May 4, 2012.

Bibliography

ABC Sports. American League Championship Series, Game 6, Angels at Red Sox, October 14, 1986, via YouTube.

———. American League Championship Series, Game 5, Red Sox at Angels, October 12, 1986, via YouTube.

———. *Monday Night Football*. Patriots at Dolphins, December 16, 1985, via YouTube.

Ash, Tyler. "Rich Gedman." Society for American Baseball Research. https://sabr.org.

Baseball-reference.com.

Basketball-reference.com.

CBS Sports. NBA Finals, Game 4, June 3, 1986, via YouTube.

———. NBA Finals, Game 6, June 8, 1986, via YouTube.

Chass, Murray. "Baylor Trade Talks Off." *New York Times*, December 14, 1985.

Craig, Jack. "NBC and NESN to Put Clemens under the Gun." *Boston Globe*, June 20, 1986, p. 47.

Finn, Chad. "How Michael Jackson Helped Save the Patriots." Boston.com, June 26, 2009.

Gosselin, Rick. "The New England Patriots Have a Sudden Concern For . . . " UPI, January 11, 1986.

"Happy Birthday Craig James." Thepostgame.com, January 2, 2015.

Jaffe, Chris. "Silver Anniversary of Bizarre Wade Boggs Injury." *The Hardball Times*, June 2011.

Kenny, Brian. *Ahead of the Curve*. New York: Simon & Schuster, 2016.

Larry Legend YouTube Channel. Highlights of Celtics vs. Mavericks, December 18, 1985.

———. Highlights of Celtics vs. Lakers, January 22, 1986.

———. Highlights of Celtics vs. Pistons, March 2, 1986.

Markusen, Bruce. "Cooperstown Confidential: The Sad Saga of Oil Can Boyd." *Fangraphs*, May 4, 2012.

McCallum, Jack. "The Cruelest Thing Ever." *Sports Illustrated* Vault, June 30, 1986. https://vault.si.com.

McDonough, Will. "Message to Boyd: It's Time to Grow Up." *Boston Globe*, August 3, 1986, p. 46.

Montville, Leigh. "Boyd Loses, 3–1, in Return." *Boston Globe*, August 6, 1986, p. 1.

NBA TV, via BTM Basketball Time Machine, via YouTube, no date given.

NBC Sports. Bengals at Patriots, December 22, 1985, via YouTube.

———. *Game of the Week*. Red Sox vs. Yankees, September 13, 1986, via YouTube.

———. Patriots at Dolphins, AFC Championship, January 12, 1986, via YouTube.

———. Patriots at Raiders, AFC Divisional Playoff, January 5, 1986, via YouTube.

———. World Series, Game Six, Red Sox vs. Mets, October 25, 1986, via YouTube.

NBCSports.com, November 3, 2011.

New England Sports Network. Red Sox vs. Blue Jays, September 28, 1986, via YouTube.

———. Red Sox vs. Mariners, April 29, 1986, via YouTube.

Pro-football-reference.com

Ryan, Bob. "Celtics Break Down in Fourth Quarter." *Boston Globe*, June 2, 1986, p. 31.

Shaughnessy, Dan. "Designated Deal—Easler-Baylor." *Boston Globe*, March 29, 1986, p. 27.

———. "A Fenway Fantasy Fulfilled." *Boston Globe*, June 30, 1986, p. 1.

———. "Red Sox Notebook." *Boston Globe*, August 17, 1986, p. 52.

Southworth YouTube Channel. "A Conversation with Roger Clemens."

Sports Channel. Celtics vs. Hawks, Game Five, May 6, 1986, via AllBasketballTV on YouTube.

"Uncle Sam's Reject Gaming." January 5, 2018, via YouTube.

UPI. "New England Patriots Owner Testified Friday That . . . " July 17, 1981.

West, Steve. "Actually Wade Boggs." Society for American Baseball Research. https://sabr.org.

Whiteside, Larry. "A Wild Night for Red Sox, Boyd." *Boston Globe,* July 11, 1986, p. 39.

Index

About the Author

Tom Van Riper covered the business of sports for *Forbes* from 2005 to 2014. Prior to that he worked the business beat for the New York *Daily News.* He lives in Floral Park, New York, with his wife, Barbara; daughters, Katie and Sarah; and son, Tommy. This is his third book.

Milton Keynes UK
Ingram Content Group UK Ltd.
UKHW011406230124
436547UK00006B/64

9 781538 175699